The Vegetarian Grill

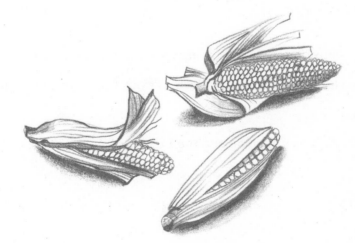

Other Cookbooks by Andrea Chesman

366 Delicious Ways to Cook Rice, Beans & Grains

Salad Suppers

Simply Healthful Skillet Suppers

Simply Healthful Pasta Salads

The Great American Dessert Cookbook
(WITH FRAN RABOFF)

Sun-Dried Tomatoes!

Salsas!

Summer in a Jar: Making Pickles, Jams, and More

Pickles and Relishes: 150 Recipes from Apples to Zucchini

By Andrea Chesman and the Editors of *Yankee Magazine*:

Yankee Church Suppers & Potluck Dinners

The Vegetarian Grill

200 Recipes for Inspired Flame-Kissed Meals

Andrea Chesman

The Harvard Common Press
Boston, Massachusetts

To a trio of great eaters: Richard, Rory, and Sam

The Harvard Common Press
535 Albany Street
Boston, Massachusetts 02118

Printed in the United States of America
Printed on acid-free paper

Library of Congress Cataloging-in-Publication Data

Chesman, Andrea.
    The vegetarian grill : 200 recipes for inspired flame-kissed meals   /
by Andrea Chesman.
      p. cm.
    Includes index.
    ISBN 1-55832-126-8 (hardcover : alk. paper). — ISBN 1-55832-127-6
(paperback : alk. paper)
      1. Vegetarian cookery. 2. Barbecue cookery. I. Title.
TX837.C454 1998
641.5'636—dc21   98-11527
                                            CIP

Cover photograph by Rita Maas
Cover design by Suzanne Noli
Text illustrations by Kathy Warriner
Text design by Joyce C. Weston

10 9 8 7 6 5 4 3 2 1

1

Grilling Basics: Equipment and Techniques

I am not the sort of cook who needs a gadget for every occasion. I am slow to buy new equipment. So for years, I got by without the one piece of equipment that makes grilling vegetables truly worthwhile—an enamel-coated metal vegetable grill rack, or grill topper, as they are sometimes called.

While getting by without the vegetable grill rack, I enjoyed grilled vegetables from asparagus season in May through the end of tomato season. I grilled slabs of eggplant and zucchini, which I then chopped and turned into ratatouille and caponata. I roasted corn and made veggie burgers. In short, I thought I was fully exploiting the possibilities of grilled vegetables.

Then I bought a vegetable grill rack and a whole new range of cooking possibilities opened up. What the vegetable grill rack does is enable you to cook vegetables that are already cut into bite-size pieces. Basically, it enables you to sauté over an open flame. With the kiss of the flame, the naturally occurring sugars in the vegetables become caramelized, adding a new layer of flavor and texture to the foods you cook. Think of the possibilities—garlic-soaked, flame-kissed zucchini whisked off the grill and tossed with just-cooked pasta; soy-marinated broccoli and tofu lightly seared over an open flame and bedded down with rice; lime-marinated peppers and onions tucked into tortillas to make rich-tasting vegetarian fajitas.

Bite-size vegetables cook faster than large slices, and yet they have a stronger grill flavor because of the increased surface area that is exposed to the heat. Because they don't have to be chopped after grilling, the vegetables are more likely to retain their heat and texture as they are moved quickly from grill to table. Veggie burgers and tofu slices, which have a tendency to fall apart on the grill, hold their shape on the vegetable grill rack.

A grill rack can be used to make pizza on the grill. The pizza cooks directly on the grill rack, which can be moved on and off the grill, eliminating the need for a baker's peel to transfer the loaded pizza. A grill rack is also wonderfully portable for campfires and barbecues at a campground. You never know what was on the grate over the fire pit before you arrived. With a vegetable grill rack, your food doesn't come in contact with the public grill grate.

A vegetable grill rack is, simply, a

Vegetable
Grill Rack

metal sheet with holes cut out of it to allow flames and smoke to touch and penetrate the food. The holes are small enough to prevent cut vegetables from falling into the fire. Griffo Grill is one brand name for this type of grill rack, but there are other brands out there as well. The shape may be square, rectangular, or curved on one side to fit a kettle-style grill. Ones with detachable handles are especially convenient for making pizza. You can find them in most kitchen stores.

So, forget about the cumbersome hinged grill baskets and the skewers. A $15 investment in a vegetable grill rack will make all the difference if you want to readily and easily enjoy the rich flavor of grilled vegetarian fare. Grill-woks are a variation on vegetable grill racks. They are made of the same enamel-coated steel with holes cut out to allow the penetration of smoke and flames. They have higher sides, which enable you to toss the vegetables with greater abandon. They also feature handles to enable you to lift the wok off the grill as needed. Unfortunately, the flat surface where the heat is most concentrated is more limited than with a vegetable grill rack, so you must work with smaller quantities of vegetables to get good results. Of course, neither the vegetable grill rack nor the grill-wok will do you any good without a grill to place it on. So let's consider grills.

Grill-Wok

Grills

The most basic of all grills is a fire pit that you dig yourself. First dig a shallow hole in the ground, clearing away nearby grass and vegetation. Then line the hole with stones or bricks and make a bit of a wall, using stones, bricks, or large logs, on which to rest a metal grate. We have a fire pit like this in our backyard—it is good for small bonfires on summer nights and we prefer it for weenie roasts, roasting marshmallows, and fire gazing. But for serious cooking, most people prefer a grill that doesn't require that you cook in a squatting position.

When buying a grill, the big question is whether to purchase a gas or a charcoal grill. Each has its advantages. I own both, but I use my gas grill more, simply because it is more convenient. If vegetables lent themselves to the same long, slow cooking of barbecued meats, there would be good cause to only consider buying a grill that could handle natural wood fuels, since it is the wood smoke that infuses the meat with flavor. But vegetables cook quickly, and most of the flavor comes from the vegetables themselves or the oils and marinades that are brushed on them, so it matters less than you might think—in terms of flavor—whether you go with gas or charcoal.

Gas Grills

In 1996, more gas grills were sold than charcoal grills—for the first time ever. Apparently, more people were guided in their choice by the convenience of backyard gas grills.

Gas grills are portable fireboxes, fueled by refillable liquid propane tanks. The gas burner is located at the bottom of the firebox. It is covered by ceramic briquettes or lava rocks. These rocks absorb the heat of the flame and radiate heat up to the food. The heat can be adjusted using the dials that regulate the

Convenience vs. Flavor

Gas versus charcoal: I can't think of another cooking situation in which the convenience versus flavor issue is so dramatically contrasted. I use my gas grill *all the time*. I grill summer and winter. I get excellent results with little fuss. I can whip up a grilled supper in less than an hour. It only takes 10 minutes to preheat a grill. The whisper of smoke adds a subtle flavor to the food I cook. Because the smoke flavor is subtle, dishes cooked on a gas grill have more flavor nuances.

Charcoal, on the other hand, requires time and patience. It can take close to an hour to get the temperature you want if the weather is at all adverse. Those big dome lids are awkward to handle and I have no convenient spot to set one on (unlike the hinged lid on the gas grill). I have to give over shed space for the charcoal, and plan ahead to be sure I have enough on hand.

But, and it is a big but, the flavor of the charcoal smoke is a stronger presence in the food. Vegetable flavor nuances may be lost, but it's hard to go wrong with that delicious smoke flavor.

People who have gas grills grill more frequently. People who have charcoal grills get more flavor from their grill. What a choice.

flow of gas into the burners. You can grill with the lid up or down. (For a discussion of whether to grill with the lid up or down, see page 11.)

You can buy stripped-down gas grills or you can buy deluxe models with electric burners on the sides, two or more tiers of grates, and shelves and cabinets. You'll enjoy having a little counter space for holding your marinade and tools, so the side shelf is handy if your cooking area doesn't already provide this convenience. As for the electric burners, you'll probably use them sometimes. But you will probably also find yourself running into the kitchen to grab more ingredients, or to use the sink, or to refill your drink, so the added convenience may not be worth the price when you may be running back and forth anyway.

Unless you regularly entertain, you don't need a huge grill, but vegetables do take up a lot of space compared to meat, so bigger grills will allow more vegetables to be cooked at a time. Small grills with just one burner are pretty limited for vegetarian grilling, since they don't seem to generate as much heat as larger grills.

It takes about 10 minutes to preheat a gas grill on its highest setting, and then you are ready to cook. For extra smoke flavor, you can presoak wood chips. Place them in the chipbox holder that some models feature. If your grill doesn't include a chipbox, place the presoaked chips in a perforated disposable metal container and place the container on a burner. This will add only a little extra flavor to a vegetarian dish since, in general, vegetables cook too quickly to benefit much from the additional smoke.

Charcoal Grills

Charcoal grills come in all sizes, from tiny apartment-size hibachis to large domed kettles on legs. The charcoal is placed in the firebox and a grate over the

---

Grilling vs. Barbecuing

Grilling is a way of cooking foods over hot coals so that the outside of the food is seared. Grilling is accomplished quickly over a hot fire. Barbecuing is a slow-cooking method in which the food is cooked by smoke and indirect heat. Barbecuing is well suited to big pieces of meat, but grilling is ideal for locking in the flavor of vegetables.

Getting Ready to Cook over Fire

'In my younger days, I never much cared to build the fire when I went camping because there was always some other camper (usually male) who had a "better way" of doing it. For all the macho mystique around fire building, there really isn't much to it. And no matter how the fire is built, or who did the building, it will take anywhere from 30 to 60 minutes to get the coals ready for cooking.

Building a Fire

To build a wood fire, start with torn paper egg cartons, crumpled newspaper, or dry pine needles, bark, or leaves. Cover these with dry, dead twigs to form a teepee over the kindling. Put a match to the paper or pine needles and hope it catches. Allow the twigs to catch on fire (blowing into the fire to add oxygen does help), then slowly and carefully add small pieces of wood that, preferably, have been split first. Gradually increase the size of the wood you are adding to the fire until you have added a few good-size chunks. Let the fire burn down so you are cooking over embers not flames.

For starting a charcoal fire, I swear by a little unit called a charcoal chimney. This two-compartment cylinder is open at both ends, with ventilation holes on the bottom. Inside, the two compartments are separated by a metal screen. You crumple a few sheets of newspaper (or use torn paper egg cartons) and stuff it into the bottom compartment, then fill the top compartment with charcoal. Light the newspaper, and the flames will reach up and ignite the charcoal. After about 10 minutes, the coals are all lit. Grab the stay-cool handle of the chimney, carefully dump out the lighted coals, pile on additional coals as needed, and your fire will be ready soon.

*Charcoal
Chimney*

I hate the smell of lighter fluid. Even if it does burn off before the food is added, the odor lingers on my clothes and in my hair. It's not necessary, and I just don't use it.

How much charcoal? You want to be able to spread out the coals to about 1 inch beyond the surface to be covered by the vegetables you are going to grill. Generally, the number of briquettes a chimney holds (35 to 40) is sufficient for a batch or two of quick-cooking vegetables, plus a dessert cooked over a low fire.

Judging When a Fire Is Ready for Cooking

There should be white ash covering all the coals. Hold the palm of your hand 5 to 6 inches above the cooking surface. If you can keep you hand there for only about 2 seconds, you have a medium-hot fire; if you can hold it there for 3 to 4 seconds, you have a medium fire; and if you can hold it for any longer, you have a low fire. Most vegetables are cooked over a medium-hot fire, but there are plenty of exceptions.

Using the Vegetable Grill Rack

Large vegetable slices and whole vegetables can be cooked directly on the grill grate without falling into the fire. Smaller cut vegetables should be cooked on a vegetable grill rack, or grill topper. It should be lightly oiled or sprayed with nonstick cooking spray, then placed on the grill and preheated for about 10 minutes before the vegetables are added.

Wood Chips for Added Smoke Flavor

You can coax a little extra flavor from your grill by adding water-soaked wood chips to the fire. The wood will smolder and produce smoke. If the food you are cooking spends more than 5 minutes on the grill, it will pick up some added smoke flavor—though not as much as you would get from food cooked in a smoker.

You can buy chips of different woods—hickory and mesquite are the most common, but you can get apple wood or pecan. Again, because of the brevity of the cooking time, I find it hard to impossible to discern flavor differences, so paying a premium price for one kind over another may not be worth it.

Soak the chips in water to cover for 30 to 90 minutes. I prefer a longer soak to prevent the possibility of the chips flaring up. Throw the soaked wood chips directly on the lit charcoal. In a gas grill, you don't want ashes to collect in the bottom of the grill, so place the soaked chips in a perforated disposable metal pan and set the pan directly on the burner. Or use the chip holder that comes with many gas grill models. The chips should start smoldering in about 5 minutes, so time your grilling accordingly.

Burners on the Side

The latest upgrade in gas grills is the inclusion of gas burners on the side of the cooking grate, so you can heat sauces or make a stove-top side dish while you grill. It's a great feature if you *really* grill a lot. But if you don't have a preparation area near the grill, you are going to have to rush in and out of the kitchen anyway, so the added convenience of the burner may not be very significant.

Grilling Vegetables

Since vegetables contain no fat, they must be brushed or tossed with an oil or marinade to provide moisture and to prevent them from sticking to the grill. Marinating for long periods of time isn't necessary because most vegetables don't absorb the marinade (eggplant and mushrooms are notable exceptions to this rule).

Vegetables should be grilled whole or cut into similar-size pieces to ensure even cooking. Just a few vegetables (artichokes, winter squash, and white potatoes) benefit from parboiling before grilling—but even these can be adapted to the grill without precooking (usually by baking on the grill wrapped in aluminum foil). Most vegetables can be cooked directly on the grill without precooking. They come out sweet and slightly crispy.

Vegetables cook quickly on the grill; most are done in 5 to 10 minutes when cooked over medium-hot coals and turned once or twice. Cooking over medium-hot coals is generally recommended to sear in flavor. Vegetables are done when they are fork tender but still juicy and lightly marked by the grill. How much a vegetable will blacken on the grill depends in part on how much natural sugar the vegetable contains and on how much sugar is in the marinade or glaze.

Grill Lid Up or Down?

Generally, the grill lid should stay up while you are grilling vegetables. Closing the lid turns the grill into an oven, trapping moist heat and smoke. The moisture is undesirable when you want a crisp texture, and the trapped smoke leaves a dull, sooty patina on the vegetables. Also, it's hard to monitor the cooking process with the lid down. However, when grilling in cold or windy weather, closing the lid may be necessary to trap the heat.

Final Words of Advice

Grilling doesn't require lots of experience, skill, or equipment, but it does help to be well organized or you will be running back and forth between grill and kitchen. Since vegetables grill quickly, you can easily burn your dinner if you have to walk away from the grill.

Grilling does require a certain amount of judgment because the times suggested in the recipes cannot cover all grilling conditions. When the weather is unusually cold, windy, or humid, the food may cook more slowly. Fully ripened vegetables cook more quickly than underripe vegetables. What is a medium fire to one person (remember we gauge it by how long you can hold your hand over the fire) may be hot to another—and gas grills do vary in how much heat is given off at the various settings.

When vegetables are grilled, the sugars naturally occurring within as well as any sugars in the marinade coating the outside will caramelize, producing a nice brown, slightly crunchy exterior. This is completely different from charring, which happens next. Charred, scorched food is bitter and unpleasant, so be prepared to remove the vegetables when they are done—and not simply when the timer goes off.

2

Simply
Vegetables

CHAPTER 2 • SIMPLY VEGETABLES

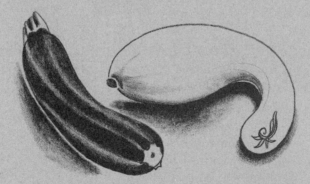

Basic Grilled Artichokes

If I had only one vegetable on which to prove my claim that grilling enhances flavor, I would probably choose to prove it with an artichoke. The nutty flavor of this green vegetable becomes even more delectable under a glaze of smoke. Serve it, if you must, with drawn butter, but I prefer it plain.

SERVES 4 TO 8

4 globe artichokes
Olive oil
Lemon wedges

1. Steam the artichokes for 25 minutes, until mostly cooked.
2. Prepare a medium-hot fire in the grill.
3. Slice the artichokes in half vertically and scrape out the feathery choke. Brush with olive oil. Grill, turning occasionally, until tender, about 10 minutes.
4. Serve hot with lemon wedges on the side.

Lemony Asparagus with Pine Nuts

Plain asparagus, lightly coated with olive oil and grilled, is sweet and delicious. Adding the tang of lemon and the buttery crunch of pine nuts elevates the dish to a celebration of spring.

SERVES 4

1¼ pounds asparagus, trimmed
2 tablespoons extra-virgin olive oil
2 tablespoons pine nuts
Juice of ½ lemon

1. Prepare a medium fire in the grill.

2. Place the asparagus in a shallow dish. Drizzle 1 tablespoon of the olive oil on top and toss to coat.

3. Grill the asparagus, turning occasionally, until tender, about 8 minutes. Remove from the grill and keep warm.

4. Heat the remaining 1 tablespoon olive oil in a small pan over low heat. Add the pine nuts and cook, stirring, just until the nuts begin to turn brown, about 3 minutes. Stir in the lemon juice, then pour over the asparagus. Serve at once.

Variations: This is also an excellent treatment for broccoli spears, long green beans, and long, thin carrots or carrot sticks.

Soy-Grilled Green Beans

Dressed in a simple soy marinade, the beans take on a slightly charred appearance. This isn't the most beautiful way to present fresh green beans, but it is among the most flavorful. I recommend using a vegetable grill rack with green beans; but if you are careful, you can lay the beans perpendicular to the grid of the grill grate and not lose too many of them into the coals.

SERVES 4

1 pound green beans, trimmed
2 tablespoons toasted sesame oil
1 tablespoon soy sauce
1 tablespoon dry sherry or Chinese rice wine
2 garlic cloves, minced

1. Prepare a medium fire in the grill with a lightly oiled vegetable grill rack or grill-wok in place.

2. Place the beans in a shallow dish. Add the sesame oil, soy sauce, sherry or rice wine, and garlic. Toss to coat.

3. Lift the beans out of the marinade with a pair of tongs. Grill the beans, tossing frequently, until tender and browned, 8 to 10 minutes.

4. Place the beans in a serving dish. Pour over any remaining marinade. Serve hot.

Variations: Substitute asparagus spears, carrot sticks, or broccoli florets for the green beans.

Simple Grilled Beets

Grilled beets? They are delicious roasted, so why not grilled? As the beets cook, you will see little beads of moisture collect on the surface and form a lovely crust on the slices. Grilled beets are delicious—and grilling is even faster than boiling. An added benefit: Grilled beets don't require peeling.

SERVES 4

8 medium-size beets (1½ to 1¾ pounds)
2 tablespoons olive or canola oil, or more as needed
Salt and black pepper

1. Prepare a medium fire in the grill. A lightly oiled vegetable grill rack is optional but recommended.

2. Scrub the beets well. Cut the tops and roots off the beets. Slice about ¼ inch thick. Place in a bowl and toss with the oil until all the surfaces are well coated.

3. Grill the beets, turning or tossing a few times and brushing with more oil if desired, for 15 to 20 minutes. The beets are done when the slices are lightly charred and flexible. Taste one to be sure.

4. Remove from the grill and place in a serving bowl. Sprinkle with salt and pepper to taste and serve hot.

Beet Packets with Balsamic Vinegar and Walnuts

Less vigilance is required when you grill-bake in a foil packet, though the time is slightly increased and the grill flavor is lessened. The walnuts and balsamic vinegar provide a nice contrast of flavors and crunch to the sweet beets. Peeling the beets is optional. When beets are baked, the skins become tender but do not slip off as they do when they are boiled.

SERVES 4

8 medium-size beets (1½ to 1¾ pounds)
¼ cup walnut pieces
1 tablespoon extra-virgin olive oil
2 teaspoons balsamic vinegar
Salt and black pepper

1. Prepare a medium-hot fire in the grill.

2. Scrub the beets well. Cut the roots off and trim them, leaving 2 inches of the beet tops. Peel, if desired. Leave baby beets whole, but cut larger beets into ½-inch-thick slices. Divide the beets and walnuts between 2 large pieces of heavy-duty foil. Drizzle ½ tablespoon of the olive oil and 1 teaspoon of the vinegar over each packet. Sprinkle generously with salt and pepper. Seal the packets so no liquid or steam will escape (see page 245).

3. Grill the beet packets for about 25 minutes. Open a packet and test with a fork to be sure the beets are tender. Baby beets should be tested for doneness after 15 minutes.

4. Serve hot. The packets will hold their heat for about 15 minutes after they are removed from the grill. Serve in the packets, or empty all the packets into a serving bowl and serve from the bowl.

On Timing

All grilling times are approximate. If the weather is very cold, or very windy, grilling times are affected. If the vegetables are dead-ripe, they will contain more water and will cook more quickly than if they are slightly underripe. Always rely on your own judgment—taste a piece of vegetable to make sure it is done before removing the food from the grill.

Roasted Bell Pepper

Roasted bell peppers, particularly red bell peppers, enhance dozens of dishes from dips to salads, from sautés to soups. Be sure to catch the juices from inside the pepper—adding them to whatever dish you are preparing will greatly increase the sweet pepper presence. This method works with any pepper, but it is particularly well suited to red bell peppers.

MAKES 1 PEPPER

1 bell pepper

1. Prepare a medium-hot fire in the grill.

2. Place the pepper on the grill and roast, turning occasionally, until completely charred, about 10 minutes. Place the pepper in a plastic or paper bag to steam for 10 minutes to loosen the skin.

3. Holding the pepper over a bowl, slit the pepper and allow the juices to drain out. Peel off the skin and discard. On a cutting board, cut the pepper in half and remove the seeds, core, and membranes from inside. Chop or slice the pepper and use in a recipe.

Variation: **Roasted Chiles.** The same method works for chiles. Because chiles are often smaller, and sometimes not waxed, they may char in less time, so watch carefully.

Grilled Bok Choy

Bok choy is a surprise vegetable for the grill, but tasting is believing. Grilling gives the slightly sweet stems a faint smoke flavor but still leaves them juicy.

SERVES 4 TO 6

4 large or 8 small stems bok choy
Toasted sesame oil
Soy sauce

1. Prepare a medium-hot fire in the grill.

2. Cut the stems from the base of the bok choy, wash well, and dry thoroughly. Brush with sesame oil.

3. Grill, turning occasionally, until tender, about 8 minutes.

4. To serve, cut each stem into 3-inch lengths or slice about ½ inch thick, depending on how you want it to look on the plate. Drizzle a little soy sauce on top and serve hot.

About Bok Choy

Bok choy, a member the Chinese cabbage family, has long white stems fringed with green leaves. Look for firm, unblemished speci-mens and avoid limp bok choy, which will be either bland-tasting or bitter.

Soy-Grilled Broccoli

This is an all-time favorite way to enjoy broccoli. Like regular stir-fried broccoli, this makes a delicious topping for rice. It goes well with grilled tofu (see
pages 50 to 51).

SERVES 4 TO 6

3 stalks broccoli
½ cup Lemon-Soy Marinade and Salad Dressing (page 278)

1. Prepare a medium-hot fire in the grill with a lightly oiled vegetable grill
rack or grill-wok in place.

2. Trim the broccoli by stripping away the leaves and tough outer peel. Cut
the stems into thin strips or slice on the diagonal about ¼ inch thick. Separate
the florets into bite-size pieces. Pour the marinade over the broccoli and toss to
coat.

3. Lift the broccoli out of the marinade with a slotted spoon and grill, tossing frequently, until tender and grill-marked, about 5 minutes.

4. Serve hot. Pour any leftover marinade into a small pitcher and pass at the
table with the broccoli.

Variations

Chinese Barbecued Broccoli. Substitute 1/2 cup Chinese Barbecue
Marinade (page 278) for the Lemon-Soy Marinade. Proceed with the
recipe as above.

Chinese Grilled Vegetables. Instead of using just broccoli with either
marinade, use 2 to 3 carrots, thinly sliced, and half of the broccoli, prepared as above. Proceed with the recipe as above.

A Fire-Starting Trick

This trick comes from Deborah Solomon, food writer for the *Burlington* (Vermont) *Free Press:* Take a cardboard egg carton and place a charcoal briquette in each egg hole. Light the carton with a match. The carton will easily ignite, which will, in turn, ignite the charcoal and your fire will be started.

Basic Grilled
Baby Carrots

Grilling carrots is a superior way to prepare them. The heat of the fire caramelizes the natural sugars in the carrots, giving them a crisp exterior. I like them slightly undercooked, but you can let them cook a bit longer if you like them soft.

SERVES 4

1 pound baby carrots
2 tablespoons extra-virgin olive oil or toasted sesame oil
Coarse salt

1. Prepare a medium fire in the grill with a lightly oiled vegetable grill rack in place.

2. Scrub the carrots. Toss with the oil to coat well.

3. Grill the carrots, tossing frequently, until tender and grill-marked, about 10 minutes. The carrots will char if you don't pay attention. Remove from the grill when they are soft enough to your liking.

4. Place in a serving bowl, sprinkle lightly with salt to taste, and serve hot.

Honey-Ginger
Glazed Carrots

The ginger, sesame, and soy give a Chinese twist to these glazed carrots, though not so definitively that you'll feel you can only serve them to accompany a stir-fry. Although I am not a big fan of cooked carrots in general, I am a very big fan of these delightful carrots.

SERVES 4

1 tablespoon toasted sesame oil
1 tablespoon honey
1 tablespoon finely minced ginger
2 garlic cloves, minced
1 teaspoon soy sauce
1 pound carrots, quartered lengthwise and cut into
*   3-inch to 4-inch lengths*

1. Prepare a medium-hot fire in the grill with a lightly oiled vegetable grill rack in place.

2. Combine the sesame oil, honey, ginger, garlic, and soy sauce and mix well. Pour over the carrots and toss to coat.

3. Grill the carrots, tossing frequently, until tender and grill-marked, about 10 minutes.

4. Place on a serving platter, drizzle any remaining glaze over the carrots, and serve hot.

Marinated Cauliflower

One might not think that cauliflower would do well on the grill, but it does. Indeed, when it comes to flavor, marinated grilled cauliflower rates far above any other more traditional preparation.

SERVES 4 TO 6

1 head cauliflower, broken into florets
¼ cup Classic Vinaigrette (page 271), Basic Herb Marinade and
  Salad Dressing (page 272), Lemon-Garlic Marinade (page
  273), Garlic-Herb Marinade (page 274), Tandoori Marinade
  (page 276), Teriyaki Marinade and Dipping Sauce (page
  277), Chinese Barbecue Marinade (page 278), Lemon-Soy
  Marinade and Salad Dressing (page 278), or your favorite
  Italian-style salad dressing

1. Combine the cauliflower and marinade in a large bowl and set aside to marinate.

2. Prepare a medium-hot fire in the grill with a lightly oiled vegetable grill rack in place (unless you plan to skewer the cauliflower).

3. Either skewer the cauliflower or lift out of marinade with a slotted spoon and grill on the vegetable grill rack. Grill the cauliflower, turning occasionally or tossing frequently, until tender and lightly grill-marked, about 10 minutes. Serve hot.

"Cauliflower is nothing but cabbage
with a college education."
—Mark Twain

Zen and the Art of Corn

It would seem that peeling back the husks and removing the silks from an ear of corn is a simple enough task. You might even be tempted to assign a child to it. But beware, a gentle touch and a conscious presence are required if the corn is, indeed, freshly picked. When the corn is fresh, the husks are crisp and likely to snap off. There is a simple solution: Replace the husks, including any broken-off ones, and secure with a piece of kitchen twine. The string will scorch but not burn, and the ears will be nicely covered.

Basic Corn-on-the-Cob

The quintessential flavor of summer—grilled corn. Roasting corn in its husk enhances its "corny" flavor. Roasting corn without its husks, as on page 28, enhances the smoke flavor. Try to find a farmstand that still grows and sells old-fashioned varieties. The new supersweet corn has sacrificed corn flavor for sweetness.

SERVES 6

6 ears corn, unhusked
Butter (optional)

1. Peel back the husks from the corn and remove the silks. Bring the husks back over the cobs. Place in water to soak for at least 10 minutes.
2. Prepare a medium-hot fire in the grill.
3. Grill the corn, turning frequently, until the husks are dry and the kernels are beginning to brown, 15 to 20 minutes.
4. Serve hot off the grill, with butter, if desired.

Variation: Corn-on-the-Cob for a Crowd. When you are grilling large quantities of corn, you don't need to bother with the silk removal, although it is a good idea to trim the silks with a pair of kitchen shears to avoid flare-ups. (But again, in really large quantities, you won't want to bother with this either.) Let the corn soak in cold water for about 1 hour or up to 6 hours. Grill the corn, turning frequently, until the husks are dry and the kernels are beginning to brown, 15 to 20 minutes.

Herb Butter–Basted Corn-on-the-Cob

This may be gilding the lily, but it is a wonderful way to enjoy fresh corn—and you need less butter than you might think. The choice of herb is limited only to what you can pluck outside your kitchen door or buy at the store.

SERVES 6

6 ears corn, unhusked
1 fresh herb sprig (such as basil, cilantro, oregano, thyme, savory,
    chives, garlic chives)
1 garlic clove
½ teaspoon salt
1½ tablespoons unsalted butter

1. Prepare a medium-hot fire in the grill.
2. Peel back the husks from the corn and remove the silks. Place in water to soak for at least 10 minutes.
3. On a cutting board or in a mortar, combine the herb, garlic, and salt. Mince finely or pulverize. Add the butter to the mortar or combine in a bowl with the herb mixture, and work until you have a smooth paste. Lightly spread on the corn. Bring the husks back over the cobs.
4. Grill the corn, turning frequently, until the husks are dry and the kernels are beginning to brown, 15 to 20 minutes. Serve hot off the grill.

Variations

Pesto-Grilled Corn. Substitute 3 tablespoons Pesto (page 282) or Cilantro Pesto (page 283) for the herb butter. Brush on the corn as above.

Jerk Corn. Substitute Jerk Paste (page 232) for the herb butter. The recipe makes enough for a dozen ears of corn.

Quick Corn

This is a quick, no-fuss way to prepare corn. If I want to add grilled corn to a salad or soup, this is the method I rely on. The corn picks up the maximum grill flavor this way.

SERVES 6

6 ears corn, husks and silks removed
Olive oil or melted butter

1. Prepare a medium-hot fire in the grill.
2. Brush the corn with the olive oil or butter.
3. Grill the corn, turning occasionally, until tender and grill-marked, about 10 minutes. Serve hot.

First Came the Corn Roast

The first European settlers in America learned to eat corn from the Native Americans. It is more than likely that their first sample was of corn grilled with the husks still on. This slow-roasting caramelizes the natural sugars in corn and is arguably the best way to enjoy this versatile vegetable.

Today, grilled corn can be found as street food around the globe. According to Elizabeth Rozin in her fascinating book *Blue Corn and Chocolate* (Alfred A. Knopf, New York, 1992), only in America is corn likely to be boiled, then brushed with butter. In Mexico, India, and Southeast Asia, husked corn-on-the-cob is roasted over charcoal, then dressed with salt, ground dried chiles, and an occasional squeeze of lemon or lime juice.

Curried Corn-on-the-Cob

The sweetness of the corn plays beautifully against the coconut-based curry baste.

SERVES 6

6 ears corn, unhusked
¼ cup thick coconut milk (see Note)
2 tablespoons chopped fresh cilantro
1 tablespoon curry powder
½ teaspoon salt
⅛ to ¼ teaspoon ground red pepper

1. Prepare a medium-hot fire in the grill.

2. Peel back the husks from the corn and remove the silks.

3. Combine the coconut milk, cilantro, curry powder, salt, and red pepper in a small bowl and mix well. Brush on the corn. Bring the husks back over the cobs.

4. Grill the corn, turning frequently, until the husks are dry and the kernels are beginning to brown, 15 to 20 minutes. Serve hot off the grill.

Note: Coconut milk is readily found in supermarkets these days. If you don't shake the can before opening, the thicker solids will float on top of the thinner milk and can be skimmed off. Thick coconut milk will enable the marinade to cling better to the corn.

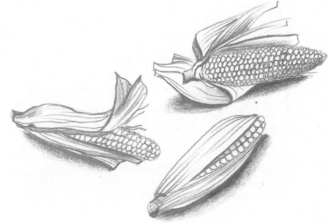

Eggplant Steaks

A good grilled eggplant steak, like a good mushroom steak, is a vegetarian's delight. The key to great flavor is to marinate the eggplant before grilling. If you choose a classic or Italian-style marinade, you can build a traditional Western-style meal around the eggplant, serving it with, say, a potato dish or a grain and a salad. Or you can work it into a sandwich with cheese and sliced tomatoes and onions. Alternatively, you can make an Asian-inspired meal out of it by marinating the eggplant in a soy-based sauce and serving it with rice and a stir-fry.

SERVES 4

1 medium-size eggplant, peeled and sliced 3/8 inch thick
⅓ cup Classic Vinaigrette (page 271), Basic Herb Marinade and
* Salad Dressing (page 272), Lemon-Garlic Marinade (page*
* 273), Garlic-Herb Marinade (page 274), Teriyaki Marinade*
* and Dipping Sauce (page 277), Chinese Barbecue Marinade*
* (page 278), Lemon-Soy Marinade and Salad Dressing (page*
* 278), or your favorite Italian-style or soy-based salad*
* dressing*

1. Prepare a medium-hot fire in the grill.
2. In a shallow bowl, combine the eggplant and marinade. Toss well to coat.

The Trouble with Eggplant

Perhaps no vegetable takes to the flame like eggplant, but no vegetable is quite as difficult to do right. When eggplant is grilled to perfection, it is slightly crusty on the outside, but very soft and moist inside. Start with slices about 3/8 inch thick (if too thin, it will char; if too thick, it will dry out). Brush it with oil *just* before grilling. Eggplant absorbs oil like a sponge, and you need the oil to be on the surface to get a nice crust. Grill over a hot fire to seal the outside. Slow-grilled eggplant becomes dry and firm—a rather unpleasant texture.

> ## About Belgian Endive
>
> These slightly bitter-tasting greens are grown in the dark so they never develop much color. The white spear-shaped leaves with yellow tips come in tightly packed heads, which make them easy to handle on the grill. Look for firm specimens; limp Belgian endive has probably sat around for a while and will be quite bitter. This green is also known as Witloof chicory.

Let the eggplant stand for at least 15 minutes to absorb the marinade.

3. Grill the eggplant, turning occasionally, until tender and grill-marked, about 10 minutes. The eggplant should be slightly crusty on the outside but soft and moist inside. Serve hot.

Basic Grilled Endive

Belgian endive makes an incredibly elegant presentation. First, there's the surprise of a grilled green. Then there is the lovely appearance on the plate. Grilled endive makes a perfect accompaniment to almost any grilled dish.

SERVES 4

4 heads Belgian endive
Extra-virgin olive oil
Coarse salt and freshly ground black pepper
Shaved Parmesan cheese or balsamic vinegar (optional)

1. Prepare a medium-hot fire in the grill.

2. Slice the endive in half lengthwise; do not trim the root end. Brush with olive oil.

3. Grill the endive until tender and lightly grill-marked, 4 to 7 minutes per side.

4. To serve, sprinkle with salt and pepper to taste. If desired, top with a sprinkling of shaved Parmesan or balsamic vinegar.

Basic Grilled Fennel

With its distinctive licorice flavor, fennel is a vegetable most people either love or abhor. When cooked, fennel's flavor is somewhat more delicate than when it is served raw. Grilling is an excellent treatment for it. When buying fennel, or finocchio, look for crisp, white bulbs, with fresh green leaves.

SERVES 4

2 fennel bulbs
2 tablespoons extra-virgin olive oil
Salt and black pepper

1. Prepare a medium-hot fire in the grill with a lightly oiled vegetable grill rack in place.

2. Cut off and discard the fennel stalks, including the feathery leaves (set aside some for a garnish, if desired). Remove any wilted outer stalks. Cut off the base. Wash well, then slice about ¼ inch thick. Transfer to a medium-size bowl, sprinkle with the oil, and toss to coat.

3. Grill the fennel, turning occasionally, until quite tender and grill-marked, 10 to 12 minutes.

4. Place the fennel in a serving bowl. Season generously with salt and pepper. Garnish with the reserved fennel leaves, if desired, and serve hot.

Grill-Roasted Garlic

Roasted garlic has an infinite number of uses. It is delicious spread on grill-toasted bread. It can be added to marinades, salad dressings, soups, and stews for additional flavor. Anywhere that garlic is good, roasted garlic is better. Roasting the garlic mellows its flavor, so a whole bulb of roasted garlic can be added where 2 to 4 raw cloves would have been more than enough.

Freshness Counts with Garlic

Garlic bulbs may be good keepers compared to most herbs, but freshness counts. Toward the end of the spring, produce sellers are offering garlic that was harvested almost a year ago, and its flavor can be harsh and bitter.

When buying garlic, look for plump, firm bulbs with dry papery skins. Avoid ones that have begun to sprout little green tips. If the garlic you bring home begins to sprout, slice each clove in half and remove the green shoot in the center. Blanching the cloves for about 3 minutes in boiling water will also help to reduce the harsh flavor.

MAKES 1 BULB

1 garlic bulb
1 tablespoon extra-virgin olive oil
Sprig of fresh thyme or rosemary (optional)

1. Prepare a medium fire in the grill.

2. Remove as much of the outer papery skin from the garlic as possible. Using a sharp knife or a pair of kitchen scissors, snip off the tips of the cloves to expose the garlic within. Place the bulb on a square of heavy-duty foil. Drizzle the olive oil over the bulb. Place the herbs, if using, on top. Wrap the bulb in the foil to form a tightly sealed packet.

3. Grill for about 10 minutes. If the bulb is easy to squeeze, remove from the heat. Otherwise continue grilling until the garlic is softened, about 5 minutes more.

4. Open the packet and allow the garlic to cool. When cool enough to handle, separate the bulb into individual cloves. Peel the cloves or squeeze out the pulp.

Vegetable Grilling Guide

Vegetable	Preparation	Approximate Grilling Time (in minutes)
Asparagus	Trim ends, leave spears whole. Brush with oil or toss with marinade.	8
Beans	Trim ends. Brush with oil or toss with marinade.	8 to 10
Beets	Slice 1/4 inch thick. Brush with oil or toss with marinade.	15 to 20
Bell and chile peppers	*Whole*: Grill until blackened all over. Steam inside a bag for 10 minutes. Peel, seed, and chop.	10
	Slices: Slice any thickness. Toss with oil or marinade.	8 to 10
Bok choy	Leave stems whole; slice baby bok choy in half lengthwise. Brush with oil or marinade.	8
Broccoli	Slice stems 1/4 inch thick. Cut florets into bite-size pieces. Toss with oil or marinade.	About 5
Carrots	Leave baby carrots whole. Slice large carrots into sticks.	10
Cauliflower	Separate head into florets. Toss with oil or marinade.	10
Corn	*With husks*: Baste with butter or oil or soak in water for 1 hour.	15 to 25
	Without husks: Brush lightly with butter or oil.	About 10
Eggplant	*Whole*: Prick several times with a fork. Drain well after grilling.	35 to 40
	Slices: Slice 3/8 inch thick. Brush with oil or marinade just before grilling.	10 to 15
Endive	Slice in half lengthwise. Brush with oil or marinade.	4 to 7
Fennel	Slice the bulb about 1/4 inch thick. Toss with oil or marinade.	10 to 12
Garlic	*Whole*: Trim the outer papery skin. Cut off the tops to expose the cloves. Brush with oil. Wrap in foil.	10 to 15
	Cloves: Skewer peeled cloves and brush with oil.	About 10
Leeks	Trim away the root ends and dark green leaves. Slice in half lengthwise and clean thoroughly. Brush with olive oil or marinade.	About 7
Mushrooms	*Whole*: Toss with oil or marinade.	About 10
	Slices: Toss with oil or marinade.	About 7

Vegetable Grilling Guide

Vegetable	Preparation	Approximate Grilling Time (in minutes)
Okra	Brush with melted butter, oil, or marinade.	8
Onions	*Thin slices*: Toss with oil or marinade.	10
	Thick slices: Brush with oil or marinade.	10 to 15
	Whole: Peel after grilling.	20
Potatoes	*Slices*: Slice 1/4 inch thick. Brush with oil or marinade.	15 to 25
	Whole: Wrap whole baking potatoes in foil.	60 to 90
Rutabagas	Slice thinly and brush with oil or melted butter.	12 to 15
Scallions	Brush with oil or marinade.	About 8
Summer squash, zucchini, or patty pan	Slice 3/8 inch thick. Brush or toss with oil or marinade.	8 to 10
Sweet potatoes	*Slices*: Slice 1/4 inch thick. Brush with oil or marinade.	15 to 20
	Whole: Wrap in foil.	About 45
Tofu	Drain. Slice 1/2 inch thick. Marinate in a soy-based marinade. Brush with glaze, if desired.	10
Tomatoes, beefsteak or plum	*Halves*: Brush cut sides with oil or marinade. Peel after grilling.	10
	Slices: Brush both sides with oil or marinade.	4 to 5 on first side, 1 to 2 on second side
Tomatoes, cherry	Slice in half. Toss with marinade or oil.	5
Winter squash	Peel. Slice 1/2 inch thick. Steam for 10 minutes. Toss with oil or marinade.	10

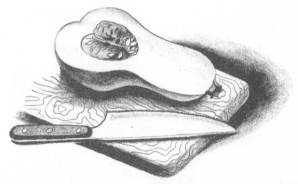

Basic Grilled Leeks

Leeks rank among the most ancient of vegetables, perhaps dating as far back as the Bronze Age. Four thousand years ago, the Assyrians were growing leeks in their gardens and recommending them as a preventative for graying hair. Leeks were among the rations given to pyramid builders in Egypt, and the Chinese included leeks in a guide to good eating that was written in about 1500 B.C. No doubt many of the ancient meals made with leeks were cooked directly over a wood fire. Try it, and you will experience a taste both ancient and contemporary.

SERVES 4

8 leeks
Extra-virgin olive oil or oil-and-vinegar based marinade
Coarse salt and freshly ground black pepper
Shaved Parmesan cheese or balsamic vinegar (optional)

1. Prepare a medium-hot fire in the grill.

2. Trim away the root ends of the leeks and all but 2 to 3 inches of the green leaves. Slice in half lengthwise and rinse under cold running water, fanning the leaves with your fingers to remove all the grit and sand. Pat dry. Brush with olive oil or marinade.

3. Grill the leeks, turning occasionally, until tender and lightly grill-marked, about 7 minutes.

4. To serve, sprinkle with salt and pepper. If desired, top with a sprinkling of shaved Parmesan or balsamic vinegar.

Sherry-Marinated Mushrooms

As fine a way to honor mushrooms as there can be. Serve these exquisite tidbits as an appetizer or a side dish. You can also fold them into an omelet, bake them in a quiche, or top a plate of buttered pasta with them. A true mushroom devotee might be content with a supper of these mushrooms on toast.

SERVES 4 TO 6

⅓ cup dry sherry
3 tablespoons extra-virgin olive oil
1 tablespoon sherry vinegar or wine vinegar
2 garlic cloves, minced
1 teaspoon dried thyme
Salt and black pepper
1½ pounds mushrooms, trimmed

1. Combine the sherry, olive oil, vinegar, garlic, thyme, and salt and pepper to taste in a large bowl. Add the mushrooms and toss to coat. Cover and let the mushrooms marinate at room temperature until most of the marinade has been absorbed, about 1 hour.

2. Meanwhile, prepare a medium-hot fire in the grill with a lightly oiled vegetable grill rack in place.

3. Grill the mushrooms, tossing frequently, until well browned, tender, and still juicy, about 10 minutes.

4. Remove the mushrooms to a bowl. Season with salt and pepper to taste and serve at once.

Variations

Mushrooms on a Stick. After marinating the mushrooms, thread them onto bamboo skewers that have been soaked in water for at least 30 minutes and grill as above. Serve as an appetizer.

Marinated Mushrooms. Substitute 1/2 cup of any marinade in Chapter 11 or your own favorite salad dressing or marinade. Grill as above.

A Field Guide to Mushrooms

Nothing takes to the grill quite so nicely as mushrooms. Their earthy flavor is the perfect match for the smoke of the grill. Exotic mushrooms are now easy to find in supermarkets, health food stores, and co-ops. Here's a guide to some of the mushrooms that are now available. Any mushroom you want to cook on the grill can be tossed with a little oil and grilled briefly until tender. Mushrooms should still be juicy when you remove them from the grill.

Button. These common white mushrooms are inexpensive, readily available, and very grill-worthy. The small ones are lovely on kabobs and the larger ones are good candidates for stuffing.

Chanterelle. Golden apricot in color, these mushrooms are delicate and expensive. They cook quickly, so stand by and be ready to remove them from the grill as soon as they are ready. You'll want to serve these pricey items plain, unadorned on garlic toasts, or tossed with pasta that has been dressed with a high-quality olive oil.

Cremini. Similar to the common white button mushroom, these mushrooms are brown and slightly more flavorful. Prepare them any way you would prepare button mushrooms.

Portobello. Portobellos are cremini mushrooms that have been allowed to keep growing and are large with open caps. Large ones can be grilled and slid between a bun just like a burger, or they can be stuffed, grilled, and served as an appetizer or main course. Their size and firm texture make them ideal for grilling, sliced or stuffed.

Shiitake. Fresh shiitake mushrooms (not dried) are another excellent candidate for the grill because they are strongly flavored and firm-textured. When buying shiitakes, look for firm, not limp, specimens. I've noticed shiitakes labeled "Oriental mushrooms" at the supermarket—which is sure to add to mushroom confusion. Discard the stems before grilling.

Basic Grilled Okra

Grilling okra is not going to make any new fans for this odd little vegetable, but those who already adore okra may be glad to have one more way to enjoy it. Grilling the pods seals in the viscous juices that are the signature of this relative of the hibiscus family.

SERVES 4

8 ounces okra pods
Melted butter
Lemon juice

1. Prepare a medium-hot fire in the grill.
2. Brush the okra pods with melted butter. Skewer or place in a hinged basket.
3. Grill until tender and grill-marked, about 4 minutes per side.
4. Toss with lemon juice and additional melted butter, if desired, and serve hot.

I Don't Do Brussels Sprouts

And I don't do parsnips. Just because a vegetable can be cooked on a grill doesn't mean it *should* be. Brussels sprouts require precooking before they can be grilled (otherwise they don't soften all the way through). But the precooking pretty much guarantees that Brussels sprouts will end up overcooked and tasting very cabbagey. Parsnips don't have enough natural sugar to benefit from the grilling process. Grilled, they taste like wanna-be carrots, decisively lacking the carrot's sweetness. Save them for soups.

Charred Onion Slivers

Grilled onion slices make a great topping for burgers, grilled mushrooms, and baked potatoes. I've even combined them in a food processor with cooked beans to create a dip strangely reminiscent of my mother's chopped liver.

SERVES 4 TO 6

*1 pound onions, thinly sliced
4 large garlic cloves, thinly sliced (optional)
2 tablespoons extra-virgin olive oil
Salt and white pepper*

1. Prepare a medium-hot fire in the grill with a vegetable grill rack in place.
2. Toss the onions and garlic, if using, with the olive oil.
3. Grill the onions and garlic, tossing frequently, until slightly charred, about 10 minutes.
4. Season with salt and pepper to taste and serve hot.

Charred-Onion Mashed Potatoes

A great complement to a grilled main dish. The onions convey just a whisper of grilled flavor.

SERVES 6

*1 large onion, thinly sliced
4 large garlic cloves, thinly sliced
1 tablespoon extra-virgin olive oil
2½ pounds potatoes, peeled and cut into small chunks
About 3 tablespoons butter, or to taste
Milk or buttermilk
Salt and white pepper*

1. Prepare a medium-hot fire in the grill with a vegetable grill rack in place.

2. Toss the onion and garlic with the olive oil.

3. Grill the onion and garlic, tossing frequently, until slightly charred, about 10 minutes. Set aside and keep warm.

4. Meanwhile, combine the potatoes with salted water to cover in a large pan. Bring to a boil and boil until very tender, about 10 minutes. Drain well.

5. Mash the potatoes, then beat in the butter and milk or buttermilk until the potatoes reach the desired consistency. Stir in the onion mixture, then season with salt and pepper to taste. Serve hot.

Herb-Grilled Potatoes

These very basic potatoes are a wonderful accompaniment to almost any food—grilled or otherwise.

SERVES 4

1½ pounds potatoes, preferably Yukon Gold
¼ cup extra-virgin olive oil
2 garlic cloves, minced
1 to 2 tablespoons chopped fresh rosemary, thyme, basil, or
*   oregano*
Salt and black pepper

1. Prepare a medium fire in the grill.

2. Peel the potatoes or scrub well, then slice ¼ inch thick. Place in a large bowl and toss with the olive oil, garlic, herbs, and salt and pepper to taste.

3. Grill the potatoes, turning frequently, until browned and tender, 15 to 25 minutes. Serve hot.

Golden Potato Wedges

You might expect that the 2 tablespoons of Louisiana-style hot sauce contribute an intense heat, but, in fact, these are just barely spicy. Instead, they are quite flavorful, and the hot sauce helps give the potatoes a golden crust.

SERVES 4

4 medium-size potatoes (1½ to 1¾ pounds)
2 tablespoons butter, melted
2 tablespoons Louisiana-style hot sauce
Salt and black pepper
Ground red pepper or paprika (optional)

1. Prepare a medium-hot fire in the grill.

2. Slice the potatoes in half lengthwise, then slice each half into 4 to 6 wedges. Combine in a bowl with the butter and hot sauce and toss to coat well. Season with salt and pepper to taste. For a little heat, dust with a little red pepper or paprika, if desired.

3. Grill the potatoes, basting with the hot sauce mixture and turning every 5 minutes, until golden and grill-marked, 15 to 25 minutes. Remove the wedges as they are done. Serve hot.

Variation: **Smoky Hot Potato Wedges.** Prepare as above, but instead of using ground red pepper, dust the potatoes with ground chipotle powder. It adds a deep smoky-hot flavor to the potatoes.

Potato Packets

As with all foil packets, the grill flavor is very subtle in this dish. Nonetheless, this is a fine and flavorful way to cook potatoes. Because the packets will hold their heat off the fire without overcooking the potatoes, it is a great side dish to choose when you are planning a meal that will involve some last-minute

Ground Chipotle Peppers

Chipotles (smoke-dried jalapeños) lend foods instant heat and smoke flavor. Ground chipotle powder can be left in a shaker bottle on the table to season grilled foods, such as grilled potatoes. A good source for ground chipotles is Penzey's Ltd., a mail-order spice company. To obtain a catalog, write Penzey's, 1921 S. West Avenue, Waukesha, WI 53186, or phone 414-574-0277.

grilling. Grill these first, then move the packets off to a cool spot on the side of the grill.

SERVES 4

> *3 tablespoons butter, melted*
> *2 tablespoons chopped fresh parsley*
> *2 garlic cloves, minced*
> *12 small red potatoes*
> *Coarse salt and black pepper*

1. Prepare a medium fire in the grill.

2. Combine the butter, parsley, and garlic in a small bowl.

3. With a sharp knife, make slits in the potatoes ⅛ inch to ¼ inch apart, cutting almost, but not quite, to the bottom of each potato so the potato stays intact. Brush the butter mixture onto the potatoes, forcing it into the slits. Divide the potatoes among 4 large pieces of heavy-duty foil. Sprinkle generously with salt and pepper. Seal the packets so no liquid or steam will escape (see page 245).

4. Grill the packets until the potatoes are tender, 15 to 20 minutes. Open one of the packets and test with a fork after about 15 minutes. Move the packets around to avoid cooking any one packet over a hot spot.

5. The packets will hold their heat off the grill for 15 to 20 minutes. Serve while still hot.

When the Lid Is Up

Though this recipe calls for grilling with the lid down, you may want to grill a second vegetable, probably with the lid up. Don't worry about it; the lid can go up—but you may need to add a little extra baking time.

Foil-Wrapped
Grill-Baked Potatoes

Never underestimate the time it takes to grill-bake a potato—usually it will take a full hour and sometimes a little more. The foil wrapping does not allow smoke flavor to penetrate the potatoes, but the method does allow you to make baked potatoes without turning on your oven and heating up your kitchen or when camping.

SERVES 4

4 medium-to-large russet potatoes
Oil or butter (optional)
*Optional toppings: Butter, sour cream, chopped chives, grated
    cheese*

1. Prepare a medium fire in the grill.

2. Scrub the potatoes and dry them thoroughly. Lightly oil or butter the skins, if desired. Wrap each potato in foil and place on the grill.

3. Grill the potatoes, with the lid down, turning occasionally, until tender when pierced with a fork or squeezed, about 60 minutes.

4. The potatoes will stay warm off the grill in their foil packets for up to 30 minutes. To serve, unwrap and return to the grill for a final 10 minutes to allow the skins to become crisp. Or fold the foil back, cut a cross on the top of each potato, and squeeze to fluff up the center. Add toppings as desired and serve hot.

Variation: **Foil-Wrapped Grill-Baked Sweet Potatoes.** Substitute sweet potatoes for the russet potatoes. Wrap in foil and grill-bake as above, but for only about 45 minutes. Serve as above.

Butter-Basted Rutabaga Chips

Rutabagas are available year-round because these yellow turnips are heavily waxed and make good keepers. However, their flavor is definitely best in the fall, when they are first harvested and taste sweetest. By summer a pretty strong cabbage flavor dominates, and this flavor is brought out by the grill. Slice as thinly as possible—less than ¼ inch thick is ideal.

SERVES 4

1 rutabaga, peeled, quartered, and thinly sliced
3 tablespoons butter, melted
Salt and black pepper

1. Prepare a medium-hot fire in the grill. A lightly oiled vegetable grill rack is optional but recommended.

2. Toss the rutabagas with the butter and sprinkle with salt and pepper to taste.

3. Grill the rutabagas, turning or tossing occasionally, until tender and grill-marked, 12 to 15 minutes. Serve hot.

Herbed
Summer Squash Chips

This basic recipe will work with zucchini, yellow summer squash, or patty pan squash. It is an appealing way to prepare these rather bland but ubiquitous summer vegetables. My son Sam calls this "the best way I ever tasted zucchini." Since we grow our own and face an overabundance every year, the compliment is high praise.

Summer squash is mostly water; it shrinks considerably as it grills. Nonetheless, cooking enough to feed four as a side dish will require all your grill space, and you may even have to grill in two batches.

SERVES 4

1½ to 2 pounds zucchini, yellow summer squash, or patty pan
squash, sliced ⅜ inch thick
3 to 4 tablespoons extra-virgin olive oil
4 garlic cloves
2 tablespoons chopped fresh herbs (such as parsley, basil,
oregano, lovage, thyme, lemon-thyme)
Salt and black pepper

1. Prepare a medium-hot fire in the grill.
2. Combine the squash, olive oil, garlic, herbs, and salt and pepper to taste. Toss gently to coat.
3. Grill the squash chips until grill-marked and tender, about 5 minutes for the first side and 4 minutes for the second side. Serve hot.

Variations: Instead of the olive oil and fresh herbs, substitute 1/4 cup of any of the oil- or soy-based marinades that appear in Chapter 11. Summer squash should be regarded as a neutral canvas on which to paint any number of flavors.

The Flying Saucer Squash

I admired the looks of patty pan squash for years before I had the courage to buy some. They are simply yellow summer squash that come in a strange shape—more like a flying saucer or a gourd than a zucchini. Inside, the flesh is very similar to yellow summer squash in both flavor and texture. The oddball shape of the slices makes them very attractive on the plate. As with all summer squash, the smaller the squash, the less watery the flesh.

Basic Grilled Sweet Potatoes

Because of its sweet, moist flesh, the Beauregard variety is my preferred sweet potato for grilling. Also, the long, narrow shape of the yam makes it perfect for slicing. This is a very simple recipe that allows the rich flavor of the sweet potato to dominate. I like the coarse crystals of kosher salt on these potatoes, but any coarse salt can be used.

SERVES 4 TO 6

2 pounds sweet potatoes
2 tablespoons vegetable oil
Coarse salt

1. Prepare a medium-low fire in the grill.
2. Scrub the potatoes well or peel them, then trim the ends and slice ¼ inch thick. Toss with the oil to coat.
3. Grill the potatoes until tender and grill-marked, 15 to 20 minutes. Check frequently; the potatoes char easily.
4. Remove from the grill, sprinkle lightly with salt, and serve hot.

Honey-Mustard
Sweet Potatoes

Mustard acts as a tangy foil for the sweetness of the potatoes, but honey mustard guarantees that the sweet flavors prevail.

SERVES 4 TO 6

2 pounds sweet potatoes
2 tablespoons canola oil
2 tablespoons honey mustard
1 tablespoon fresh lemon juice
½ teaspoon dried thyme
¼ teaspoon black pepper
Coarse salt

1. Prepare a medium-low fire in the grill.

2. Scrub the potatoes well or peel them, then trim the ends and slice ¼ inch thick.

3. Combine the canola oil, mustard, lemon juice, thyme, and pepper in a medium-size bowl. Add the sweet potato slices and toss to coat.

4. Grill the potatoes, turning occasionally, until tender and grill-marked, 15 to 20 minutes. Check frequently; the potatoes char easily.

5. Remove from the grill, sprinkle lightly with salt, and serve hot.

Sweet Potatoes with Maple-Lime Marinade

Some vegetables are just meant to be roasted over a flame, and sweet potatoes definitely fall into that category. Here they are first immersed in the flavors of maple and lime, the fruity sweet essence of which acts as a foil for the smoke. Although usually served as a side dish, sweet potato slices also make a delicious appetizer.

SERVES 4 TO 6

2 pounds sweet potatoes
1 recipe Maple-Lime Marinade (page 275)

1. Scrub the potatoes well or peel them, then trim the ends and slice horizontally into ¼-inch-thick rounds. Place in a large bowl, add the marinade, and toss to coat each slice.

2. Prepare a medium-low fire in the grill.

3. Lift the sweet potatoes out of the marinade with a slotted spoon and grill, turning occasionally and basting with the remaining marinade, until tender when pierced with a fork, 15 to 20 minutes. Serve hot.

Super Sweet Potatoes

One sweet potato contains only 140 calories yet provides twice the recommended daily allowance of vitamin A and almost half the needed vitamin C. It is an excellent source of calcium, iron, and thiamin. Sweet potatoes are low in sodium and a good source of fiber—with the skin, a sweet potato has more fiber than a bowl of oatmeal. It is considered the most nutritious of vegetables and has been cited as one of the top four cancer-fighting foods. The truly amazing thing is that sweet potatoes are delicious—and they taste even better grilled.

Basic Grilled Tofu

Tofu is easy to prepare on the grill, provided you take the time to press out the excess moisture. Grilling on a vegetable grill rack will ensure that the tofu doesn't fall apart and into the fire. A light coating of oil will yield a nice crust. But grilled tofu alone is boring, so plan to make a mushroom gravy or serve with a soy-based dipping sauce, such as Teriyaki Marinade and Dipping Sauce (page 277).

SERVES 4 TO 6

2 pounds firm or extra-firm tofu
1 tablespoon soy sauce
1 tablespoon toasted sesame oil or peanut oil

1. Wrap the tofu in a clean cotton kitchen towel. Place a heavy weight on top (such as a cutting board weighted with a heavy juice can). Set aside for at least 30 minutes to allow the excess water to drain from the tofu.

2. Prepare a medium-hot fire in the grill with a lightly oiled vegetable grill rack in place.

3. Slice each block of tofu into ½-inch-thick slices. Combine the soy sauce and oil and brush on the tofu.

4. Grill the tofu until browned and a slight crust forms, about 5 minutes per side. Serve hot.

Variations

Basic Grilled Marinated Tofu. Replace the soy sauce and oil with 1/2 cup Chinese Soy–Black Bean Marinade and Dressing (page 280) or Spicy Chinese Marinade and Dressing (page 280). Pour over the sliced tofu and let sit for about 30 minutes to allow the marinade to be absorbed. Then grill as above.

Teriyaki Tofu. Replace the soy sauce and oil with 1/2 cup Teriyaki Marinade and Dipping Sauce (page 277). Brush onto the sliced tofu, then grill as above. Additional marinade can be served as a dipping sauce at the table.

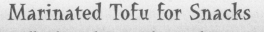

Marinated Tofu for Snacks

Whenever you grill tofu, make extra for snacking on. My kids and I especially enjoy grilled marinated tofu, right out of the refrigerator. We snack on it the way you might grab a piece of cheese when you want a protein snack to keep you going.

Basic Grilled
Tomato Slices

I prefer to use plum tomatoes for grilled slices as they hold their shape best, but you can use regular beefsteak-type tomatoes. The trick is to grill the tomatoes until pretty much done on the first side, then flip and grill very briefly on the second side. Don't overcook or the tomato will fall apart. A vegetable grill rack, which isn't 100 percent necessary, enables you to slip the spatula under the tomatoes without damaging the soft flesh.

SERVES 4

4 to 8 medium-size to large tomatoes, sliced ¼ to ⅓ inch thick
*3 to 4 tablespoons extra-virgin olive oil or ¼ cup Classic
        Vinaigrette (page 271), Basic Herb Marinade and Salad
        Dressing (page 272), Lemon-Garlic Marinade (page 273),
        Garlic-Herb Marinade (page 274), or your favorite Italian-
        style salad dressing*
Salt and black pepper (optional)

1. Prepare a medium-hot fire in the grill. A lightly oiled grilled rack is optional but recommended.

2. Brush the tomatoes with the olive oil or marinade.

3. Grill the tomatoes until tender and grill-marked, about 5 minutes. Then flip carefully and grill on the second side until lightly grill-marked, 1 to 2 minutes more. Avoid overcooking.

4. Remove from the grill, taste, and add salt and pepper if needed. Serve hot.

Basic Grilled Cherry Tomatoes

Although you can grill these little marbles on skewers, they will absorb more flavor from the smoke and marinade if they are halved and grilled on a vegetable grill rack.

SERVES 4

1 pint cherry or yellow pear tomatoes
2 tablespoons Basic Herb Marinade and Salad Dressing (page 272), Classic Vinaigrette (page 271), Lemon-Garlic Marinade (page 273), Garlic-Herb Marinade (page 274), or Lemon-Soy Marinade and Salad Dressing (page 278)
Salt and black pepper (optional)

1. Prepare a medium-hot fire in the grill with a lightly oiled vegetable grill rack in place.

2. Toss the tomatoes with the marinade. Lift them out of the marinade with a slotted spoon and grill, flipping carefully with a spatula once or twice, until tender and grill-marked, about 5 minutes. Avoid overcooking; the tomatoes should still retain their rounded shape.

3. Remove from the grill, taste, and add salt and pepper, if needed. Serve hot.

Variation: Cherry Tomato Kabobs. You can grill cherry tomatoes, whole or halved, on kabob skewers. If you cut them in half first and toss them with the marinade, they will have more flavor than if you leave them whole, but either way works. Grill the tomatoes until tender, 3 to 5 minutes, turning a few times.

Basic Grilled
Winter Squash

Although it is possible to grill winter squash slices from start to finish without precooking, I prefer to steam the squash first; this results in a slightly moister squash. Winter squash skins are not edible; for the grill they are peeled before steaming. Easy-to-peel types include buttercup, butternut, banana, and delicata.

SERVES 4 TO 6

1 medium-size winter squash (1½ to 2 pounds)
2 tablespoons vegetable oil
Coarse salt

1. Prepare a medium-low fire in the grill with a lightly oiled vegetable grill rack in place.

2. Peel the squash, cut in half horizontally, remove the fibers and seeds, and slice about ½ inch thick.

3. Steam the squash over boiling water until the flesh is just tender, about 10 minutes. Toss with the oil to coat well.

4. Grill the squash, turning occasionally, until tender and grill-marked, about 10 minutes. Check frequently; squash will char easily.

5. Remove from the grill, sprinkle lightly with salt, and serve hot.

Using Leftover Marinades

It is completely safe to take a marinade that has been used with a vegetable and serve it at the table as a dipping sauce. Indeed, soy-based marinades are delicious poured over rice and served alongside soy-grilled vegetables. Don't try this with meat, however. Any marinade that has come in contact with raw meat is a potential carrier of bacteria and must be boiled for 10 minutes before reusing or discarded.

Grilled Butternut Squash with Maple-Lime Glaze

Butternut squash is my favorite squash for just about any cooking purpose. It is perfect for the grill because it is easy to peel with a vegetable peeler and because the flesh retains a lovely moist texture, even when subjected to the drying heat of a fire.

SERVES 4 TO 6

1 medium-size butternut squash (1½ to 2 pounds)
1 recipe Maple-Lime Glaze (page 284)

1. Prepare a medium-low fire in the grill.

2. Peel the squash, cut in half horizontally, remove the fibers and seeds, and slice about ½ inch thick.

3. Steam the squash over boiling water until the flesh is just tender, about 10 minutes. Brush the marinade onto the warm squash.

4. Grill until grill-marked on the bottom side, about 5 minutes. Check frequently; squash will char easily. If there are hot spots, you may want to rotate the positions of the pieces. Brush with the glaze, turn each slice, and grill until tender throughout and grill-marked on both sides.

5. Remove from the grill, and brush on any remaining glaze. Serve hot.

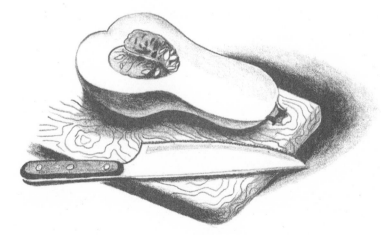

The Surprise Vegetables

Everyone knows that the standard kabob vegetables—onions, mushrooms, peppers, and summer squash—lend themselves to grilling. Their juicy textures make them self-basting. But the surprise is that most every vegetable benefits from grilling—and that includes many greens (radicchio, bok choy, endive), broccoli and cauliflower, and, especially, most root vegetables, such as rutabagas and beets. If you've ever had a roasted vegetable you enjoyed, expect that you will also appreciate it grilled.

3

Appetizers
and Soups from
the Grill

Bruschetta

Bread grilled lightly, rubbed with garlic, then topped with high-quality olive oil is the starter for many meals in Italy. You can stop right there and enjoy grilled food at its most simple and basic best. Or you can add toppings, such as the ones listed below.

Start with high-quality coarse-crumbed Italian bread, sliced at least ½ inch thick. Grill over a medium fire until lightly toasted, about 2 minutes per side. Then rub with a cut clove of garlic.

Top with any one or a combination of the following, if desired:

* Sliced fresh tomatoes, with or without a sprinkling of chopped fresh basil
* Pesto (page 282)
* Sliced fresh mozzarella
* Shaved Parmesan cheese, with or without a little chopped arugula
* Goat cheese with grilled peppers or zucchini
* Grilled sliced mushrooms and a shaving of Parmesan cheese
* Grill-Roasted Garlic (page 32)
* Grilled marinated mushrooms and artichoke hearts. (Grill on skewers, as specified in the recipe on page 67, or on top of a vegetable grill rack, then use as a topping.)
* Grilled vegetable slices, such as eggplant, zucchini, onions, or tomatoes
* Olivada (page 177)
* Marinated Roasted Pepper and Olive Salad (page 100), with or without a little Parmesan cheese
* Grilled Red Pepper Relish (page 126), with or without goat cheese

Cheese Quesadillas with Grilled Peppers

Quesadillas are nothing more than flour tortillas stuffed with melted cheese and other fillings, then folded over or left flat and topped with another tortilla. They make great snacks for kids and go wonderfully well with an icy cold beer or chilled white wine while the rest of the dinner grills. For more heat in the tortillas, use more jalapeños; for a child-safe version, use just one.

SERVES 4 TO 6

2 green bell peppers, julienned
1 to 3 jalapeños, seeded and julienned
1 onion, cut into thin slivers
1 tablespoon olive oil
8 ounces Monterey Jack cheese, grated
6 10-inch flour tortillas

1. Prepare a medium-hot fire in the grill with a lightly oiled vegetable grill rack in place.

2. Toss the bell peppers, jalapeños, and onions with the olive oil.

3. Grill the bell peppers, jalapeños, and onions, tossing frequently, until tender and lightly charred, about 7 minutes.

4. Cool down the grill to low by spreading out the coals or reducing the flame.

5. Coat one side of 3 of the tortillas with nonstick cooking spray. Place the tortillas, coated side down, on a work surface. Spread a third of the vegetables on each tortilla. Top each with a third of the Monterey Jack. Place another tortilla on top of each and press firmly together. Mist the top tortillas with nonstick spray.

6. Grill each quesadilla until the cheese is melted and the tortilla is lightly toasted, about 4 minutes. Flip and grill on the other side for 2 to 3 minutes more. Remove from the grill and keep warm. Repeat with the remaining quesadillas. Depending on the size of your grill, you may be able to grill them two at a time.

7. Cut the warm quesadillas into wedges and serve at once.

Variation: **Campfire Cheese Quesadillas.** Quesadillas make wonderful campfire fare. For a quick version, to keep hungry hikers happy, omit the peppers, jalapeños, and onions and go straight to the cheese filling, adding canned roasted chiles if desired. The tortillas can be lightly moistened using a paper towel dipped in a little oil, instead of using nonstick cooking spray.

Smoky Poblano Cheese Quesadillas

Poblano chiles are mild, flavorful chiles that are perfect to use when you want just a hint of heat and a lot of flavor. If you can't find them, substitute 1 small green bell pepper and 1 jalapeño for 2 poblanos.

SERVES 4 TO 6

4 plum tomatoes, halved lengthwise
1½ tablespoons olive oil
1 red bell pepper, julienned
1 to 2 poblano chiles, seeded and julienned
4 scallions, chopped
6 10-inch flour tortillas
8 ounces smoked cheddar cheese, grated

1. Prepare a medium-hot fire in the grill with a lightly oiled vegetable grill rack in place.

2. Brush the cut side of the tomatoes with olive oil. Toss the bell peppers, chiles, and scallions with the remaining olive oil.

3. Grill the tomatoes, cut side down, until soft and lightly charred, about 10 minutes. Grill the bell peppers, chiles, and scallions, tossing frequently, until tender and grill-marked, about 7 minutes.

Fire Your Imagination

Sometimes the best heat is provided by the hot sauce that accompanies grilled foods. Asian chili pastes, sweet Caribbean hot sauces, and Mexican salsas all have their place on the picnic table next to the grilled food. If your local specialty food stores don't carry enough selection, here are some great hot sauce resources:

Chile Pepper
P.O. Box 769
Mt. Morris, IL 61054
800-959-5468
Bimonthly magazine

Chile Today–Hot Tamale
919 Highway 33, Suite 47
Freehold, NJ 07228
800-468-7377
Catalog

Hot Sauce Club of America
P.O. Box 5784
Baltimore, MD 21224
800-728-2328
Catalog; newsletter for club
   members

Mo Hotta Mo Betta
P.O. Box 4136
San Luis Obispo, CA 93403
800-462-3220
Catalog

4. Peel and chop the tomatoes and combine with the other grilled vegetables in a medium-size bowl.

5. Cool down the grill to low by spreading out the coals or reducing the flame.

6. Coat one side of 3 of the tortillas with nonstick cooking spray. Place the tortillas, coated side down, on a work surface. Spread a third of the vegetables on each tortilla. Top each with a third of the cheddar. Place another tortilla on top of each and press firmly together. Mist the top tortillas with nonstick spray.

7. Grill each quesadilla until the cheese is melted and the tortilla is lightly toasted, about 4 minutes. Flip and grill on the other side for 2 to 3 minutes more. Remove from the grill and keep warm. Repeat with the remaining quesadillas. Depending on the size of your grill, you may be able to grill them two at a time.

8. Cut the warm quesadillas into wedges and serve at once.

Black Bean and Goat Cheese Quesadillas

Black beans and goat cheese make a surprisingly successful culinary marriage. These tasty quesadillas do quite well as a light lunch and as an appetizer. However you serve them, they are guaranteed to disappear quickly.

SERVES 6 AS AN APPETIZER;
SERVES 4 AS A MAIN COURSE

1½ cups cooked black beans (or 1 15-ounce can), drained
½ cup salsa (homemade or store-bought)
Salt
4 10-inch flour tortillas
4 ounces soft goat cheese
2 tablespoons chopped fresh cilantro

1. Prepare a low fire in the grill.

2. In a food processor fitted with a steel blade, combine the beans and salsa. Process until well mixed but not completely smooth. Taste and season with salt and additional salsa to taste.

3. Coat one side of 2 of the tortillas with nonstick cooking spray. Place the tortillas, coated side down, on a work surface. Spread half of the bean mixture evenly on each tortilla. Top each with half of the goat cheese and sprinkle with half of the cilantro. Place another tortilla on top of each and press firmly together. Mist the top tortillas with nonstick spray.

4. Grill each quesadilla until the cheese is melted and the tortilla is lightly toasted, about 4 minutes. Flip and grill on the other side for 2 to 3 minutes more. Remove from the grill and keep warm. Repeat with the remaining quesadilla. Depending on the size of your grill, you may be able to grill them both at the same time.

5. Cut the warm quesadillas into wedges and serve at once.

Sushi Rice Squares

The delicious seasoned rice used for sushi is pressed into squares and grilled. It is surprisingly simple to make despite the lengthy instructions.

MAKES 32 SQUARES

RICE SQUARES

3 cups uncooked short-grain white rice
3¾ cups water
2 tablespoons mirin (sweet rice wine)
½ cup rice vinegar
2 tablespoons sugar
2 teaspoons salt
1 sheet nori (dried seaweed)
1 carrot, finely grated
2 scallions, finely chopped

GLAZE AND DIPPING SAUCE

3 tablespoons mirin (sweet rice wine)
2 tablespoons tamari
2 tablespoons toasted sesame oil

¼ cup pickled ginger (optional)

1. Combine the rice, water, and mirin in a medium-size saucepan. Cover, bring to a boil, reduce the heat, and boil gently until the rice is tender and the water is absorbed, 12 to 15 minutes.

2. In a small saucepan, combine the vinegar, sugar, and salt and bring to a boil.

3. Transfer the rice to a shallow bowl or pan. Gradually pour the hot vinegar mixture over the rice and toss with a spoon or rice paddle held in one hand while fanning the rice with the other hand. (Alternatively, set the rice in front of a fan and let the fan cool the rice while you toss.) Continue until the rice is cool to the touch and appears glossy, 10 to 20 minutes.

4. Hold the nori over an open flame until toasted, about 1 minute per side. Crumble and add to the rice along with the carrot and scallions. Mix well.

5. Line an 8-inch square baking dish with plastic wrap. Spoon the rice mixture into the pan. Cover with plastic wrap. Place another baking dish on top and press to compress the rice and make the top level. Refrigerate until the rice is firm enough to cut, at least 4 hours.

6. Prepare a medium-hot fire in the grill with a lightly oiled vegetable grill rack in place.

7. To make the glaze and dipping sauce, combine the mirin, tamari, and sesame oil in a small bowl. Mix well to combine.

8. Invert the rice onto a cutting board; remove the pan and plastic wrap. Cut the rice into quarters, then cut each quarter in half horizontally. Cut each of the 8 pieces into quarters to make 32 squares. Brush the squares with the glaze.

9. Grill the rice squares, turning once, until heated through and grill-marked, about 8 minutes.

10. To serve, arrange the rice squares on a platter. Garnish the plate with the pickled ginger, and pass the remaining glaze as a dipping sauce.

Serving Suggestions: This makes a delicious hors d'oeuvre for a party, but it can also be served instead of plain white rice as a base for a vegetable dish. Try it with Teriyaki Vegetable Kabobs (page 214) or Simple Grill-Wok Stir-Fry (page 219).

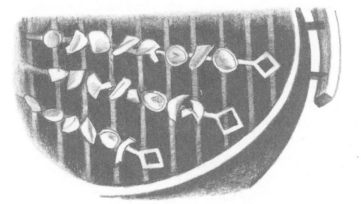

Tortellini Kabobs with Roasted Tomato Dipping Sauce

This is one of those "If you can boil water…" recipes—it is a simple recipe that produces delicious and beautiful results. The dipping sauce is optional but quick to make, and it does enhance the dish.

SERVES 4 TO 8

TORTELLINI

12 ounces fresh or frozen cheese tortellini
1 tablespoon extra-virgin olive oil

ROASTED TOMATO DIPPING SAUCE

1 tomato, halved horizontally
Olive oil
2 garlic cloves
6 basil leaves
½ cup sour cream (nonfat sour cream is acceptable)
Salt and black pepper

1. Prepare a medium-hot fire in the grill.
2. Bring a large pot of salted water to a boil for the tortellini.
3. Cook the tortellini according to the package directions. Drain well. Toss with the olive oil.
4. Brush the cut side of the tomato halves with a little olive oil. Grill, cut side down, until tender and grill-marked, about 10 minutes.
5. Peel the tomato. On a cutting board, in a mortar and pestle, or in a food processor, chop the tomato, garlic, and basil until you have a fine paste. Stir into the sour cream. Add salt and pepper to taste.
6. Thread the tortellini onto skewers. They will stay on the skewers best if they are threaded through the filled part of the tortellini. Grill, turning once, until lightly charred, about 2 minutes per side.
7. Serve the kabobs at once, passing the dipping sauce on the side.

Variation: Mini Ravioli Kabobs. You can often find fresh or frozen mini ravioli in the same supermarket case as the tortellini. Cook according to the package directions. Weave onto the skewers, trying to pierce each ravioli twice as it is threaded on. Grill and serve with the sauce as above.

Marinated Artichoke and Mushroom Kabobs

Here's another utterly simple-to-make appetizer that is absolutely delicious.

SERVES 4 TO 8

4 ounces mushrooms, trimmed
2 7-ounce jars marinated artichoke hearts
2 garlic cloves, minced
Salt and black pepper

1. Combine the mushrooms, artichokes and their liquid, and garlic in a large bowl. Season with salt and pepper to taste. Set aside to marinate for at least 30 minutes or up to 8 hours.

2. Prepare a medium-hot fire in the grill.

3. Thread the mushrooms and artichoke hearts onto skewers. Grill, turning occasionally, until the mushrooms are tender and grill-marked, about 10 minutes.

4. Serve hot or at room temperature.

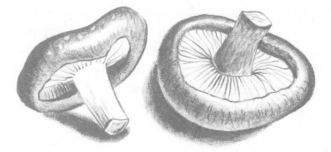

Little Mushroom Bites

When you are preparing grilled hors d'oeuvres to show off the versatility of the vegetarian grill, these are a sure winner. The basic recipe focuses on the distinct flavor of the grilled mushroom, but plenty of flavor variations are possible (see the Variations). The mushrooms can be partly grilled and stuffed ahead of time, then grilled to finish cooking and heat through at the last minute.

SERVES 4

12 ounces mushrooms, trimmed
2 tablespoons extra-virgin olive oil
Salt and black pepper
2 garlic cloves
¾ cup fresh bread crumbs
¼ cup grated cheese (such as Parmesan or provolone)
2 tablespoons sherry

1. Prepare a medium-hot fire in the grill with a vegetable grill rack in place.

2. Remove the stems from the mushrooms and hollow out the caps, reserving the stems and trimmings. Brush both sides of the mushroom caps with olive oil and sprinkle the inside of the caps with salt and pepper to taste.

3. Grill the mushrooms, hollow side down, until partially cooked, about 5 minutes. Set aside.

4. Combine the reserved mushroom stems and trimmings with the remaining olive oil and the garlic and toss to coat. Grill, tossing frequently, until lightly cooked, about 5 minutes.

5. Finely chop the mushroom pieces and garlic by hand or in a food processor. Combine in a medium-size bowl with the bread crumbs, cheese, and sherry. Season with salt and pepper to taste. Stuff into the mushroom caps, mounding up the filling and pressing with your fingers to pack tightly.

6. Grill the stuffed mushrooms, stuffing side up, until the mushrooms are completely cooked and the cheese is melted, about 10 minutes.

7. Serve hot or warm.

Variations: This is a rather simple recipe, and the flavors can be varied as desired. A tablespoon of chopped fresh herbs is a lovely addition, or a teaspoon of dried herbs can be used. More garlic or a shallot can be grilled with the mushroom trimmings. Any wine or stock can be used instead of the sherry. The bread crumbs can be made with any high-quality white or whole-grain bread.

Roasted Pepper and Zucchini Antipasto

Be sure to choose young zucchini for this appetizer—the young squash hold their shape better than older ones, which have more developed seeds.

SERVES 4 TO 6

2 red bell peppers
2 yellow or orange bell peppers
1 recipe Lemon-Garlic Marinade (page 273)
3 small zucchini, cut into quarters or eighths and sliced
     into 4-inch-long spears
2 tablespoons drained capers
6 basil leaves, cut into thin ribbons

1. Prepare a medium-hot fire in the grill.

2. Roast the peppers, turning occasionally, until completely charred, about 10 minutes. Place in a plastic or paper bag to steam for 10 minutes to loosen the skin. Cut slits in the pepper, then drain briefly into the bowl with the marinade to catch any juices. Peel and seed the pepper, then cut into long, thin strips.

3. Brush the marinade onto the zucchini. Grill, turning occasionally, until tender and lightly charred, about 5 minutes.

4. Mound the pepper strips in the center of a platter and arrange the zucchini spears around the edges. Scatter the capers and basil on top. Drizzle a few tablespoons of the remaining marinade on top. Serve at room temperature, accompanied by fresh or grilled Italian bread.

Grape Leaves Stuffed with Brie

Simple and delicious are these little morsels of melted Brie wrapped inside a grape leaf. Although you can harvest your own grape leaves, then blanch them in boiling water, it is far easier to buy them brined in jars. The bottled leaves also tend to be easier to handle. Other cheeses can be substituted for the Brie, but I like the Brie–grape leaf combination best.

SERVES 6

9 large or 18 small jarred grape leaves, patted dry
8 ounces Brie cheese, cut into 1-inch cubes
Olive oil

1. Prepare a medium fire on the grill.

2. Cut off any grape leaf stems and, if the leaves are large, cut in half. Lay a leaf flat on a work surface. Place a piece of cheese on top. Fold up from the bottom, then the sides, then roll into a tight packet. Brush with olive oil.

3. Grill the grape leaf bundles until the edges of the leaves brown and the cheese softens, 1 to 2 minutes per side. Serve hot off the grill.

Roasted Chestnuts

Chestnuts roasting in a covered grill. Kinda makes you want to burst into song, doesn't it? These chestnuts are delicious to eat out of hand, when you can find them, which is usually around Christmas time. The great thing about chestnuts is that they are surprisingly low in fat—there are only 3 grams of fat in a cup of roasted chestnuts, compared to 63 grams of fat in a cup of cashews.

SERVES 6

1 pound chestnuts

1. Prepare a medium-hot fire in the grill.
2. Score each chestnut with an X on the flat side to allow steam to escape.
3. Place the chestnuts directly on the grill grate. Unless they are unusually small, they should stay on the grate and not fall into the coals. Close the lid on the grill and allow the chestnuts to roast until they smell toasted and are beginning to curl at the cuts, about 10 minutes.
4. Allow to cool just enough to handle comfortably. Peel and eat while still warm.

Veggie Chips with Horseradish Cream Sauce

This is a great appetizer to serve when you want to prove that just about any vegetable can be grilled, even rutabagas. The vegetables look lovely and taste delicious. The only drawback is that the vegetables take up a lot of grill space, so you can't easily double the recipe.

SERVES 6

HORSERADISH CREAM SAUCE

*½ cup plain yogurt
¼ cup sour cream (nonfat sour cream is acceptable)
1 tablespoon snipped fresh chives
2 teaspoons prepared horseradish
Salt and black pepper*

VEGGIE CHIPS

*1 baking potato, peeled and sliced ¼ inch thick
1 sweet potato, peeled and sliced ¼ inch thick
1 rutabaga, peeled, quartered, and sliced ¼ inch thick
4 medium-size beets (about ¾ pound), sliced ¼ inch thick
3 tablespoons extra-virgin olive oil
½ teaspoon dried thyme
Coarse salt and freshly ground black pepper*

1. Prepare a medium fire in the grill. A lightly oiled vegetable grill rack is optional but recommended.

2. To make the horseradish cream sauce, combine the yogurt, sour cream, chives, horseradish, and salt and pepper to taste in a small bowl. Set aside.

3. To make the veggie chips, place the potatoes, sweet potatoes, and rutabagas in one bowl and the beets in another. (Keeping the beets separate prevents them from staining the other vegetables.) Add 2 tablespoons of the olive oil and the thyme to the potato mixture and the remaining 1 tablespoon olive oil to the beets. Toss to coat well.

4. Grill the vegetables, turning occasionally, until tender and lightly grill-marked, 15 to 25 minutes for the baking potato, 15 to 20 minutes for the sweet potato, rutabaga, and beets. Try to avoid placing the sweet potatoes over the hottest area on the grill, as they are the most likely to char. Remove the vegetables from the grill as they are done and arrange on a serving platter.

5. Season the chips with salt and pepper. Serve the horseradish cream sauce alongside for dipping.

Smoky Tomato Salsa

The complexity of flavors in this salsa delights me every time I make it. First there is the mild heat of the poblanos and the more assertive smoky heat from the chipotles. The lime juice contributes a floral note that is enhanced by the smoky-floral flavor of the cilantro and the smoky-sweet charred tomatoes. The onion and garlic add an underlying herbal essence. This is a wonderfully balanced salsa that is great as a dip with chips or as a condiment with grilled foods.

MAKES ABOUT 4 CUPS

2½ pounds vine-ripened tomatoes
4 garlic cloves
2 poblano chiles
½ red bell pepper
½ green bell pepper
Extra-virgin olive oil
1 cup finely diced Vidalia or other sweet onion
¼ cup chopped fresh cilantro
1 teaspoon minced chipotle en adobo, or more to taste
3 tablespoons fresh lime juice
Salt

1. Prepare a medium-hot fire in the grill.

2. Slice the tomatoes in half. Peel and skewer the garlic. Brush the tomatoes, garlic, chiles, and bell peppers with olive oil.

3. Grill the vegetables, turning occasionally, until tender and slightly charred, 5 to 10 minutes. Remove the vegetables as they are done. Place the chiles and bell peppers in a plastic or paper bag to steam for 10 minutes to loosen the skins.

4. Peel the chiles, tomatoes, and bell peppers if you wish. Finely chop the vegetables. Combine in a bowl and stir in the onion, cilantro, chipotles, lime juice, and salt to taste.

5. Transfer the salsa to a serving bowl and let stand for at least 1 hour at room temperature to allow the flavors to blend before serving. This salsa is best the day it is made.

Serving Suggestions: Serve with chips as an appetizer or serve the salsa as a relish on top of burgers or to accompany other grilled foods, especially burritos and tacos.

Charred Corn Salsa

In order to bring out the flavor of the flame, you really must char the corn. Without the charring, however, it's still a great-tasting fresh salsa. It really does take a while for the flavors to develop in this salsa, so don't panic if you taste little more than the heat of the jalapeño when this is first made.

SERVES 10 TO 12

*2 garlic cloves
4 ears corn, husks and silks removed
1 pound vine-ripened tomatoes, halved
1 jalapeño, or more to taste
½ red bell pepper
¼ red onion
1 to 2 tablespoons extra-virgin olive oil
2 tablespoons chopped fresh cilantro
Juice of 1 lime
1 teaspoon red wine vinegar
Salt*

1. Prepare a medium-hot fire in the grill.

2. Skewer the garlic. Brush the garlic, corn, tomatoes, jalapeño, bell pepper, and onion with the olive oil.

3. Place the vegetables on the grill, arranging the tomatoes cut side down. Grill, turning occasionally, until the vegetables are charred, 8 to 10 minutes. Remove the vegetables from the grill as they are done.

4. Peel the tomatoes and bell pepper, if desired. Seed the jalapeño.

5. In a food processor fitted with a steel blade, combine the onion, jalapeño, bell pepper, and garlic and process until finely chopped. Add the

Baba Ghanouj

Get out the wood chips for this one. Slow-roasting the eggplant in a closed grill with smoldering wood chips guarantees a rich smoky flavor that greatly adds to this classic Middle Eastern dip.

SERVES 6

1 large eggplant
2 garlic cloves, minced
3 tablespoons fresh lemon juice
2 tablespoons tahini (sesame paste)
2 tablespoons extra-virgin olive oil
2 tablespoons chopped fresh parsley
1 teaspoon salt, or more to taste
Flatbread or sesame crackers (optional)

1. Prepare a medium-low fire in a grill. If you have them, add soaked wood chips to the fire (see page 10).

2. Prick the eggplant with a fork in several places on all sides. Place on the grill, cover with the lid, and grill, turning occasionally, until completely soft and collapsed, 40 to 60 minutes. Place the eggplant in a colander and let drain and cool for about 30 minutes.

3. Remove the eggplant flesh from the skin and mash with a fork or puree in a food processor. Combine in a bowl with the garlic, lemon juice, tahini, olive oil, parsley, and salt and mix well. Taste and adjust the seasonings.

4. Cover and let stand at room temperature for at least 30 minutes to allow the flavors to blend. Serve at room temperature with flatbreads or sesame crackers for scooping up the dip, if desired.

Eggplant Caviar

Another great dip from the Middle East.

SERVES 4 TO 6

1 large eggplant
2 onions, quartered
4 garlic cloves
1 red bell pepper, halved
¼ cup extra-virgin olive oil
¼ cup chopped fresh parsley
¼ cup snipped fresh chives
2 tablespoons chopped fresh cilantro
3 tablespoons fresh lemon juice, or more to taste
Salt and black pepper
Flatbread or sesame crackers (optional)

1. Prepare a medium-low fire in a grill. If you have them, add soaked wood chips to the fire (see page 10).

2. Prick the eggplant with a fork in several places on all sides. Skewer the onions and garlic. Brush the onions, garlic, and pepper with olive oil.

3. Place the eggplant on the grill, cover with the lid, and grill, turning occasionally, until completely soft and collapsed, 40 to 60 minutes. About 10 minutes before the eggplant is done, lift the grill lid and add the onions, garlic, and pepper. Grill until tender and grill-marked. Place the eggplant in a colander and let drain and cool for about 30 minutes.

4. Scrape the eggplant flesh onto a cutting board and chop. Finely chop the onions, garlic, and pepper. Combine the chopped vegetables in a bowl with the parsley, chives, and cilantro. Beat in the remaining olive oil and lemon juice. Season with salt and pepper to taste.

5. Cover and let stand at room temperature for at least 30 minutes to allow the flavors to blend. Season to taste with more salt, pepper, and lemon juice. Serve with flatbread or sesame crackers, if desired.

Holiday Chestnut-Mushroom Pâté

You'll only find fresh chestnuts in the stores around holiday time. By roasting the chestnuts and mushrooms on the grill, you can sing along with Nat King Cole as you prepare this luxurious spread.

SERVES 6 TO 8

8 ounces fresh chestnuts in their shell
12 ounces mixed wild and domestic mushrooms, trimmed
2 large garlic cloves, minced
1 teaspoon fresh thyme leaves
3 tablespoons extra-virgin olive oil
1 tablespoon sherry
2 tablespoons cream cheese
Salt and black pepper
Crackers or sliced French bread (optional)

1. Prepare a medium-hot fire in the grill with a lightly oiled vegetable grill rack in place on one side of the grill.

2. Score each chestnut with an X on the flat side to allow steam to escape. In a medium-size bowl, combine the mushrooms, garlic, thyme, and olive oil and toss to coat well.

3. Place the chestnuts directly on the grill grate. Unless they are unusually small, they should stay on the grate and not fall into the coals. Place the mushrooms on the vegetable grill rack and grill, tossing the mushrooms frequently, until tender, about 8 minutes. Remove the mushrooms from the grill and set aside. Close the lid and continue to roast the chestnuts until they smell toasted and are beginning to curl at the cuts, 2 to 7 minutes more. Remove from the grill.

4. When the chestnuts are cool enough to handle, peel them, making sure to remove the inner paper shell inside the hard shell.

5. In a food processor fitted with a steel blade, combine the chestnuts and mushrooms. Add the sherry and cream cheese and process until smooth. Season with salt and pepper to taste.

6. Transfer the mixture to a serving bowl, cover, and refrigerate for several hours. Serve the pâté with crackers or as a spread for French bread, if desired.

Chilled Garden-to-Grill Soup

There comes a time in most every gardener's season when the tomatoes and zucchini threaten to overwhelm. This is a lovely soup to make, inspired by gazpacho but more flavorful because of the touch of the grill.

SERVES 4 TO 6

3 shallots
3 garlic cloves
¼ cup olive oil
2 pounds very ripe tomatoes, halved
2 small to medium-size zucchini, sliced lengthwise
*   ¼ inch thick*
1 red bell pepper, halved
1 slice country-style French bread or 2 slices from a baguette
2 cucumbers, peeled, seeded, and finely chopped
2 cups canned tomato juice
2 tablespoons sherry
Salt and black pepper

Planning a Party Menu with Grilled Food

Backyard barbecues are a great way to entertain in the summer, but timing is everything. Unless you have a gas grill, you may find the fire in a pit or even in a kettle barbecue isn't ready when you are. And then there is the problem that vegetables take up a lot of room and generally need to be served in large quantities to fill up hungry guests. Therefore, it is a good idea to include on your menu foods that don't come directly off the grill, or ones that can be grilled in advance. A chilled gazpacho, such as the Chilled Garden-to-Grill Soup on this page, makes a great start and will keep your guests happy while the rest of the meal cooks on the grill.

1. Prepare a medium-hot fire in the grill.

2. Skewer the shallots and garlic. Brush the olive oil on the shallots, garlic, tomatoes, zucchini, pepper, and bread.

3. Place the tomatoes, cut side down, along with the shallots, garlic, tomatoes, zucchini, and pepper on the grill and grill until tender and grill-marked, 5 to 10 minutes, turning a few times. Grill the bread until lightly toasted, about 2 minutes per side.

4. Peel and chop the tomatoes. Dice the zucchini and pepper. Very finely chop the shallots, garlic, and bread. Combine in a large bowl with the cucumbers, tomato juice, sherry, and salt and pepper to taste.

5. Chill for at least 2 hours before serving. Season to taste with more sherry, salt, and/or pepper.

Minestrone with Grilled Vegetables

Serve this hearty soup with a loaf of bread and a green salad for a fine fall meal.

SERVES 4 TO 6

¼ cup extra-virgin olive oil
1 garlic bulb, loose papery peel removed
2 pounds tomatoes, halved
1 red bell pepper, halved
1 green bell pepper, halved
1 onion, halved
1 medium-size zucchini, quartered lengthwise
1 carrot, quartered lengthwise
4 ounces green beans, trimmed
4 cups vegetable or chicken stock or broth
1 tablespoon tomato paste
1 teaspoon dried thyme
1 teaspoon dried oregano
2 bay leaves
½ cup small pasta shapes (such as ditalini, orzo, or tubettini)

1½ cups cooked cannellini beans (or 1 15-ounce can), drained
Salt and black pepper
¼ cup Pesto (page 282)

1. Prepare a medium-hot fire in the grill.

2. Brush the oil on the garlic bulb, tomatoes, peppers, onion, zucchini, carrot, and green beans.

3. Grill the garlic until softened and the cloves easily pop out of their skins, about 20 minutes. Grill the vegetables, turning occasionally, until tender and grill-marked, 10 to 15 minutes for the tomatoes, peppers, and onion; about 5 minutes for the zucchini, carrot, and green beans. Remove the vegetables from the grill as they are done.

4. Pop the garlic cloves out of their skins and blend with half of the tomatoes to make a puree. Chop or dice the peppers, onion, zucchini, carrot, and green beans.

5. Combine the garlic-tomato puree and chopped vegetables in a soup pot. Add the stock, tomato paste, thyme, oregano, and bay leaves. Bring to a boil and let simmer until the flavors have blended, 20 to 30 minutes. Return to a boil and stir in the pasta and beans. Cook until the pasta is tender, about 15 minutes. Remove the bay leaves. Season to taste with salt and pepper.

6. To serve, ladle the soup into bowls and swirl a little pesto into each serving. (The soup will thicken as it stands and may need to be thinned with additional broth or water before reheating. If you do need to thin it, taste and adjust the seasonings before serving.)

Split Pea Soup
with Grilled Vegetables

It's hard to conceive of a rich pea soup without some smoked flavor. Meat-eaters get that traditional smoky flavor by adding a ham bone to the pot. Vegetarians should try adding grilled vegetables.

2 cups dried split peas, rinsed
8 cups water
2 onions
2 carrots
2 celery ribs, quartered
1 bay leaf
1 red bell pepper, diced
8 ounces mushrooms, diced
3 tablespoons extra-virgin olive oil
4 garlic cloves, minced
1 tablespoon snipped fresh dill
Salt and black pepper

1. Combine the peas and water in a large soup pot and bring to a boil. When the water comes to a boil, reduce the heat to a simmer and skim off any foam that rises to the top of the pot. Cut 1 onion and 1 carrot into quarters. Add the celery, the quartered onion and carrot, and the bay leaf. Simmer for 1 hour.

2. Remove the soup from the heat to cool slightly. Remove the bay leaf and process the soup in a blender until smooth. Return to the pot.

3. Meanwhile, prepare a medium-hot fire in the grill with a lightly oiled vegetable grill rack in place.

4. Dice the remaining carrot and onion and combine in a large bowl with the pepper and mushrooms. Add the olive oil, garlic, and dill and toss to coat.

5. Divide the vegetables into two batches. Grill each batch of vegetables, tossing frequently, until tender and grill-marked but not charred, 6 to 8 minutes.

6. Add the grilled vegetables to the pureed soup. Season to taste with salt and pepper. Let stand for at least 1 hour to allow the flavors to develop.

7. Before serving, thin with water, if needed, and season to taste with salt and pepper. Reheat gently and serve hot.

New England–Style Grilled Corn Chowder

Flame-charred corn adds a depth of flavor to this classic chowder. This hearty soup makes a wonderful main course when accompanied with grilled bread. I especially like to serve slabs of cornbread, brushed with butter and grilled lightly, with this soup.

SERVES 6 TO 10

1 pound potatoes, peeled and diced
2 cups water, or more to cover
1 leek (white part only), halved lengthwise
6 ears corn, husks and silks removed
1 red bell pepper, halved
2 garlic cloves
2 tablespoons butter, melted
2 cups whole milk
1 teaspoon fresh savory or thyme leaves, or more to taste
Salt and black pepper

1. Prepare a medium-hot fire in the grill.

2. Combine the potatoes and water in a medium-size saucepan. If necessary, add just enough more water to cover the potatoes. Bring to a boil and boil until the potatoes are tender, about 5 minutes. Remove from the heat and set aside; do not drain.

3. Brush the leeks, corn, pepper, and garlic with the butter.

4. Grill the vegetables, turning occasionally, until tender and grill-marked, about 8 minutes for the leeks; about 10 minutes for the corn, peppers, and garlic.

5. Scrape the corn kernels from the cobs into the pot with the potatoes. Using the dull side of a knife, scrape the cobs over the pot to extract all the "milk." Dice the leeks and peppers and mince the garlic, then add to the potatoes. Stir in the milk and savory or thyme. Simmer over medium heat until the flavors have blended, at least 15 minutes; do not allow the soup to boil.

6. Remove 2 cups of the soup from the pot and puree in a blender. Return to the pot and season to taste with more savory or thyme, salt, and pepper.

7. Simmer for 5 minutes more. Serve hot.

Tex-Mex–Style Grilled Corn Chowder

This soup follows along the theme of the previous soup—a corn chowder with added depth of flavor from the grilled vegetables. I think the combination of poblano chiles and jalapeños adds just the right mix of chile flavor and mild heat to this cream soup, but feel free to experiment with other chiles, too.

SERVES 6 TO 10

1 pound potatoes, peeled and diced
Approximately 2 cups water
2 garlic cloves, minced
1 teaspoon ground cumin
3 tablespoons canola or olive oil
6 ears corn, husks and silks removed
1 red or yellow bell pepper, halved
1 green bell pepper, halved
2 green chiles, preferably 1 poblano and 1 jalapeño
2 cups whole milk
1 tablespoon chopped fresh cilantro, or more to taste
Salt and black pepper

1. Prepare a medium-hot fire in the grill.

2. Combine the potatoes and water in a medium-size saucepan. If necessary, add just enough more water to cover the potatoes. Bring to a boil and boil until the potatoes are tender, about 5 minutes. Remove from the heat and set aside; do not drain.

3. Combine the garlic, cumin, and oil in a small bowl. Brush on the corn, bell peppers, and chiles.

Grill Cover Up or Down?

When it comes to grilling, like all cooking, intuition has its role to play. Whether the grill lid is up or down depends in part on outdoor conditions and on the effect you are looking for. If the outdoor temperature is not abnormally cold or windy and the grill is working properly and retaining its heat, then the grill lid can be left up. The heat of the fire will sear the food, and you will be able to monitor the food as it cooks, which is especially important with cut vegetables.

With the lid down, a large piece of food, such as a whole squash, will bake without charring, which is probably desirable. The food will also taste smokier, which may also be desirable.

4. Grill the corn, bell peppers, and chiles, turning occasionally, until tender and grill-marked, about 10 minutes.

5. Scrape the corn kernels from the cobs into the pot with the potatoes. Using the dull side of a knife, scrape the cobs over the pot to extract all the "milk." Dice the bell peppers and chiles, then add to the potatoes. Stir in the milk and cilantro. Simmer over medium heat until the flavors have blended, at least 15 minutes; do not allow the soup to boil.

6. Remove 2 cups of the soup from the pot and puree in a blender. Return to the pot, season to taste with more cilantro, salt, and pepper.

7. Simmer for 5 minutes more. Serve hot.

4

Great Grilled
Salads

Green Salad with Marinated Grilled Vegetables

This is a terrific salad and a great introduction to the joys of grilled vegetables. The fire leaves the vegetables crunchy enough to satisfy any salad lover while adding a tremendous amount of flavor.

SERVES 4 TO 6

1 cup broccoli and/or cauliflower florets
1 red bell pepper, julienned
1 carrot, julienned
4 ounces green beans, trimmed and cut into 2-inch lengths
1 small onion, slivered
12 small mushrooms, trimmed
1 recipe Basic Herb Marinade and Salad Dressing (page 272) or
⅓ cup Italian-style salad dressing
1 pint cherry or yellow pear tomatoes, halved
8 ounces fresh mozzarella cheese, diced
6 slices French bread (sliced on the diagonal)
1 garlic clove, halved
12 cups mixed salad greens
½ cup imported brine- or oil-cured black olives

1. In a large bowl, combine the broccoli or cauliflower, pepper, carrot, green beans, onion, and mushrooms. Add the marinade and let stand for 30 minutes at room temperature or up to 8 hours in the refrigerator.

2. Prepare a medium-hot fire in the grill with a lightly oiled vegetable grill rack in place.

3. Lift the vegetables out of the marinade with a slotted spoon. Grill, tossing frequently, until tender and grill-marked, about 7 minutes. Set aside.

4. Toss the cherry tomatoes with the remaining marinade. Lift out with a slotted spoon and grill, tossing frequently, until tender, about 5 minutes. Set aside.

5. Stir the mozzarella into the remaining marinade and set aside.

Best Fire Starter

Consumer demand has forced many egg producers in Vermont, where I live, to switch from Styrofoam to cardboard egg cartons on the grounds that Styrofoam is a petroleum-based product made from nonrenewable resources and that Styrofoam is not biodegradable. This is great for both the environment and the griller—because nothing starts a fire better than cardboard egg cartons. Use torn paper egg cartons instead of crumpled newspaper when starting your next fire and you will see superior fire-starting qualities. Perhaps you should start a similar consumer movement in your state.

6. Grill the bread until toasted, about 2 minutes per side. Rub both sides with the cut side of the garlic.

7. To serve, arrange a bed of greens on 4 dinner plates or 6 salad plates. Place the garlic toasts on the side of each plate. Arranged the grilled vegetables on top of the greens. Spoon the mozzarella cubes and any remaining marinade over the salad. Garnish with the olives. Serve at once.

Escalivada

From Spain, a grilled vegetable salad. The name comes from the verb *escalivar,* which means to cook over hot embers. The salad is quite simple—really just a platter of grilled vegetables, so make sure you use fresh, fresh vegetables and an excellent quality olive oil. This makes a wonderful first course served with French bread; it also makes a great sandwich filling.

SERVES 4 TO 6

3 medium-size onions, unpeeled
2 green bell peppers
2 red bell peppers
1 medium-size eggplant
3 tablespoons extra-virgin olive oil
Coarse salt and freshly ground black pepper
French bread

1. Prepare a medium-hot fire in the grill.
2. Place the onions, peppers, and eggplant on the grill. Cover and grill until the vegetables are well browned and very soft, about 10 minutes for the peppers and 20 minutes for the onions and eggplant. Turn and rotate positions every 5 minutes or so. Remove the vegetables from the grill as they are done. Place the peppers in a plastic or paper bag to steam for 10 minutes to loosen their skins. Allow all the vegetables to cool to room temperature.
3. Peel and cut the grilled vegetables into 3-inch-long thin strips. Arrange on a serving platter or in a shallow bowl, drizzle the olive oil on top, and season with salt and pepper to taste.
4. Serve at room temperature accompanied with slices of French bread. The bread can be served fresh or lightly toasted on the grill, if the grill is still warm.

Mediterranean
Grilled Vegetable Salad

This recipe is similar to the previous one, with the rich sunny flavors of the Mediterranean intensified by the smoky essence of the grill. However, in this vegetable mélange, the flavors are made somewhat more complex with the addition of tomatoes, basil, and garlic. The grill flavor is intensified because the vegetables are sliced before they are grilled, increasing the surface area exposed to the smoke, whereas in the previous recipe, the vegetables are grilled whole and unpeeled.

SERVES 4 TO 6

1 eggplant, sliced lengthwise ⅜ inch thick
1 onion, quartered
1 red bell pepper, halved
1 small zucchini, sliced lengthwise ½ inch thick
1 small yellow summer squash, sliced lengthwise ½ inch thick
About ⅓ cup extra-virgin olive oil
1 pound plum tomatoes, halved lengthwise
2 tablespoons chopped fresh basil
2 tablespoons balsamic vinegar
2 garlic cloves, minced
Salt and black pepper

1. Prepare a medium-hot fire in the grill.

2. Brush the eggplant, onion, pepper, zucchini, and summer squash with most of the olive oil, reserving a little for the tomatoes. Skewer the onion.

3. Grill the vegetables, turning occasionally, until well browned, about 10 minutes. Do not crowd the vegetables; do this step in two batches if your grill surface is limited. Remove to a large cutting board.

4. Brush the cut side of the tomatoes with the remaining olive oil and grill cut side down until lightly charred, about 10 minutes.

5. Chop the eggplant, onion, pepper, zucchini, and summer squash into bite-size pieces. Peel and chop the tomatoes. Combine in a large bowl with the

basil, vinegar, and garlic. Season with salt and pepper to taste.

6. Let stand for at least 30 minutes to allow the flavors to develop. Serve warm or at room temperature.

Serving Suggestions: The salad can be served as an antipasto, salad, relish, or sandwich filling. Try it with toasted French bread as in Escalivada (page 91).

Asparagus Salad with Garlic Toasts and Shaved Parmesan

This hearty salad makes a delicious light meal, especially when accompanied with a soup. Use more or less greens, depending on how central the role of the salad is to the meal.

SERVES 4

1 red bell pepper
1 pound asparagus, trimmed
1 recipe Classic Vinaigrette (page 271)
4 to 8 cups mesclun or mixed salad greens
Shaved Parmesan cheese
8 Garlic Toasts (page 167)

1. Prepare a medium-hot fire in the grill.
2. Roast the pepper, turning occasionally, until completely charred, about 10 minutes. Place in a plastic or paper bag to steam for 10 minutes to loosen the skin. Peel and seed, then very finely chop.
3. Brush the asparagus with the vinaigrette. Grill, turning occasionally, until tender, about 8 minutes. Meanwhile, prepare the garlic toasts.
4. To serve, make a bed of greens on each plate. Arrange the asparagus on top. Sprinkle with the roasted pepper. Drizzle the remaining vinaigrette on top. Garnish with the shaved Parmesan, and serve at once with the garlic toasts on the side.

Asparagus Salad with
Roasted Pepper Vinaigrette

This is a handy little three-for-one recipe because both the simply grilled asparagus and the roasted pepper vinaigrette can be served separately. Grilling asparagus adds a smoky crispness to the vegetable without masking its unique spring-grass flavor. The roasted pepper vinaigrette makes a delicious dressing for other grilled vegetables, especially leeks, carrots, and zucchini. It can also be used to dress green salads.

SERVES 4

ROASTED PEPPER VINAIGRETTE

1 red bell pepper
2 tablespoons extra-virgin olive oil
2 garlic cloves
1 tablespoon red wine vinegar
1 tablespoon chopped fresh basil
Salt and black pepper

SALAD

2 tablespoons extra-virgin olive oil
1¼ pounds asparagus, trimmed
Butterhead lettuce
Shaved Parmesan cheese

1. Prepare a medium-hot fire in the grill.

2. To make the roasted pepper vinaigrette, roast the pepper, turning occasionally, until completely charred, about 10 minutes. Place in a plastic or paper bag to steam for 10 minutes to loosen the skin. Cut slits in the pepper, then drain briefly into a blender or the bowl of a food processor to catch any juices. Peel and seed the pepper, then coarsely chop and add to the blender or food processor. Add the olive oil, garlic, vinegar, and basil and process until smooth. Season with salt and pepper to taste. Set aside.

3. Drizzle the olive oil over the asparagus and toss to coat.

4. Grill the asparagus, turning occasionally, until tender, about 8 minutes.

5. To serve, arrange a bed of lettuce on a platter or on individual salad plates. Spoon the vinaigrette over the lettuce. Arrange the asparagus on top and sprinkle with the shaved Parmesan. Serve at room temperature.

Arugula and Grilled Mushroom Salad

This salad is simply delicious. It works well as an appetizer for a formal dinner. The mushrooms are served warm on top of the salad, but they hold their heat long enough for you to finish preparing a few other dishes before you serve this as a first course.

SERVES 4

1 pound mixed button, shiitake, and oyster mushrooms
1 recipe Lemon-Garlic Marinade (page 273)
1 bunch arugula, stemmed and leaves torn
Shaved Parmesan cheese

1. Prepare a medium-hot fire in the grill with a lightly oiled vegetable grill rack in place.

2. Trim the mushrooms and discard any tough stems. Slice about ¼ inch thick. Reserve 2 tablespoons of the marinade and pour the rest over the mushrooms. Toss to coat well.

3. Lift the mushrooms out of the marinade with a slotted spoon. Grill the mushrooms, tossing frequently, until tender and grill-marked, about 8 minutes.

4. In a large bowl, toss the arugula with the remaining marinade.

5. To serve, arrange the arugula on salad plates and scatter the mushrooms on top. Top with a few curls of shaved Parmesan.

Judging Mushrooms for Doneness

Perfectly grilled mushrooms will be grill-marked and slightly crisp on the outside and completely juicy on the inside. Overcooked mushrooms will be crisp or chewy all the way through. To tell if your mushrooms are done, cut (or bite) into one and see if it is juicy all the way through. Most whole mushrooms will roll right off a pancake turner, so use your tongs to remove them from the grill.

Soy-Grilled Green Bean and Mushroom Salad

Here's a great make-ahead salad, rich with smoke and soy, but it's not a last-minute dish. The marinade has many layers of distinctively Chinese flavors, and it pairs beautifully with the green beans. If you don't have black beans with chili sauce, you can substitute chili paste with garlic for similar results.

SERVES 4

1 pound green beans, trimmed
1 recipe Chinese Soy–Black Bean Marinade and Dressing
    (page 280)
8 ounces shiitake mushrooms, stems discarded and caps
    sliced ¼ inch thick
1 scallion, finely chopped
2 tablespoons chopped fresh cilantro

1. Prepare a medium-hot fire in the grill with a lightly oiled vegetable grill rack or grill-wok in place.

2. Place the beans in a shallow dish. Pour about half of the marinade over the beans and toss to coat. Place the mushrooms in another bowl, pour the remaining marinade on top, and toss to coat.

3. Lift the green beans from the marinade with a pair of tongs. Grill, tossing

frequently, until the beans are tender and browned, 8 to 10 minutes. Remove to a large salad bowl.

4. Lift the mushrooms from the marinade with a slotted spoon. Grill, tossing frequently, until the mushrooms are tender and grill-marked, about 5 minutes. Add to the beans.

5. Pour any remaining marinade over the salad. Add the scallion and cilantro.

6. Toss just before serving at room temperature.

Beet and Endive Salad with Maple-Balsamic Vinaigrette

The grilled vegetables hold up well at room temperature for more than an hour, so this salad makes a fine accompaniment to other grilled dishes. It is also delicious proof that there's more to vegetable grilling than onions, mushrooms, and zucchini.

SERVES 4

VINAIGRETTE

1 tablespoon pure maple syrup
2 tablespoons balsamic vinegar
2 garlic cloves, minced
3 tablespoons extra-virgin olive oil

SALAD

8 medium-size beets (1½ to 1¾ pounds)
About 3 tablespoons olive oil
2 heads Belgian endive
2 tablespoons pine nuts, toasted (see Note)
Salt and black pepper

1. Prepare a medium-hot fire in the grill. A lightly oiled vegetable grill rack is optional but recommended.

2. To make the vinaigrette, combine the maple syrup, balsamic vinegar, and garlic in a small jar. Add the olive oil, close tightly, and shake until the oil is emulsified. Set aside.

3. Scrub the beets. Trim off the tops and roots and cut the beets into slices about ¼ inch thick. Place in a bowl and toss with 2 tablespoons of the olive oil. Slice the endives in half lengthwise and brush with olive oil.

4. Grill the beets, turning occasionally and brushing with olive oil as needed, until lightly charred and tender all the way through, 15 to 20 minutes. Place the beets in a salad bowl.

5. Shake the vinaigrette to remix, pour over the beets, and toss to coat.

6. Grill the endive until tender and lightly charred, 4 to 7 minutes per side. Place the endive on a cutting board.

7. Just before serving, slice the endive about ¼ inch thick and add to the beets along with the pine nuts. Toss briefly. Season generously with salt and pepper. Serve at once.

Note: To toast pine nuts, place them in a dry skillet over medium heat and toast, stirring constantly, until the nuts begin to color, about 3 minutes. Do not allow the nuts to scorch or they will taste bitter.

Leeks Vinaigrette

This salad makes a particularly appealing addition to a buffet table. It goes nicely with many other flavors and holds up well at room temperature.

SERVES 4

8 leeks, each about 1½ inches in diameter
2 tablespoons balsamic vinegar
2 garlic cloves, minced
3 tablespoons extra-virgin olive oil
Salt and black pepper
1 red bell pepper
⅓ cup Niçoise or other small imported brine- or oil-cured
*   black olives*
Tomato wedges (optional)

1. Prepare a medium fire in the grill.

2. Trim away the root ends of the leeks and all but 2 to 3 inches of the green leaves. Slice in half lengthwise and rinse under cold running water, fanning the leaves with your fingers to remove all the grit and sand. Pat dry.

3. Combine the vinegar and garlic in a bowl. Whisk in the olive oil until emulsified. Season with salt and pepper to taste. Brush generously onto the leeks.

4. Roast the pepper, turning occasionally, until completely charred, about 10 minutes. Place in a plastic or paper bag to steam for 10 minutes to loosen the skin. Meanwhile, grill the leeks, turning occasionally, until tender and grill-marked, about 8 minutes.

5. Cut slits in the pepper, then drain briefly into the bowl with the remaining marinade to catch any juices. Peel and seed the pepper, then julienne.

6. Combine the pepper and leeks on a platter or in a shallow serving bowl. Scatter the olives on top. If desired, arrange the tomato wedges around the edge of the platter or bowl for more color. Drizzle the remaining marinade on top.

7. Set aside for about 30 minutes to allow the flavors to blend. Serve at room temperature.

Variation: Asparagus Vinaigrette. In Europe, leeks are sometimes called the "poor man's asparagus." Substitute asparagus for the leeks in this dish and you'll see how well these vegetables can be exchanged.

Marinated Roasted Pepper and Olive Salad

This recipe is an absolutely necessary addition to any vegetarian repertoire. The variations and serving possibilities are endless (see the Serving Suggestions).

SERVES 4 TO 6

2 green bell peppers
2 red bell peppers
2 yellow bell peppers
8 ounces fresh mozzarella cheese, cubed
½ cup brine- or oil-cured black olives
2 tablespoons extra-virgin olive oil
1 tablespoon red wine vinegar
1 tablespoon chopped fresh basil
Salt and black pepper

1. Prepare a hot fire in the grill.

2. Roast the peppers, turning occasionally, until completely charred, about 10 minutes. Place in a plastic or paper bag to steam for 10 minutes to loosen the skins.

3. Cut slits in the peppers, then drain briefly into a large bowl to catch any juices. Peel and seed the peppers, julienne, and add to the bowl. Add the mozzarella, olives, olive oil, vinegar, basil, and salt and pepper to taste. Toss to combine.

4. Let stand at room temperature for at least 30 minutes to blend the flavors. Serve at room temperature.

What Makes a Salad a Salad?

Generally it is the bed of lettuce lining the plate that makes a dish a salad. You can take almost any grilled vegetable combination and put it on a bed of lettuce and you will have a salad. Try topping a bed of greens with Grilled Ratatouille (page 235) or Grilled Chakchouka (page 236) for starters. Any of the stuffed vegetables in Chapter 6 can also be arranged on a bed of lettuce for a delicious "warm" salad.

Serving Suggestions: This salad is so versatile, it's hard to know where to begin when it comes to serving suggestions. You can make a whole meal out of this salad with the addition of crusty French bread, some sliced tomatoes, and perhaps some grilled corn for heartier appetites. You can serve it as a topping for warm pasta—or as a dressing for a cold pasta salad—or serve it simply as an appetizer with sliced French or Italian bread. It also makes a great addition to a spread of antipasto dishes. Without the olives, it makes a fine sandwich filling.

Variation: Marinated Roasted Peppers. Omit the olives and mozzarella and you have Marinated Roasted Peppers, which will keep for up to a week in the refrigerator. The peppers can be used to top other grilled vegetable combinations, to dress up burgers or sandwiches, or to add a sweet, smoky flavor to sauces and salad dressings.

A Guide to Salad Greens

When putting together a blend of greens for a salad plate, look for a balance of tastes and textures and a variety of colors. A generous base of lettuce will provide a mild, sweet, crunchy background against which you can play the peppery greens (arugula, dandelion greens, and watercress), the cabbage family greens (cabbages, bok choy, mustard greens, mizuna), and the bitter chicories (Belgian endive, curly endive, radicchio). Here's a list of some of the greens you are most likely to encounter.

Arugula. With a distinctively peppery and slightly bitter flavor, arugula stands out in a salad mix. It has small, lobed dark green leaves on stems that should be discarded if tough. Arugula is quite perishable and will keep in the refrigerator for two to three days. It is not available year-round (watercress can be substituted as needed). Arugula is the Italian name for this trendy green; also look for it under the names "rocket" and "roquette."

Curly endive. These days you may see this frizzy-leafed green go by its French name, "frisée," or it may be labeled "chicory." By any name, it has a loose head with dark frilly leaves on the outside and paler leaves toward the center. The flavor is quite bitter; select pale-colored heads for milder flavor.

Escarole. This member of the chicory family has broader leaves than curly endive but a similar flavor. Like curly endive, the leaves on the outer edge of the rosette are darker and more strongly flavored.

Lettuce. There are dozens of different lettuce varieties sold by specialty growers, but they all fall into four general types.

Crisphead lettuces, such as iceberg, have firm, round heads and can be held for up to a week in the refrigerator. Each head contains about 90 percent water by weight, which accounts for its bland taste. Crisphead lettuce alone makes a bland salad, but in a mix of greens it adds a crisp texture and sweet flavor.

Cos, or romaine-type, lettuces have long narrow leaves, with dark outer leaves and lighter, crisper leaves at the interior of the head. They have more flavor than crisphead lettuces, while still offering crisp texture and a relatively sweet flavor.

Butterhead lettuces include Boston lettuce, butter lettuce, Bibb lettuce, and Kentucky limestone lettuce. The leaves are distinctively soft and crumpled and have a mild, sweet flavor and soft, buttery texture. Butterhead lettuces are quite delicate and wilt almost as soon as they are dressed.

Loose-leaf lettuces offer the most variety in terms of leaf shape and color. At the supermarket you may find just "red-leaf lettuce" and "green-leaf lettuce." At a farm-stand you may be regaled with Salad Bowl, Ruby, Oak Leaf, Lolla Rossa, and Lolla Bianco. In general, these lettuces are mild, sweet, and somewhat crisp, with colors ranging from pale green to deep red.

Mâche. This green is also known as corn salad or field lettuce (because it is found wild in corn fields) and lamb's lettuce (because the small, tender, velvety leaves are said to resemble a lamb's tongue). The flavor is delicate and rather nutty. You will pay a premium price for mâche because it is extremely perishable.

Mesclun. From a Niçoise word meaning "mixture," mesclun (or sometimes "mesclum") is a mixture of baby greens and herbs usually found only in specialty markets. You pay a premium price for the mixture—because it involves extra work for the farmer, and because the farmer harvests the leaves when very small, thus reducing the yield per acre—but the price is usually worth it. The mix may include butterhead lettuce, mâche, arugula, red-leaf lettuce, baby mustard leaves, spinach, and edible herbs, such as chervil. A very easy-to-make salad supper is a bed of lightly dressed mesclun topped with an assortment of grilled vegetables.

Radicchio. Perhaps the most beautiful "green" in the salad bowl, radicchio has brilliant ruby-colored leaves with white veins that form a small, tight head. The leaves can be used as natural bowls for holding dips. Radicchio adds a cabbagey taste and lots of color to a salad.

Spinach. Tender young spinach with dark green, glossy leaves and slightly astringent flavor are a familiar sight in the salad bowl, alone or mixed with other greens. The crinkly leaves of certain varieties are excellent dirt catchers, so wash thoroughly. Discard large stems, which are stringy and tough.

Watercress. This spicy-flavored green with dark-green lobed leaves adds a distinctive flavor to any salad. Although it has its own peppery flavor, you can substitute watercress for the more difficult to find arugula in most salads.

Tomato Salad with Corn, Roasted Peppers, and Smoked Cheese

A fresh feast of sweet corn, vine-ripened tomatoes, and fragrant basil is the perfect way to end a hot summer day—but don't even think of making this recipe until the local harvest is ready. Sharp-tasting arugula provides a peppery contrast to the sweetness of the vegetables.

SERVES 4 TO 6

6 ears fresh corn, unhusked
2½ pounds vine-ripened tomatoes, chopped
1 Vidalia or other sweet onion, thinly sliced
2 large garlic cloves, minced
½ cup chopped fresh basil
3 tablespoons extra-virgin olive oil
2 tablespoons balsamic vinegar
Salt and black pepper
2 yellow bell peppers
8 slices French or whole-wheat bread
4 cups chopped arugula
8 ounces smoked cheese (such as mozzarella, Gouda, or cheddar),
cubed

1. At least 1 hour before serving, peel back the husks from the corn and remove the silks. Soak the corn in water to cover.

2. In a medium-size bowl, combine the tomatoes, onions, garlic, basil, 2 tablespoons of the olive oil, and the vinegar. Season with salt and pepper to taste. Set aside.

3. Prepare a medium-hot fire in the grill.

4. Grill the soaked corn until tender and slightly charred, about 15 minutes. Shuck the corn and remove the kernels from the cob using a sharp knife. Add to the tomato salad.

5. Roast the peppers, turning occasionally, until completely charred, about 10 minutes. Place in a plastic or paper bag to steam for 10 minutes to loosen the

skins. Cut slits into the peppers, then drain briefly into the bowl with the tomato salad to catch any juices. Peel, seed, and chop the peppers, then add to the tomato salad.

6. Brush the bread with the remaining 1 tablespoon olive oil. Toast over the coals, turning once, until golden. Cut into cubes.

7. Just before serving, add the arugula and bread cubes to the salad and toss to combine. Spoon the salad onto individual salad plates or a large serving plate. Top with the cheese and serve immediately.

Spring Asparagus and New Potato Salad

This is a wonderful way to usher in the season of light suppers from the garden—yours or the farmers' in the hills. There is a natural sweetness in both fresh asparagus and new potatoes that is enhanced by grilling. Served on a bed of greens with a lemony vinaigrette, the vegetables are transformed into a feast of spring.

SERVES 4 TO 6

6 tablespoons extra-virgin olive oil
Juice of 1 lemon
2 garlic cloves, minced
Salt and black pepper
1½ pounds new potatoes, halved or quartered if large
1 pound asparagus, trimmed
12 to 16 cups mesclun or other mixed salad greens
Coarse-grated Parmesan cheese

1. Prepare a medium fire in the grill.

2. In a shallow dish, combine the olive oil, lemon juice, garlic, and salt and pepper to taste. Mix well. Add the potatoes and asparagus and toss to coat.

3. Grill the potatoes, turning every 10 minutes or so, until golden, about 30 minutes. Grill the asparagus until limp and lightly grill-marked, about 8 minutes.

4. Arrange the greens on individual salad plates. Top with the grilled asparagus and potatoes. Drizzle the remaining olive oil and lemon juice mixture on top. Sprinkle with the Parmesan and serve at once.

Chunky Potato Salad

Olives and cherry tomatoes are a wonderful complement to the flame-tossed potatoes and peppers. This is a rich salad. Accompanied by a green salad and a flatbread, this potato salad could make a satisfying main course.

SERVES 4 TO 6

DRESSING

¼ cup extra-virgin olive oil
2 tablespoons balsamic vinegar
1 teaspoon chopped fresh oregano, or ½ teaspoon dried
1 garlic clove, minced
½ teaspoon salt
¼ teaspoon black pepper

POTATO SALAD

2 pounds new potatoes, cut into bite-size wedges
1 green or yellow bell pepper, cut into ½-inch pieces
1 red bell pepper, cut into ½-inch pieces
1 cup imported brine- or oil-cured black olives, pitted and halved
1 cup imported brine-cured green olives, pitted and halved
1 cup halved cherry tomatoes
2 scallions, chopped
Salt and black pepper

1. To make the dressing, whisk together the olive oil, vinegar, oregano, garlic, salt, and pepper in a large bowl.

2. Steam the potatoes over boiling water until just tender, about 12 minutes. Drain well. Add to the dressing and toss to coat.

3. Prepare a medium-hot fire in the grill with a lightly oiled vegetable grill rack in place.

4. Lift the potatoes from the dressing with a slotted spoon. Grill, tossing frequently, until completely tender and grill-marked but not mushy, about 8 minutes. Remove from the grill and place in a large salad bowl.

5. Add the peppers to the dressing and toss to coat. Lift from the dressing with a slotted spoon. Grill, tossing frequently, until just tender and lightly browned, about 3 minutes. Remove from the grill and add to the potatoes.

6. To serve, add the olives, tomatoes, and scallions to the potatoes. Add the remaining dressing and toss gently to mix. Season with salt and pepper to taste. Serve at once.

Grilled Potato and Carrot Salad

In this salad, the potatoes are cut as French fries and steamed to ensure they are thoroughly cooked. The dressing is a more traditional mayonnaise dressing, but it is applied with a very light hand so as not to overwhelm the delicate smokiness of the grilled vegetables.

SERVES 4 TO 6

1¾ pounds potatoes (such as chefs', red, or Yukon Gold), peeled,
  if desired, and cut like French fries
3 tablespoons extra-virgin olive oil
1 tablespoon chopped fresh rosemary
Salt and black pepper
2 large or 4 medium-size carrots, cut into 2-inch by ⅜-inch sticks
4 to 6 scallions, cut into 2-inch lengths, or ½ Vidalia or other
  sweet onion, sliced
2 tablespoons mayonnaise
2 tablespoons plain yogurt
2 tablespoons white wine vinegar
1 teaspoon Dijon mustard
3 tablespoons chopped fresh parsley

1. Steam the potatoes over boiling water until just tender, about 12 minutes. Drain well.

2. Prepare a medium-hot fire in the grill with a lightly oiled vegetable grill rack in place.

3. Place the potatoes in a large bowl and drizzle 2 tablespoons of the olive oil on top. Sprinkle with the rosemary and season with salt and pepper to taste. Toss to coat. In another bowl, combine the carrots and scallions or onion. Drizzle the remaining 1 tablespoon of olive oil on top and toss to coat.

4. Grill the potatoes, tossing frequently, until tender and grill-marked, about 8 minutes. Return to the large bowl. Grill the carrots and scallions or onion, tossing frequently, until tender and grill-marked, about 4 minutes. Add to the potatoes.

5. In a small bowl, combine the mayonnaise, yogurt, vinegar, mustard, and parsley. Mix well. Add to the potato mixture and toss to coat. Season with salt and pepper to taste.

6. Serve warm or at room temperature.

Tuscan Bread Salad
with Grilled Vegetables

This recipe is either the ultimate in frugal-housewife cookery, or it is a frank admission that everyone's favorite part of the salad is the bite of bread that mops up the last drop of dressing in a bowl. The more rustic the loaf, the better the salad. A bread salad calls for a bread of distinction, with a coarse crumb and a chewy texture. A soft loaf will yield a soggy salad.

SERVES 6 TO 8

½ cup extra-virgin olive oil
¼ cup red wine vinegar
Salt and black pepper
1 medium-size zucchini, sliced lengthwise
1 yellow summer squash, sliced lengthwise
1 1-pound loaf stale country bread, cut into 1-inch cubes

1 red bell pepper
1 yellow bell pepper
1 green bell pepper
1 pound tomatoes, diced
½ cup diced Vidalia or other sweet onion
1 bunch arugula, stemmed and leaves torn
Shaved Parmesan cheese (optional)

1. Prepare a medium-hot fire in the grill.

2. In a large bowl, whisk together the olive oil, vinegar, and salt and pepper to taste. Brush on the zucchini and summer squash.

3. Add the bread to the remaining oil and vinegar dressing. Toss to coat. Set aside, stirring occasionally while you prepare the rest of the salad.

4. Roast the peppers, turning occasionally, until completely charred, about 10 minutes. Place in a plastic or paper bag to steam for 10 minutes to loosen the skins. Grill the zucchini and summer squash, turning once, until tender and grill-marked, about 5 minutes.

5. Slice the zucchini and summer squash into bite-size pieces and add to the bread. Peel and seed the peppers, then dice and add to the bread salad. Add the tomatoes and onion to the salad and toss to mix well.

6. Just before serving, add the arugula and toss again. Season with salt and pepper to taste. Serve garnished with the shaved Parmesan, if desired.

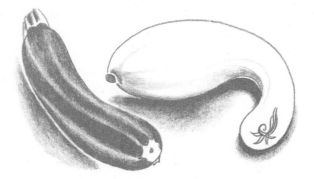

Minty Couscous Salad with Grilled Asparagus

Couscous makes a perfect background for the mustard-marinated grilled asparagus, salty feta and olives, and fresh-tasting mint.

SERVES 4 TO 6

1½ cups instant couscous
½ teaspoon salt
2¼ cups boiling water
¼ cup fresh lemon juice
½ teaspoon Dijon mustard
⅓ cup extra-virgin olive oil
1 pound asparagus, trimmed and cut into 2-inch lengths
¾ cup crumbled feta cheese
½ cup imported brine- or oil-cured black olives
¼ cup chopped fresh mint
Salt and freshly ground black pepper

1. Prepare a medium fire in the grill with a lightly oiled vegetable grill rack in place.

2. Combine the couscous, salt, and boiling water in a large bowl. Cover and let stand until the couscous is tender and the water is absorbed, about 10 minutes. Fluff with a fork.

3. Meanwhile, whisk together the lemon juice and mustard in a medium-size bowl. Slowly pour in the olive oil and whisk constantly until the oil is emulsified. Add the asparagus and toss to coat.

4. Lift the asparagus from the marinade with a slotted spoon and grill, tossing occasionally, until tender, about 8 minutes.

5. Add the grilled asparagus to the couscous along with the feta, olives, mint, and any remaining marinade. Season with salt and pepper to taste.

6. Serve at room temperature.

Variations: Broccoli or green beans can be substituted for the asparagus.

Grilled Vegetable Pasta Salad

The trick to making pasta salads with great flavor is to coat the cooked pasta with a little olive oil so it doesn't absorb all the dressing. And, of course, grilling the vegetables rather than tossing them in raw doesn't hurt either.

SERVES 4 TO 8

1 pound small pasta (such as farfalle, shells, twists, or orecchiette)
3 tablespoons extra-virgin olive oil or herb-flavored oil
2 garlic cloves
½ to 1 teaspoon crushed fresh rosemary
1 small head radicchio, sliced ¼ inch thick
1 small onion, cut into slivers
1 red bell pepper, julienned
1 green bell pepper, julienned
1 pound asparagus or other vegetable (such as green beans or zucchini), trimmed and julienned
½ cup loosely packed chopped fresh basil
Juice of 1 lemon, or more to taste
Salt and black pepper

1. Prepare a medium-hot fire in the grill with a lightly oiled vegetable grill rack in place.

2. Bring a large pot of salted water to a boil. Add the pasta and cook until just tender. Drain and rinse thoroughly to cool. Place in a large bowl and toss with 1 tablespoon of the oil.

3. Combine the remaining 2 tablespoons oil, the garlic, and rosemary in a large bowl. Add the radicchio, onion, peppers, and asparagus or other vegetable and toss to coat.

4. Grill the vegetables, tossing frequently, until lightly charred, about 5 minutes.

5. Toss the vegetables with the pasta, basil, and lemon juice. Season with salt and pepper to taste.

6. Serve at room temperature.

Zucchini Pasta Salad with Feta Cheese and Olives

There's no rule that says a pasta salad must have an oil- or mayonnaise-based dressing. In this salad, ketchup adds a wonderful background flavor to the dressing. The result is a "barbecued" pasta salad.

SERVES 4 TO 8

1 pound small pasta (such as farfalle, shells, twists, or
 orecchiette)
3 tablespoons extra-virgin olive oil or herb-flavored oil
2 garlic cloves
1 tablespoon ketchup
3 small zucchini, quartered and sliced
1 red bell pepper, julienned
1 carrot, julienned
½ cup crumbled feta cheese
½ cup Kalamata olives
¼ cup diced red onion
¼ cup chopped fresh parsley
2 tablespoons red wine vinegar
Salt and black pepper

1. Prepare a medium-hot fire in the grill with a lightly oiled vegetable grill rack in place.

2. Bring a large pot of salted water to a boil. Add the pasta and cook until just tender. Drain and rinse thoroughly to cool. Place in a large bowl and toss with 1 tablespoon of the oil.

3. Combine the remaining 2 tablespoons oil, the garlic, and ketchup in a large bowl. Add the zucchini, peppers, and carrots and toss to coat.

4. Grill the vegetables, tossing frequently, until lightly charred, about 5 minutes.

5. Toss the vegetables with the pasta, feta, olives, onion, parsley, and vinegar. Season with salt and pepper to taste.

6. Serve at room temperature.

Chinese Sesame Noodles with Grilled Broccoli and Tofu

Although Chinese sesame noodles are typically served as an appetizer at restaurants, here they make a main course with the addition of grilled broccoli and tofu. The instructions say to combine the dressing with the noodles and serve at once, and that is not an exaggeration. The noodles will soak up the dressing, and although the flavor holds up, the texture becomes a bit dry after the salad has sat around for a while. It is easy, however, to prepare all the ingredients in advance, and then to dress the salad just before sitting down.

SERVES 4 TO 6

SALAD

1 pound firm or extra-firm tofu
2 tablespoons toasted sesame oil
1 tablespoon soy sauce
2 garlic cloves, minced
1 tablespoon minced fresh ginger
1 pound broccoli, cut into florets, stems julienned
1 pound fresh Chinese wheat noodles or linguine

DRESSING

3 tablespoons toasted sesame oil
½ cup smooth peanut butter
½ cup vegetable or chicken stock or broth, brewed black tea,
    or water
¼ cup soy sauce
1 tablespoon Chinese black vinegar or Worcestershire sauce
1 to 2 teaspoons chili paste with garlic
2 tablespoons sugar, or to taste

¼ cup minced scallions

1. To make the salad, wrap the tofu in a clean cotton kitchen towel. Place a heavy weight on top (such as a cutting board weighted with a heavy juice can). Set aside for at least 30 minutes to allow the excess water to drain from the tofu. Cut into ½-inch cubes.

2. Combine the sesame oil, soy sauce, garlic, and ginger in a large bowl. Add the broccoli and tofu and toss to coat.

3. Bring a large pot of salted water to a boil. Add the noodles and cook until just tender. Drain and rinse thoroughly to cool. Transfer to another large bowl.

4. To make the dressing, combine the sesame oil, peanut butter, and stock, broth, tea, or water, with the soy sauce, vinegar or Worcestershire, chili paste, and sugar in a blender and blend well. If you have used a natural unsweetened peanut butter, you may need a little more sugar. Set aside.

5. Prepare a medium-hot fire in the grill with a lightly oiled vegetable grill rack in place.

6. Grill the broccoli and tofu, tossing frequently, until tender and grill-marked, about 8 minutes, turning occasionally.

7. Just before serving, toss the dressing with the noodles. Transfer to a large serving bowl or platter. Arrange the broccoli and tofu on top and sprinkle with the scallions. Serve at once.

Variations: Asparagus or green beans can be substituted for the broccoli.

Vietnamese Noodle Salad
with Grilled Vegetables

This is a great salad. It would be a good salad even without the grilled vegetables, but the smoky asparagus and carrots are delightful in this very light noodle dish. The dressing is made with *nuoc mam* or *nam pla,* a flavoring sauce that is an essential ingredient in Thai and Vietnamese cuisines. Made from an extract of anchovies and sea salt, this pungent, salty sauce is aged and refined to a clean, amber liquid. Without the sauce, which strict vegetarians often avoid, you can't achieve the quintessential flavor of Southeast Asia. Fish sauce is available wherever Asian foods are sold.

SERVES 4 TO 6

DRESSING

⅓ cup fish sauce
¼ cup white vinegar
3 tablespoons sugar
1 garlic clove, minced

8 ounces rice vermicelli
1 pound asparagus, trimmed and cut into 2-inch lengths
2 large carrots, julienned
1 to 2 tablespoons peanut or canola oil
3 tablespoons chopped fresh mint
3 tablespoons chopped fresh cilantro
3 tablespoons chopped roasted peanuts

1. To make the dressing, combine the fish sauce, vinegar, sugar, and garlic in a small saucepan. Heat gently, stirring constantly, until the sugar is dissolved. Set aside to cool.

2. Bring a large pot of water to a boil. Add the noodles and cook until tender but firm, about 5 minutes. Drain and rinse thoroughly to cool.

3. Prepare a medium-hot fire in the grill with a lightly oiled vegetable grill rack in place.

Keep Fresh Herbs Fresh

When you buy a bunch of basil or cilantro with their roots still attached, place them, roots down, in a jar of water, and leave in a sunny window. I have kept vases of these herbs going for months in my kitchen, changing the water every few days. Store parsley and other herbs without roots in the refrigerator. A fresh bunch can be placed in a jar of water with a plastic bag covering the leaves and then refrigerated. If the herbs are already washed and bagged in airtight bags or a plastic box, open the containers to allow a little air circulation, then refrigerate.

4. Combine the asparagus, carrots, and oil. Toss to coat.

5. Grill the vegetables, tossing frequently, until tender and grill-marked, about 8 minutes.

6. To serve, place the rice vermicelli in a large bowl and pour half of the dressing on top. Toss well. Arrange the noodles on a large platter or on individual plates. Arrange the asparagus and carrots on top. Drizzle the remaining dressing over the vegetables. Sprinkle the mint, cilantro, and peanuts on top. Serve at once.

5

Sensational Sandwiches and Burgers

CHAPTER 5 • SENSATIONAL SANDWICHES AND BURGERS

Stuffed Picnic Loaf
with Pesto, Grilled Vegetables, and
Provolone Cheese

Have you ever gone to an outdoor classical music concert, where you were surrounded by music lovers serving elegant gourmet picnics on designer blankets, and suffered alternate bouts of envy and fits of amusement? Well, this outstandingly easy and flavorful recipe may be your best response. Grilled vegetables, pesto, and provolone cheese melted together inside a loaf of Italian bread makes outstanding picnic fare. Just wrap the warmed loaf in several thicknesses of foil, then transport it in an insulated picnic basket to keep it warm. Be sure to bring along wine and plenty of napkins.

SERVES 4

6 tablespoons extra-virgin olive oil
4 garlic cloves, minced
1 large eggplant, peeled and sliced ⅜ inch thick
1 red or green bell pepper, quartered
1 Vidalia or other sweet onion, sliced ½ inch thick
1 large loaf Italian or French country bread (1¼ to 1½ pounds)
½ cup Pesto (page 282)
2 large vine-ripened tomatoes, sliced
5 ounces provolone cheese, sliced

1. Prepare a medium-hot fire in the grill.

2. Combine the olive oil and garlic in a small bowl and brush on the eggplant, pepper, and onion.

3. Grill the vegetables, turning occasionally, until well browned, 10 to 15 minutes. Remove the vegetables from the grill as they are done.

4. Reduce the temperature of the grill by spreading out the coals or by reducing the flame on a gas grill to low.

5. Slice the bread in half horizontally. Remove some of the interior of the loaf to create a hollow space for stuffing the vegetables. Brush the inside of the loaf with the remaining olive oil and garlic, then spread with the pesto. Layer

one-half of the provolone, the grilled vegetables, the tomatoes, and the remaining provolone on the bread. Position the top half of the loaf in place. Wrap the loaf in foil.

5. Place the loaf on a low-heat spot on the grill, away from direct heat, cover the grill, and bake until the bread is lightly toasted and the cheese is melted, about 10 minutes. Do not allow the bread to scorch.

6. To serve, unwrap the loaf. Slice into wedges and serve hot.

Make Ahead Notes: The sandwich loaf can be assembled up to a day in advance and refrigerated in its foil wrapper. To heat, bake over low coals, turning occasionally, for about 30 minutes. Or heat in the oven at 350°F for about 30 minutes.

Variations: Possible variations on this theme are infinite. Substitute Grilled Red Pepper Relish (page 126) or olivada (see page 177) for the pesto. Use different vegetables, replacing some or all of the ones specified with grilled zucchini, yellow summer squash, and mushrooms. Cheddar, fontina, Monterey Jack, Colby, Gouda—any semihard cheese with good melting properties—can replace the provolone. Or use goat cheese and omit the pesto and provolone.

The Greek Salad Complement

The Greek salad used in the following recipe can be used to complete the menu of many grilled meals. For starters, just about any grilled vegetable or veggie burger—commercial or homemade—tastes better in a pita pocket stuffed with Greek salad. A meal of grilled potatoes and Greek salad, with perhaps some grilled zucchini on the side, makes a summery feast. As long as the meal includes either potatoes or bread, as well as the salad, any grilled vegetable can be added to make a satisfying meal.

Greek Salad Pita Pockets with Grilled Eggplant

A great way to make a meal out of a Greek salad. This is a delicious combination.

SERVES 4 TO 6

1 head lettuce, torn into bite-size pieces
½ English cucumber, sliced
2 large vine-ripened tomatoes, chopped
1 Vidalia or other sweet onion, thinly sliced
2 tablespoons plus ⅓ cup extra-virgin olive oil
2 tablespoons fresh lemon juice
½ cup Greek black olives
4 ounces feta cheese, crumbled
2 garlic cloves, minced
1 tablespoon chopped fresh thyme or lemon thyme
½ teaspoon salt
¼ teaspoon black pepper
1½ pounds eggplant (preferably Japanese or Chinese), peeled, if
*   desired, and sliced ⅜ inch thick*
6 pita pockets

1. Combine the lettuce and cucumbers in a large salad bowl and refrigerate. In a medium-size bowl, combine the tomatoes, onion, 2 tablespoons of the olive oil, the lemon juice, olives, and feta. Set aside to marinate at room temperature.

2. Prepare a medium fire in the grill.

3. Combine the remaining ⅓ cup olive oil, garlic, thyme, salt, and pepper. Brush on the eggplant. Cut the pitas in half to form 2 pockets and wrap in foil.

4. Grill the eggplant, turning once, until quite brown and tender, 10 to 15 minutes. Warm the pitas off to the side of the grill, turning occasionally.

5. Add the marinated tomato mixture to the salad bowl and toss.

6. Serve the warmed pitas, grilled vegetables, and Greek salad at the table, and allow diners to assemble their own sandwiches.

Pita Pockets Stuffed with
Greek-Style Grilled Vegetables

Feta cheese has a wonderful creamy consistency when warmed. Here the feta cheese is stuffed into warmed pita pockets along with lemony, oregano-scented vegetables. The result is a delicious and practical sandwich that can hold its heat wrapped in foil by the side of the grill while you make the perfect accompaniment—Herb-Grilled Potatoes (page 41). The pita pockets are not overfilled, so one could also stuff in a burger—vegetarian or otherwise—if so inclined.

SERVES 4

*3 tablespoons extra-virgin olive oil
2 tablespoons fresh lemon juice
2 garlic cloves, minced
1 tablespoon chopped fresh oregano, or 1 teaspoon dried
2 medium-size zucchini, sliced ¼ inch thick
1 green bell pepper, julienned
1 red bell pepper, julienned
1 large onion, cut into slivers
4 pita pockets
4 ounces feta cheese, crumbled*

1. Prepare a medium-hot fire in the grill with a lightly oiled vegetable grill rack in place.

2. In a large bowl, combine the olive oil, lemon juice, garlic, and oregano. Add the zucchini, peppers, and onion and toss to coat. Cut the pitas in half to form 2 pockets and wrap in foil.

3. Warm the pitas off to the side of the grill, turning occasionally. Grill the zucchini, peppers, and onion, tossing frequently, until grill-marked and tender, 5 to 10 minutes. Remove the vegetables from the grill as they are done and return to the bowl. Immediately sprinkle the feta over the warm vegetables and toss to mix.

4. Serve the warm vegetable mixture and pitas at the table, and allow diners to assemble their own sandwiches. Or stuff the vegetable mixture into the pita

halves, wrap each half in foil, and return to the grill over low heat briefly to heat through.

Pitas with Red Pepper Hummus and Grilled Vegetables

You've had grilled vegetables in pitas before. You've had hummus in pitas before. But have you ever had pitas with grilled vegetables *and* hummus? And have you ever made a particularly delicious version of hummus with grilled red peppers? This is an outstanding flavor combination.

SERVES 4

RED PEPPER HUMMUS

2 red bell peppers
2 garlic cloves
¼ cup chopped fresh parsley leaves
1½ cups cooked chickpeas (or 1 15-ounce can), drained
¼ cup tahini (sesame paste)
3 tablespoons fresh lemon juice
Salt and black pepper

⅓ cup extra-virgin olive oil
2 garlic cloves, minced
1½ tablespoons chopped fresh mint, or 2 teaspoons dried
1 medium-size eggplant, peeled and sliced ⅜ inch thick
1 small zucchini, halved lengthwise and sliced ⅜ inch thick
1 onion, sliced
1 green bell pepper, sliced
4 pita pockets

1. Prepare a medium-hot fire in the grill with a lightly oiled vegetable grill rack in place.

2. Roast the peppers, turning occasionally, until completely charred, about

10 minutes. Place in a plastic or paper bag to steam for 10 minutes to loosen the skins.

3. Place the garlic and parsley in a food processor fitted with a steel blade. Process until finely chopped. Add the chickpeas, tahini, and lemon juice and process until smooth. Cut slits in the peppers, then drain briefly into the food processor bowl to catch any juices. Peel and seed the peppers, then chop and add to the chickpea mixture. Process until smooth. Season to taste with salt and pepper. Set aside. (The hummus can be made up to 3 days in advance and stored in an airtight container in the refrigerator. However, it should be served at room temperature.)

4. Combine the olive oil, garlic, and mint in a small bowl. Brush on the eggplant. Combine the zucchini, onion, and pepper in a large bowl. Add the remaining olive oil mixture and toss to coat. Cut the pitas in half to form 2 pockets and wrap in foil.

5. Grill the vegetables, turning occasionally, until tender and grill-marked, 10 to 15 minutes for the eggplant slices; 8 to 10 minutes for the zucchini, onion, and pepper. Warm the pitas off to the side of the grill, turning occasionally.

6. Serve the warmed pitas, hummus, and grilled vegetables at the table, and allow diners to assemble their own sandwiches.

Lentil-Stuffed Pita Pockets
with Grilled Onions

You could enjoy the lentil, grilled onion, and goat cheese combination as a salad, served on a bed of arugula or lettuce. But my favorite way to enjoy this sublime combination is stuffed in a warmed pita pocket. Don't substitute another type of lentil for the French green *lentilles du Puy;* these are the only ones that have a sufficiently mild flavor and firm texture.

SERVES 4

1 cup French green lentils
4 onions, cut into slivers
2 tablespoons extra-virgin olive oil

½ teaspoon dried thyme
1 red or yellow bell pepper
4 ounces soft goat cheese, crumbled
1½ tablespoons balsamic vinegar
Salt and black pepper
4 pita pockets
1 bunch arugula, stemmed and leaves torn

1. Boil the lentils in 6 cups of salted water until tender but not mushy, about 25 minutes. Drain and place in a large bowl.

2. Meanwhile, prepare a medium-hot fire in the grill with a lightly oiled vegetable grill rack in place.

3. In a large bowl, combine the onions, olive oil, and thyme and toss to coat.

4. Grill the onions, turning occasionally, until completely tender and well browned, 10 to 12 minutes. Roast the pepper, turning occasionally, until completely charred, about 10 minutes. Place in a plastic or paper bag to steam for 10 minutes to loosen the skin.

5. Cut slits in the pepper, then drain briefly into the bowl with the lentils to catch any juices. Peel and seed the pepper, then dice it. Add the pepper and onions to the lentils and toss to mix. Add the goat cheese, vinegar, and salt and pepper to taste. Toss gently to mix.

6. To serve, warm the pitas on the grill for about 3 minutes, watching carefully to avoid scorching them. Cut the pitas in half and stuff each with some arugula, then with the lentil mixture. Serve at once.

Goat Cheese and Grilled
Red Pepper Relish Sandwiches

While toasted cheddar cheese sandwiches say "lunch" or "campfire fare," goat cheese sandwiches say "casual al fresco dining." Be sure to add chilled wine, deck or porch, and summer breeze.

SERVES 4 TO 6

GRILLED RED PEPPER RELISH

2 red bell peppers
1 onion, quartered
4 garlic cloves
Olive oil
1 tablespoon balsamic vinegar
Salt and black pepper

1 large loaf of Italian or French country bread or
  1 baguette, sliced
8 ounces soft goat cheese

1. Prepare a medium-hot fire in the grill.

2. Roast the peppers, turning occasionally, until completely charred, about 10 minutes. Place in a plastic or paper bag to steam for 10 minutes to loosen the skins. Meanwhile, skewer the onion and garlic, brush lightly with olive oil and grill, turning occasionally, until lightly charred, about 10 minutes.

3. Cut slits in the peppers, then drain briefly into the bowl of a food processor to catch any juices. Peel and seed the peppers, then chop and add to the juice. Add the onion and garlic and pulse to finely chop. Add the vinegar and salt and pepper to taste and pulse to combine.

4. Grill the bread until toasted, about 2 minutes per side. Spread the goat cheese on the warm bread, top with some of the relish, and cover with the final slice of bread. Repeat with the remaining slices. Slice the sandwiches in half and serve at once.

101 Uses for Grilled Red Pepper Relish

If you find yourself with leftover relish (perhaps you only wanted to make 4 sandwiches), consider yourself lucky as there are plenty of ways to enjoy this condiment. Consider the sandwich possibilities alone: on any sort of grilled cheese sandwich, on any grilled mushroom or grilled eggplant sandwich, on any burger, vegetarian or otherwise. It makes a fine dip for raw vegetables and a great spread for crackers. Use it as a topping for pizza, bruschetta, or pasta tossed with olive oil and Parmesan. Or mix a little into your favorite potato salad, pasta salad, or chicken salad. Puree it with some olive oil and add more vinegar to taste, and you'll have an instant red pepper vinaigrette for salad or to top grilled vegetables. A spoonful added to a chilled or hot vegetable soup or a tomato sauce adds a subtle sweet-sour note. I could extend this list to reach 101 uses, but I'll leave the rest to your imagination.

Portobello Mushroom and Goat Cheese Sandwiches

These sandwiches are at their best when served while the mushrooms are still hot off the grill; the warm mushrooms make the goat cheese more creamy. But you can assemble the sandwiches, wrap them, and take them on a picnic, and they will hold up admirably. If you take them with you when meeting a group of friends, as we recently did, be prepared for trading....

SERVES 4

3 tablespoons olive oil
2 garlic cloves, minced
8 large portobello mushrooms, sliced ½ inch thick
4 hard white or wheat rolls, halved, or 8 slices whole-wheat bread
8 ounces soft goat cheese

2 medium-size tomatoes, sliced
Small bunch arugula or watercress

1. Prepare a medium-hot fire in the grill with a lightly oiled vegetable grill rack in place.

2. Combine the olive oil and garlic. Drizzle over the mushrooms and toss to coat.

3. Grill the mushrooms, tossing frequently, until tender and grill-marked, about 10 minutes. If you are going to serve the sandwiches at once, lightly toast the rolls or bread, if desired, for about 2 minutes per side.

4. To assemble the sandwiches, spread the goat cheese on both sides of the rolls or on each slice of bread. Arrange the mushrooms over the goat cheese. Top with tomatoes, then the arugula. Close up the sandwiches, slice in half, if desired, and serve.

Why Grilled Sandwiches?
Read M. F. K. Fisher

M. F. K. Fisher, one of America's most admired food writers, writes about a "Railroad Sandwich," which was invented and enjoyed by her family, consisting of a hollowed-out loaf of French bread, a slathering of butter and mustard, and a layering of ham. The loaf was wrapped first in waxed paper or foil, then in a clean towel. "Then, and this is the Secret Ingredient, call up a serene onlooker (a broad or at least positive beam adds to the quick results, and here I do not refer to a facial grimace but to what in other dialects is called a behind-derrière-bum-ass-seat-etc.) to sit gently but firmly upon this loaf for *at least* twenty minutes."

For melting the butter and melding the ingredients together, personally, I prefer the grill.

> ## Bread for Grilled Sandwiches
>
> Your sandwich is only as good as the bread you select. If you don't make your own bread, or if your specialty is a soft loaf-style sandwich bread, check out the offerings at your nearest artisan bakery. Look for European-style coarse-textured white loaves. When sliced, a coarse-textured bread gives a slightly uneven surface, which results in lots of bumps to catch on the garlic clove or olive oil that you rub on the surface. It won't grill evenly, but that is part of its charm and flavor. Toast lightly; you don't want the bread to be brittle.

Barbecued Mushroom Sandwiches

A great barbecue sandwich, with portobello mushrooms providing the "meat" of the sandwich. Serve with traditional barbecue fixings, especially cole slaw, pickles, and potato salad.

SERVES 4

8 large portobello mushrooms, sliced ½ inch thick
4 ½-inch-thick onion slices
½ cup Barbecue Glaze (page 280) or any tomato-based barbecue
*   sauce*
4 whole-wheat rolls, halved, or 8 slices whole-wheat bread
Lettuce leaves

1. Prepare a medium fire in the grill.
2. Brush the mushrooms and onion with some of the barbecue sauce.
3. Grill the mushrooms and onion, turning occasionally, until tender and grill-marked, about 10 minutes. Grill the rolls or bread until lightly toasted, about 2 minutes per side.
4. To assemble the sandwiches, lightly brush the toasted bread with the remaining barbecue sauce. Arrange the mushrooms on 4 roll halves or bread slices. Arrange the onions on the mushrooms, then top with lettuce. Close up the sandwiches, slice in half, if desired, and serve at once.

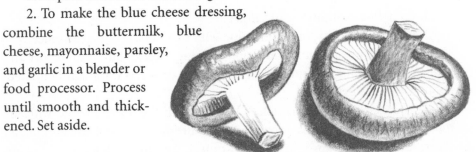
Mushroom Steak Sandwiches
with Blue Cheese Dressing

"What are in these sandwiches?" my husband asked the first time I made them. I counted off: blue cheese dressing, greens, tomatoes, and grilled mushrooms and onions. "And...?" he asked, "What's the meat?" I know it is a cliché to say that a grilled mushroom sandwich tastes like it contains meat, but it *really* does.

SERVES 4

BLUE CHEESE DRESSING

¼ cup buttermilk
3 tablespoons crumbled blue cheese
2 tablespoons mayonnaise (reduced-fat is acceptable)
2 tablespoons chopped fresh parsley
1 small garlic clove

8 large portobello mushrooms, sliced ½ inch thick
4 ¾-inch-thick onion slices
2 tablespoons extra-virgin olive oil
8 large slices of high-quality white bread (such as French, Italian, sourdough)
1 garlic clove, halved
1 tomato, sliced
1 bunch arugula or watercress, stemmed, or 2 cups mesclun

1. Prepare a medium fire in the grill.

2. To make the blue cheese dressing, combine the buttermilk, blue cheese, mayonnaise, parsley, and garlic in a blender or food processor. Process until smooth and thickened. Set aside.

Blue Cheese Dressing Notes

The blue cheese dressing for this recipe can be made several days in advance and stored in an airtight jar in the refrigerator. In fact, the dressing can be made in double or triple batches and used as a salad dressing. It also makes a great dip for raw or grilled vegetables. Try it instead of the Horseradish Cream Sauce with the Veggie Chips (page 71).

3. Brush the mushrooms and onions lightly with olive oil.

4. Grill the mushrooms and onions, turning occasionally, until tender and grill-marked, about 10 minutes. Grill the bread until lightly toasted, about 2 minutes per side.

5. To assemble the sandwiches, rub the toasted bread with the garlic. Spread the blue cheese dressing on the bread. Arrange the mushrooms on 4 slices. Separate the onions into rings and place over the mushrooms. Top with tomatoes and greens. Cover with the remaining slices of bread, slice in half, if desired, and serve at once.

Variation: Mushroom Steak Sandwiches with Goat Cheese Dressing. Replace the blue cheese in the dressing with crumbled soft goat cheese. Proceed with the recipe as above.

Rich Man's Subs

When I was in college, a "poor man's sub" was simply sauce, canned mushrooms, and cheese on a sub roll—for those of us too poor to afford the dollar extra for the meatballs or belonging to that curious breed of vegetarians who deserved sympathy for the deprivations they surely endured. This submarine is proof no deprivation is involved at all when it comes to a good vegetarian sandwich.

SERVES 4

*1 pound mushrooms (preferably portobellos), sliced
1 large onion, thinly sliced
1 large green bell pepper, julienned
1 large red bell pepper, julienned
¼ cup extra-virgin olive oil
4 garlic cloves, minced
1 tablespoon chopped fresh rosemary, or 1 teaspoon dried
Salt and black pepper
2 cups well-seasoned tomato sauce, heated
4 submarine rolls or small baguettes
4 ounces provolone cheese, thinly sliced*

1. Prepare a medium fire in the grill with a lightly oiled vegetable grill rack in place.

2. Toss the mushrooms, onion, and peppers with the olive oil, garlic, and rosemary. Season to taste with salt and pepper.

3. Divide the vegetables into two batches and grill, tossing and turning frequently, until tender and grill-marked, about 10 minutes per batch.

4. Reduce the heat in the grill by spreading out the coals or adjusting the gas flame.

5. To assemble the subs, brush a little tomato sauce inside each roll. Stuff the grilled vegetables inside. Top with about ½ cup tomato sauce per roll. Divide the provolone among the sandwiches and stuff into the rolls. Close up each sub so as little cheese peeks out as possible and tightly wrap in foil.

6. Return the subs to the low fire and bake until the rolls are crispy and the cheese is melted, about 10 minutes. Serve warm, with plenty of napkins.

Falafel

Traditionally this classic street food of the Middle East is made with deep-fried balls made from chickpeas and served in pita pockets with a tahini-based sauce. In this version, the bean patties are grilled. There's no loss of flavor, only a significant reduction in fat. With the help of a food processor and the use of canned beans, this lengthy-looking recipe is actually quick to prepare.

SERVES 4

SAUCE

½ cup tahini (sesame paste)
½ cup plain nonfat yogurt
1 tablespoon honey
1 tablespoon fresh lemon juice
1 tablespoon water, or more as needed

RELISH

2 plum tomatoes, sliced
½ English cucumber, sliced
½ green or red bell pepper, sliced
¼ cup diced Vidalia or other sweet onion
1 tablespoon lemon juice
Salt and black pepper

FALAFEL

3 cups cooked chickpeas (or 2 15-ounce cans), drained
4 slices sandwich bread, preferably whole-wheat
8 scallions, trimmed
¼ cup chopped fresh cilantro
¼ cup chopped fresh parsley
2 garlic cloves
2 teaspoons ground cumin
1 teaspoon ground coriander
¼ teaspoon ground red pepper, or to taste
Salt and black pepper
2 tablespoons olive oil
4 pita pockets

1. To make the sauce, combine the tahini, yogurt, honey, lemon juice, and water in a small bowl and mix well. Set aside.

2. To make the relish, combine the tomatoes, cucumber, pepper, and onion in a food processor fitted with a steel blade. Pulse to finely chop. Mix in the lemon juice and season to taste with salt and pepper. Pour into a bowl and set aside. Don't wash the food processor bowl; it will be used again.

3. Prepare a medium fire in the grill. A lightly oiled vegetable grill rack is optional but recommended.

4. To make the falafel, puree the chickpeas and bread in a food processor. Remove to a large bowl. Then puree the scallions, cilantro, parsley, and garlic. Add to the chickpea mixture along with the cumin, coriander, red pepper, and salt and pepper to taste. Knead with your hands to combine.

5. Form the chickpea mixture into patties about 2½ inches in diameter. Brush the olive oil on both sides. Cut the pitas in half to form 2 pockets and wrap in foil.

6. Grill the falafel until lightly browned, about 4 minutes per side. Warm the pitas off to the side of the grill, turning occasionally.

7. Serve the relish and sauce alongside the falafel and warmed pitas at the table, and allow diners to assemble their own sandwiches.

Barbecued Tempeh Sandwiches

Who first thought to boil soybeans, chop them up, press them into cakes, and then allow the cakes to ferment until they develop a downy white coating (like certain cheeses), a soft chewy texture, and a yeasty flavor? That's how tempeh is made, and it was developed in Indonesia where it is stir-fried and used instead of meat in curries.

This recipe is particularly good for those who have never eaten tempeh before, or have not yet acquired a taste for it. The strong flavor of the glaze masks some of the yeasty, beany flavor of tempeh. And why try tempeh in the first place? Well, curiosity must be satisfied, particularly when the food in question is very high in protein and low in fat.

Tempeh Tips

You can find tempeh in most natural food stores, where they often sell both plain tempeh and tempeh cakes extended with other grains. The cakes with additional grains have a milder flavor, and most people prefer them. Keep them refrigerated and use within a week of purchase.

SERVES 4

1 8-ounce package tempeh, sliced into ⅜-inch-thick strips
½ cup Barbecue Glaze (page 280) or any tomato-based barbecue
  sauce
8 slices whole-wheat bread or 4 whole-wheat rolls, halved
Lettuce leaves
Tomato slices
Onion slices

1. Combine the tempeh and barbecue sauce in a large bowl and toss to coat. Set aside to marinate.

2. Prepare a medium-hot fire in the grill. A lightly oiled vegetable grill rack is optional but recommended.

3. Grill the tempeh until heated through and crusty, 4 to 6 minutes per side. Lightly toast the bread on the grill, about 2 minutes per side.

4. To assemble the sandwiches, brush a little barbecue glaze on the bread. Arrange the tempeh, lettuce, tomatoes, and onions on the bottom slice or half. Close up each sandwich and serve.

Variation: Pita Pockets Stuffed with Barbecued Tempeh. Grill the tempeh as above. Stuff into pita pockets along with Grilled Onion Dip (page 288) or Tomato-Cucumber Relish (page 143).

Basic Bean-and-Grain Burgers

This is a very easy recipe to put together on a busy weeknight. You are likely to have the ingredients on hand and it is all quickly prepared in a food processor. These burgers are great served plain. But the usual burger fixings—ketchup, relish, pickles, onion slices, etc.—don't hurt a bit. Choose a whole-wheat roll, preferably toasted, because the texture of the burger is too soft for the traditional hamburger bun.

MAKES 8 BURGERS

⅔ cup uncooked bulgur
1⅓ cups boiling water
4 slices stale or toasted whole-wheat bread
1½ cups cooked red kidney, pinto, or black beans
    (or 1 15-ounce can), drained
¼ cup chopped fresh parsley
2 garlic cloves, minced
1 large egg
2 tablespoons tomato paste
1 tablespoon soy sauce
1 tablespoon chili powder
Salt and black pepper
8 whole-wheat rolls, halved

Lose the Bun! Toast the Bread!

Supermarket hamburger buns will do little to enhance most vegetarian burgers. The buns are just too soft. If you want to make a burger sandwich, opt for a chewy, rustic loaf, like rye or whole-wheat. Consider toasting the bread to give your teeth something firm to bite into.

Binders for Burgers

Vegetarian burgers generally need an ingredient that will absorb any excess liquid and bind all the ingredients together. My binder of choice is dry bread crumbs—preferably made from a good bakery or homemade whole-grain bread. A light white bread won't add much flavor, a sourdough may add too much of the wrong kind, so choose wisely. Four slices of thinly sliced toasted bread whirled in a food processor will give you about 1 1/2 cups of bread crumbs.

Oats, partially ground in a blender, are often used in burgers, but I think they contribute a gummy texture and a slightly chalky flavor.

1. Combine the bulgur and boiling water in a bowl, cover, and set aside to steam for 10 minutes.

2. Process the bread in a food processor fitted with a steel blade until you have about ½ cup crumbs. Set aside. Don't wash the food processor bowl; it will be used again.

3. Combine the beans, parsley, and garlic in the food processor and process until you have a fairly smooth mixture. Drain the bulgur of any excess water and stir into the bean mixture. Add the bread crumbs, egg, tomato paste, soy sauce, chili powder, and salt and pepper to taste. Set aside for 30 minutes. The mixture will thicken as it stands.

4. Prepare a medium fire in the grill with a lightly oiled vegetable grill rack in place.

5. Form the bean mixture into eight 3-inch burgers. Mist both sides with nonstick spray.

6. Grill the burgers until crisp, about 5 minutes per side.

7. Briefly toast the rolls on the grill. Stuff with the burgers and serve immediately.

Variation: Burger Burritos. Form the burger mixture into 2-inch or 4-inch sausages and grill as above. Wrap up in heated flour tortillas with provolone cheese. Top with salsa if desired.

Barbecued Bean Burgers Deluxe

The secret to these fantastic bean burgers is the wheat berries in the burger mix, which give them a pleasingly chewy texture. The mustardy cole slaw—my Mom's recipe—takes them over the top, adding crunch and spark to the barbecue sauce–flavored burgers. You may never eat a plain burger again!

MAKES 6 BURGERS

⅓ cup wheat berries
3 cups water
1 tablespoon extra-virgin olive oil
1 medium-size onion, diced
10 stems fresh parsley
1½ cups cooked red kidney beans (or 1 15-ounce can), drained
2 tablespoons tomato-based barbecue sauce
1 teaspoon dried thyme
1 egg
½ to ¾ cup dry whole-wheat bread crumbs
Salt and black pepper
6 hard rolls, halved

SLAW

4 cups finely grated green cabbage
2 carrots, finely grated
¼ cup minced onion
1 cup mayonnaise (fat-free mayonnaise is acceptable)
3 tablespoons yellow ballpark mustard
Salt and black pepper

1. Rinse the wheat berries under running water. In a medium-size saucepan, combine the wheat berries and water. Cover, bring to a boil, reduce the heat, and simmer until the wheat berries are tender, 1¼ to 1½ hours. (You can reduce the cooking time to 50 to 60 minutes by soaking the berries overnight before cooking.) Drain off any excess water.

Burger or Burrito?

Everyone loves a burger, right? We love its hand-held convenience, its aptitude for a variety of condiments. The only drawback to a bean burger is that its texture isn't quite complemented by traditional soft burger buns. You can't make a bean burger with the same chewy texture of meat, but you can rethink the bun.

I happen to think that veggie burgers are often best complemented by either pita pockets or tortilla wraps. Pita pocket halves hold a burger nicely. For tortillas, form your burger mix into sausage shapes, grill, then wrap them in heated flour tortillas. Cheese is always nice in a burrito with a veggie burger. So are either the traditional burger fixings or salsa and chopped chiles and onions.

2. Meanwhile, make the slaw by combining the cabbage, carrots, onion, mayonnaise, mustard, and salt and pepper to taste. Set aside.

3. Heat the olive oil in a medium-size skillet. Add the onion and cook, stirring, until soft and golden, about 5 minutes. In a food processor fitted with a steel blade, combine the onion and parsley and process until finely chopped. Add the beans, barbecue sauce, thyme, and egg and process until you have a fairly smooth mixture. Remove to a bowl. Stir in the wheat berries, ½ cup of the bread crumbs, and salt and pepper to taste. Continue to add crumbs, as needed, to make the mixture stiff enough to form into burgers.

4. With wet hands, form the mixture into six 3-inch burgers. Mist both sides with nonstick spray.

5. Prepare a medium fire in the grill with a lightly oiled vegetable grill rack in place.

6. Grill the burgers until crisp, about 5 minutes per side.

7. Serve the burgers on the rolls topped with the slaw. Pass the extra slaw at the table.

Black Bean–Mushroom Burgers

If you like black beans, you'll find these burgers irresistible. The grill adds just a touch of smoke to the beans, while the chopped mushrooms that bind them give them a pleasingly earthy flavor. The goat cheese added to the burger mix is optional—it just happens that black beans, goat cheese, and cilantro is one of my favorite flavor combinations.

MAKES 6 BURGERS

1 tablespoon olive or canola oil
1 onion, finely chopped
8 ounces mushrooms, finely chopped
2 garlic cloves, minced
½ teaspoon ground cumin
1½ cups cooked black beans (or 1 15-ounce can), drained
¼ cup packed fresh cilantro leaves
2 ounces soft goat cheese, crumbled (optional)
*4 slices stale or toasted sandwich bread, processed to make
    bread crumbs*
Salt and black pepper
6 hamburger buns or hard rolls
Salsa

1. Prepare a medium-hot fire in the grill with a lightly oiled vegetable grill rack in place.

2. Heat the oil in a large skillet over medium-high heat. Add the onion and cook, stirring, until golden, about 4 minutes. Add the mushrooms, garlic, and cumin and cook, stirring, until the mushrooms have released their juices, about 5 minutes.

3. Spoon the mixture into the food processor. Add the beans and cilantro and process briefly until well combined but still chunky. Spoon into a bowl, stir in the goat cheese, if using, and bread crumbs. Season generously with salt and pepper.

4. With wet hands, form the mixture into 6 burgers. Mist both sides with nonstick spray.

> ### Stocking Up on Bread Crumbs
>
> Since bread crumbs are my binder of choice for burgers, I don't like to run short. When the ends of a loaf of good bakery bread begin to go stale, or when I find myself with the stump end of a baguette, I save the bread in a plastic bag in the freezer. Two turns through the toaster defrosts and toasts a slice of frozen bread. Then I chop or tear the bread in bits and grind it to crumbs in a food processor. You can also process the bread before freezing to save freezer space.

5. Grill the burgers until crisp and heated through, about 5 minutes per side.
6. Serve the burgers on the buns, passing salsa at the table.

Dilled and Grilled Veggie Burgers

Grilled vegetables form the basis of these burgers, with some cooked wheat berries thrown in for a little texture.

MAKES 6 BURGERS

1 medium-size eggplant, peeled and sliced ⅜ inch thick
2 plum tomatoes, sliced ⅓ inch thick
1 onion, quartered
1 russet or baking potato, peeled and sliced ¼ inch thick
⅓ cup extra-virgin olive oil
4 slices stale or toasted sandwich bread
4 garlic cloves
½ cup cooked wheat berries (about 3 tablespoons uncooked),
    see Note
1 tablespoon snipped fresh dill
Salt and black pepper
6 pita pockets or rolls, halved
6 lettuce leaves
6 tomato slices

Commercial Burgers Fail the Test

One evening I gathered twelve friends at my home to taste commercial vegetarian burgers. One of the tasters was a buyer for a natural food store, two were farmers. Half were vegetarians, half meat-eaters. All were dedicated to eating well.

On a scale of 1 to 10, with 10 being "delicious; would stock it in my kitchen," the highest score mustered was a 7.3. This was for Gardenburger (Zesty), a bean burger with a nice Mexican spicing—but more suitable for a tortilla wrap and salsa than a burger bun and ketchup. The other "relatively" high scorers were vegetable burgers that looked and tasted like they were made from vegetables. The burgers that attempted to look like meat engendered such comments as "Terrible! McDonald's is better" and "Sawdust and slime fast food." The meat lovers were offended by the flavor and texture of the pseudo-meat burgers and the vegetarians were just grossed out.

Most people observed that the burgers tasted "factory produced." Some remarked they had been taken in by clever packaging at one time or another but had been disappointed. No one in the tasting group wanted to run out and buy these burgers to have on hand in the freezer.

1. Prepare a medium-hot fire in the grill.

2. Brush the eggplant, tomatoes, onion, and potato with the olive oil.

3. Grill the vegetables, turning occasionally, until tender and lightly charred, 10 to 15 minutes. Remove the vegetables from the grill as they are done.

4. Process the bread in a food processor until you have fine crumbs. Transfer to a bowl. Process the garlic until finely chopped, then add the grilled vegetables and process until you have a fairly smooth mixture. Stir into the bread crumbs along with the wheat berries, dill, and salt and pepper to taste.

5. Form the mixture into 6 burgers. Mist both sides with nonstick spray.

6. Grill the burgers until crisp and heated through, about 5 minutes per side.

7. Serve the burgers between pitas or rolls with a lettuce leaf and tomato slice on each.

Note: To cook wheat berries, combine 1 part berries with 6 parts water. Bring to a boil, then reduce the heat and simmer until the berries are tender but still chewy, 1¼ to 1½ hours. Drain off any excess water. (You can reduce the cooking time to 50 to 60 minutes by soaking the berries overnight in water to cover.)

Lentil Burgers with Tomato-Cucumber Relish

I like to serve these curry-flavored brown-rice-and-lentil burgers in pita pockets stuffed with a relish of tomatoes, cucumbers, and cilantro. But they go just as well with a Greek salad, such as the one found on page 121. Either way, a moist topping counteracts the slightly dry texture of the burgers.

SERVES 6

½ cup dried green or brown lentils, rinsed
½ cup uncooked brown rice
1 medium-size onion, chopped
1 carrot, grated
4 garlic cloves, minced
4 teaspoons ground cumin
1 teaspoon ground coriander
1 teaspoon salt
2½ cups water
6 pita pockets

TOMATO-CUCUMBER RELISH

1 large cucumber, peeled, if desired, and diced
1 large ripe tomato, diced
1 cup plain yogurt
1 tablespoon chopped fresh cilantro
2 garlic cloves, minced
Salt

Burgers to Go

When vegetarians are invited to a barbecue, they are often expected to satisfy themselves on salads or bring their own burgers. Given that most homemade vegetarian burgers are rather fragile in their uncooked state, I recommend precooking the burgers in a skillet, wrapping them individually in plastic film or bags, and freezing them for up to 3 months. Then, whenever you need a burger-to-go, grab a frozen one. If it doesn't defrost in transit, it can be cooked frozen. Because the burger is precooked, the grilling will just heat it through and add a touch of grill flavor.

1. Combine the lentils, brown rice, onion, carrot, garlic, cumin, coriander, and salt in a medium-size saucepan. Add the water. Cover and bring to a boil, then reduce the heat and boil gently until the rice and lentils are tender and all the liquid is absorbed, about 40 minutes. Drain in a colander to remove any excess liquid. Let cool slightly, then process in a food processor fitted with a steel blade until you have a fairly smooth mixture. Form into 6 burgers.

2. Prepare a medium-hot fire in the grill with a lightly oiled vegetable grill rack in place.

3. To make the tomato-cucumber relish, combine the cucumber, tomato, yogurt, cilantro, garlic, and salt to taste in a medium-size bowl. Mix gently. Set aside at room temperature to allow the flavors to develop.

4. Mist both sides of the burgers with nonstick spray. Cut the pitas in half to form 2 pockets and wrap in foil.

5. Grill the burgers until crisp, about 5 minutes per side. Warm the pitas off to the side of the grill, turning occasionally.

6. To serve, stuff the burgers into the pitas. Pass the relish at the table.

6

Wrapped and Stuffed

CHAPTER 6 • WRAPPED AND STUFFED

Chile-Rubbed Veggie Burritos

I often think food tastes better encased in a tortilla or wrapper of some sort. In this burrito, grilled vegetables are combined with refried beans and cheese to make a delicious hand-held burrito.

SERVES 4 TO 8

2 tablespoons extra-virgin olive oil
1 teaspoon chili powder
6 plum tomatoes, halved lengthwise
1 green or red bell pepper, halved
1 small zucchini, sliced lengthwise ¼ inch thick
½ onion, sliced
1 to 2 jalapeños, halved and seeded, or 1 to 2 teaspoons minced
    chipotle en adobo (optional)
2 garlic cloves
Salt and black pepper
2 tablespoons chopped fresh cilantro
¼ cup chopped black olives
8 10-inch flour tortillas
2 cups refried beans, heated
8 ounces Monterey Jack cheese, grated

1. Prepare a medium fire in a grill with a lightly oiled vegetable grill rack in place.

2. Combine the oil and chili powder. Lightly brush on the tomatoes, pepper, zucchini, onion, jalapeños, and garlic. Sprinkle with salt and pepper to taste.

3. Grill the vegetables, turning occasionally, until tender and lightly charred on all sides, 10 to 12 minutes for the tomatoes, pepper, onion, jalapeños, and garlic; 5 to 8 minutes for the zucchini. Remove the vegetables from the grill as they are done.

4. Peel the pepper and tomatoes, if desired. Chop all the vegetables. In a medium-size bowl, combine the chopped vegetables, cilantro, and olives. Season with more salt and pepper, if desired, and chipotle en adobo, if using.

5. To assemble, heat 1 flour tortilla directly over the grill (or over a gas burner or in a dry skillet over medium-high heat), turning to warm both sides. As each tortilla becomes warm and pliable, place on a work surface. Spread about ½ cup of the beans on the tortilla. Spoon about ¼ cup of the chopped vegetables over the beans. Sprinkle with about ¼ cup of the Monterey Jack. Fold in the sides and roll up the tortilla to enclose the filling. Place in a baking pan. Repeat with the remaining tortillas.

6. Cover the burritos with foil and heat on the grill over indirect heat or on a raised rack (or in a 300°F oven) until the cheese is melted and the filling is heated through, about 10 minutes. Serve hot.

Black Bean Burritos

The grill can serve as an adjunct to the kitchen—for casual al fresco dining, as well as for keeping the heat out of the kitchen. In this recipe, the grilled vegetables do add an extra sparkle of flavor, but combined with the other ingredients, it is not the grill flavor that dominates. I think what I enjoy most about this particular recipe is the ease with which it can be prepared outdoors.

SERVES 4 TO 8

1 green or purple bell pepper, julienned
1 red or yellow bell pepper, julienned
1 poblano chile or 2 jalapeños, julienned
1 onion, thinly sliced

Veggie Burger Burritos

Have you tried any of the veggie burgers in Chapter 5 wrapped in a tortilla? They make great burritos. Indeed, I find the bean burgers a trifle mushy for the traditional hamburger bun. But the texture is perfectly pleasing in a tortilla wrap, and salsa makes a great accompaniment.

A Cure for What Ails You

Herbalists agree that garlic is a strong antibacterial and antifungal agent. It has also been shown to lower cholesterol, reduce the size of cancerous tumors, and enhance the immune system.

Have you had your garlic today?

2 garlic cloves, minced
½ teaspoon ground cumin
3 tablespoons extra-virgin olive oil
6 plum tomatoes, halved lengthwise
8 10-inch flour tortillas
1½ cups cooked black beans (or 1 15-ounce can), drained
1 avocado, diced
Salt and black pepper
8 ounces Monterey Jack or cheddar cheese, grated

1. Prepare a medium fire in a grill with a lightly oiled vegetable grill rack in place.

2. In a large bowl, combine the peppers, poblano or jalapeños, onion, garlic, cumin, and 2 tablespoons of the olive oil. Toss to coat. Brush the cut side of the tomatoes with the remaining 1 tablespoon olive oil. Wrap the tortillas in foil.

3. Grill the peppers, poblano or jalapeños, onion, and garlic, tossing frequently, until tender and grill-marked, 8 to 12 minutes. Remove the vegetables from the grill and return to the bowl as they are done.

4. Meanwhile, grill the tomatoes cut side down, until tender and grill-marked, about 10 minutes. Warm the tortillas on a raised rack off to the side of the grill, turning occasionally.

5. Peel the tomatoes, if desired, chop, and add to the vegetables. Add the beans and mix well. Add the avocado and toss lightly. Season to taste with salt and pepper.

6. To assemble, spread about ¼ cup of the cheese down the center of a tortilla. Cover with a heaping ½ cup of the vegetable-bean mixture. Fold in the

sides and roll up the tortilla to enclose the filling. Place in a baking pan. Repeat with the remaining tortillas.

7. Cover the burritos with foil and heat on the grill over indirect heat or on a raised rack (or in a 300°F oven) until the cheese is melted and the filling is heated through, about 10 minutes. Serve hot.

Grilled Portobello Burritos with Jalapeño Sauce

These are the hit of the party each time they are served. Portobello mushrooms, with their firm texture, are ideal for grilling and make a surprisingly substantial filling for a burrito.

SERVES 4

4 medium-to-large portobello mushrooms
⅓ cup Barbecue Glaze (page 280) or any tomato-based
    barbecue sauce
8 10-inch flour tortillas

JALAPEÑO SAUCE

3 tablespoons butter, softened
1 fresh jalapeño, finely chopped
3 ounces cream cheese
1 egg yolk
1 tablespoon lemon or lime juice
¼ teaspoon salt

1. Prepare a medium fire in the grill.

2. Trim the mushrooms, leaving 1 inch of stem, and slice ½ inch thick. Brush with the barbecue sauce and set aside. Wrap the tortillas in foil.

3. To make the jalapeño sauce, melt 1 tablespoon of the butter in a small saucepan over low heat. Add the jalapeños and cook, stirring, until softened, about 2 minutes. Meanwhile, combine the remaining 2 tablespoons butter, the cream cheese, egg yolk, lemon or lime juice, and salt in a small bowl. Add to the

pan and cook, stirring constantly, until the sauce thickens, about 2 minutes. Do not allow the sauce to boil. Remove to a bowl and cover with plastic wrap.

4. Grill the mushrooms, basting with additional barbecue sauce and turning frequently, until tender, about 10 minutes. Warm the tortillas off to the side of the grill, turning occasionally.

5. To assemble, spread about 1 tablespoon of the jalapeño sauce slightly off center on a tortilla and cover with a few mushroom slices. Roll up part way and fold in the sides. Finish rolling and place on a warm plate, seam side down. Repeat with the remaining tortillas.

6. Serve at once, passing additional sauce on the side.

Chimichangas
on the Grill

Traditionally, chimichangas are deep-fried or pan-fried burritos. But there's no need for frying when the heat of the grill can brown the tortilla and give it a lovely crispy texture. A spoonful of chipotle en adobo gives the black beans a special smoky flavor. Chimichangas should be cooked over a low fire. If you like, keep the fire hot for grilling potatoes or corn as an accompaniment, and grill the chimichangas off to the side, away from the intense heat.

SERVES 4 TO 8

3 tablespoons canola or olive oil
2 garlic cloves, minced
1 teaspoon ground cumin
3 cups cooked black beans (or 2 15-ounce cans), drained
1½ cups diced fresh or canned tomatoes
1 tablespoon minced chipotle en adobo, or to taste
Salt and black pepper
8 10-inch flour tortillas
8 ounces Monterey Jack cheese, grated
¼ cup chopped fresh cilantro (optional)
Salsa

The Magic Ingredient: Chipotles en Adobo

Chipotles en adobo (pronounced chih-POHT-lays en a-DO-bo) is the magical ingredient in these beans and in many other Mexican dishes. The magic comes from the smoke flavor—chipotles are smoke-dried jalapeños. You can find them in the dried form or conveniently rehydrated in a tomato-vinegar sauce, which is adobo. You should be able to find chipotles en adobo wherever Mexican foods are sold. A good mail-order source is: Nancy's Specialty Market, P.O. Box 530, Newmarket, NH 03857; 800-462-6291.

1. Heat 2 tablespoons of the canola or olive oil in a medium-size skillet or saucepan. Add the garlic and cumin and cook, stirring, until the oil smells fragrant, about 2 minutes. Add the beans and tomatoes and cook until heated through, about 10 minutes. Using a potato masher, mash the beans. Then stir with a wooden spoon to make a fairly smooth mixture. Stir in the chipotle en adobo and season to taste with salt and pepper.

2. Prepare a medium-low fire in the grill.

3. Heat 1 flour tortilla directly over a gas burner or in a dry skillet over medium-high heat, turning to warm both sides. Sprinkle about ¼ cup of the Monterey Jack in a line across the center of the tortilla. Spread about ⅓ cup of the beans on top. Sprinkle with the cilantro, if using. Fold in the sides and roll up the tortilla to enclose the filling. Place on a baking sheet, seam side down. Repeat with the remaining tortillas. Brush the tortillas with the remaining 1 tablespoon oil.

4. Transfer the tortillas, seam side down, to the grill and grill, turning occasionally, until heated through and browned, 15 to 20 minutes.

5. Serve hot, passing salsa on the side.

Vegetarian Fajitas
with Chipotle Sour Cream

It's the fixin's that make fajitas so appealing. Here's a version where the fixings are so delicious, no one will notice that the tough meat is missing. Other accompaniments you might want to include are grated cheese and a chopped lettuce, tomato, and onion salad lightly dressed with oil and lemon or lime juice.

SERVES 4

GUACAMOLE

2 ripe avocados
1 garlic clove, minced
2 to 4 tablespoons Smoky Tomato Salsa (page 73)
    or store-bought salsa
Lime juice
Salt and black pepper

CHIPOTLE SOUR CREAM

1 cup sour cream (nonfat sour cream is acceptable)
1 to 2 teaspoons chipotle en adobo
Salt

FAJITAS

2 onions, thinly sliced
2 bell peppers (red, yellow, green, or a combination), julienned
1 to 2 large mild chiles, such as poblanos, julienned
2 small to medium-size zucchini, julienned
2 tablespoons extra-virgin olive oil
1 tablespoon fresh lime juice
Salt and black pepper
8 10-inch flour tortillas
Smoky Tomato Salsa (page 73) or store-bought salsa

1. Prepare a medium fire in the grill with a lightly oiled vegetable grill rack in place.

2. To make the guacamole, mash the avocados with a fork or puree them in a food processor. Combine with the garlic, salsa, lime juice, and salt and pepper to taste. Cover and set aside.

3. To make the chipotle sour cream, combine the sour cream, chipotle en adobo, and salt to taste. Cover and set aside.

4. To make the fajitas, combine the onions, peppers, chiles, and zucchini, olive oil, lime juice, and salt and pepper to taste. Toss to coat and set aside. Wrap the flour tortillas in foil.

5. Divide the vegetables into 2 batches. Grill each batch, tossing frequently, until tender and grill-marked, about 8 minutes. Warm the tortillas off to the side of the grill, turning occasionally.

6. Serve the warmed tortillas, salsa, guacamole, chipotle sour cream, and grilled vegetables at the table, and allow diners to assemble their own fajitas.

Potato-Cheese Tacos

ⓜ

These soft tacos are filled with a mixture of potatoes, cheese, and chiles, then grilled. My husband called them a "Mexican potato knish"—and ate them with relish.

SERVES 4

3 large baking potatoes (2½ to 3 pounds)
1 green bell pepper
2 jalapeños
1 cup grated sharp cheddar cheese
1 egg, lightly beaten
2 tablespoons minced fresh cilantro
Salt and black pepper
10 to 12 6-inch corn tortillas
1 tablespoon olive or canola oil
Salsa

Holy Guacamole

My friend M. L. receives a case of avocados from her parents every spring, when their 26 trees produce a bounty they must harvest and give away as quickly as possible. Though avocados have many uses and have been made into everything from creamed soup to ice cream, the best way to enjoy a good avocado is in guacamole, or *ahuacamolli* as the Aztecs called it, literally "avocado mixture." The Aztecs made their guacamole with green chiles, tomatoes, and herbs. M. L., like many cooks today, also adds a little lime juice and some chopped onions or garlic.

Guacamole is the perfect accompaniment to every burrito, taco, and fajita recipe in this chapter.

1. Prepare a medium fire in the grill.

2. Prick each potato several times with a fork and wrap in foil. Place the potatoes, pepper, and jalapeños on the grill. Roast the peppers, turning occasionally, until completely charred, about 10 minutes. Remove the peppers and jalapeños from the grill and place in a plastic or paper bag to steam for 10 minutes to loosen the skins. Close the grill lid and continue roasting the potatoes, rotating every 10 minutes or so to ensure even cooking, until fork-tender, about 45 minutes more.

3. Peel, seed, and finely chop the peppers. Set aside in a medium-size bowl.

4. When the potatoes are tender, remove from the grill and unwrap. When cool enough to handle, cut in half and scrape out the flesh. Add the flesh to the peppers along with the cheddar, egg, and cilantro. Season generously with salt and pepper and mix well.

5. To assemble the tacos, set a tortilla on a work surface. Spoon about 2 tablespoons of the filling onto one side of the tortilla. Fold over and press gently to seal. Repeat until all the tacos are filled. Brush each taco with the oil.

6. Place the tacos on the grill. Grill until the outside is crisp and grill-marked and the inside is heated through, about 3 minutes per side.

7. Serve immediately, passing salsa on the side.

Refried Bean Tacos

It is important to use fresh, pliable tortillas for these soft tacos. Stale tortillas will crack and break when they are folded. If the tortillas seem stiff, steam them briefly or heat them in a microwave until they are pliable.

SERVES 4

10 to 12 6-inch corn tortillas
1½ cups refried beans (homemade or store-bought)
1½ cups grated Monterey Jack or cheddar cheese
1 tablespoon olive or canola oil
Salsa

1. Prepare a medium fire in the grill.
2. Set a tortilla on a work surface. Spoon about 2 tablespoons of the beans and 2 tablespoons of the cheese onto one side of the tortilla. Fold over and press gently to seal. Repeat until all the tacos are filled. Brush each taco with the oil.
3. Place the tacos on the grill and grill until the outside is crisp and grill-marked and the inside is heated through, about 3 minutes per side.
4. Serve immediately, passing salsa on the side.

Twice-Grilled Corn

In this recipe, grilled corn is removed from the cob, seasoned, then wrapped inside corn husks and grilled again. You may want to double this recipe for a party because the presentation is so special and most of the work can be done in advance. Also in its favor: The corn packets will hold their heat for up to 30 minutes, allowing you time to grill other dishes. Does it go without saying that this is a delicious way to enjoy fresh corn?

SERVES 4

4 ears corn
2 tablespoons extra-virgin olive oil
1 teaspoon chili powder
½ teaspoon ground cumin
1 green bell pepper, diced
1 onion, diced
¼ cup sliced pimiento-stuffed green olives
2 tablespoons chopped fresh cilantro (optional)
Salt and black pepper

1. Peel back the husks from the corn cobs and remove the silks. Break off the ear of corn, leaving the husks still attached to the stem. Blanch the husks in boiling water for 3 minutes. Drain well.

2. Prepare a medium-hot fire in the grill with a lightly oiled vegetable grill rack in place.

3. Combine the olive oil, chili powder, and cumin in a medium-size bowl. Brush onto the ears of corn. Add the pepper and onion to the oil remaining in the bowl and toss to coat.

4. Grill the corn, turning occasionally, until tender and grill-marked, about 10 minutes. Grill the pepper and onion, tossing frequently, until tender and grill-marked, about 5 minutes. Return the pepper and onion to the bowl.

5. Cut the kernels off the cobs and add to the bowl along with the olives and cilantro, if using. Season to taste with salt and pepper. Divide the corn mixture among the 4 corn husks. Close up the husks to completely enclose the vegetables. Use kitchen twine to secure the open ends.

6. Grill the corn husk packages, turning occasionally, until well browned and heated through, about 15 minutes.

7. Serve immediately or hold for up to 30 minutes before serving.

Meaty Portobellos

Mushrooms have a quality that the Japanese call *umami*, which means meatlike. No mushroom exemplifies that concept more than portobellos, which are inevitably described as meaty, rich-tasting, and satisfying. These giant mushrooms are perfect for grilling. When buying portobellos, look at the gills. The ones that are pink-beige are younger and fresher than ones that are dark brown. Avoid ones with damp or bruised gills. When you get the mushrooms home, remove them from the plastic bag or wrap. Spread them out on a tray or basket, cover with a towel, and refrigerate. They will last for several days if they started out fresh.

Kasha-Stuffed Portobellos

The earthy flavor of kasha is perfectly complemented by the mushrooms in this dish.

SERVES 4

4 large portobello mushrooms
1 tablespoon extra-virgin olive oil, plus more for brushing
2 shallots, finely chopped
½ red bell pepper, finely chopped
2 garlic cloves, minced
⅔ cup uncooked kasha (toasted buckwheat groats)
1⅓ cups boiling water
1 teaspoon salt, plus more to taste
Black pepper

1. Prepare a medium-hot fire in the grill.

2. Remove the stems from the mushrooms. Brush the caps with olive oil. Finely chop the stems.

3. Heat the oil in a large skillet over medium heat. Add the chopped mush-

room stems, shallots, pepper, garlic, and kasha and cook, stirring, until the vegetables are softened and the kasha smells toasted, about 5 minutes. Add the water and salt. Return to a boil, cover, reduce the heat, and simmer until the liquid is absorbed and the kasha is tender, about 15 minutes. Season to taste with more salt, if needed, and pepper.

4. Grill the mushrooms caps, gill side down, for 2 minutes. Turn and grill until tender and juicy throughout, about 5 minutes.

5. Remove the mushrooms from the grill and mound the kasha mixture on top. Serve immediately.

Cheese-Stuffed Chiles

Stuffed chiles make a delicious appetizer or accompaniment to a meal of chili or tacos. Which chiles to choose for stuffing depends on your palate and tolerance for heat.

SERVES 4 AS AN APPETIZER OR SIDE DISH

*4 large chiles (such as mild Italian frying peppers, Cubanelles, or
   Hungarian hot wax) or 8 medium-size chiles (such as poblanos)*
8 ounces Monterey Jack cheese, grated

1. Prepare a medium-hot fire in the grill.

2. Roast the chiles, turning occasionally, until completely charred, about 10 minutes. Place in a plastic or paper bag to steam for 10 minutes to loosen the skins.

3. Peel and cut a slit down the length of each chile. Remove the seeds and membranes and stuff each with the Monterey Jack. Secure with toothpicks to hold the chiles closed. Wrap the chiles in a foil packet (see page 245), completely enclosing them. Return to the grill to heat through, about 10 minutes.

4. Before serving, open the foil packet and let the chiles cool for about 5 minutes. The cheese will firm up slightly, making the chiles easier to handle. Remove the toothpicks and place the chiles on individual plates or a serving platter. Serve warm.

Stuffed Grilled Peppers

Stuffed peppers work surprisingly well on the grill, though the grilling process is somewhat different from oven baking. Instead of standing the peppers up on the grill, you secure the tops with toothpicks and lay the peppers on their sides. This version of stuffed peppers uses a rice-and-bean filling with Southwestern flavors, but the possibilities for other grain stuffings are infinite.

**SERVES 2 AS A MAIN COURSE;
SERVES 4 AS A SIDE DISH**

4 large green bell peppers
2 cups cooked white or brown rice
1 cup cooked black beans
1 cup Smoky Tomato Salsa (page 73) or store-bought salsa
½ cup fresh or frozen corn kernels
¼ cup chopped scallions
¼ cup chopped fresh cilantro
1 teaspoon minced chipotles en adobo or to taste
Salt and black pepper

1. Prepare a medium-low fire in the grill.
2. Cut the top off each pepper and remove the seeds and core. Reserve the tops.
3. In a medium bowl, combine the rice, beans, salsa, corn, scallions, cilantro, chipotles, and salt and pepper to taste. Stuff in the peppers. Return the tops to the peppers and secure with toothpicks.
4. Place the peppers on their sides and grill with the lid down, turning every 10 minutes or so until tender and browned, 40 to 60 minutes. Do not allow the peppers to char.
5. Serve immediately or remove from the grill, lightly cover, and hold for up to 30 minutes before serving.

Twice-Grilled Stuffed Sweet Potatoes

Once-baked sweet potatoes are delicious. Twice-baked sweet potatoes are even more so. Cheese and chiles transform ordinary sweet potatoes into a fiesta of flavors.

SERVES 4

4 medium-size sweet potatoes (1½ to 1¾ pounds)
1 poblano chile or jalapeño
4 scallions, trimmed
Olive oil
4 tablespoons butter
½ cup grated Monterey Jack cheese
Salt and black pepper

1. Prepare a medium-hot fire in the grill. Wrap each potato in foil.

2. Grill the potatoes with the lid down, turning occasionally, until tender, about 45 minutes.

3. While the potatoes are grilling, grill the pepper until blackened and blistered all over, about 10 minutes. Place in a paper or plastic bag to steam for 10 minutes to loosen the skins. Meanwhile, brush the scallions with oil and grill, turning occasionally, until tender and grill-marked, about 8 minutes. (Don't worry about opening the grill to grill the chile pepper and scallions.)

4. Peel, seed, and finely chop the pepper. Finely chop the scallions.

5. When the potatoes are cooked through, partially unwrap and make a large slit in the top of each one. When cool enough to handle, fluff the flesh with a fork. Mix in 1 tablespoon of the butter, 2 tablespoons of the Monterey Jack, one-quarter of the peppers, and one-quarter of the scallions. Mix in salt and pepper to taste. Close up the potato and rewrap in the foil. Repeat with the remaining potatoes.

6. Return the potatoes to the grill and heat until the cheese is melted and the potatoes are hot, 10 to 20 minutes. Serve immediately.

Pesto-Stuffed Plum Tomatoes

Plum tomatoes are the tomatoes of choice for stuffing because their firm, meaty texture allows them to hold their shape better than other tomatoes.

SERVES 4 AS A SIDE DISH

4 large plum tomatoes
Extra-virgin olive oil
Salt and black pepper
½ cup Pesto (page 282) or Cilantro Pesto (page 283)
½ cup freshly grated Parmesan (if using Pesto) or Monterey Jack
*   cheese (if using Cilantro Pesto)*

1. Prepare a medium-hot fire in the grill.

2. Slice the tomatoes in half lengthwise. With the tip of a spoon, scoop out the seeds from the tomatoes. Brush the cut sides with olive oil and sprinkle with salt and pepper.

3. Grill the tomatoes, cut side down, until soft and grill-marked, about 8 minutes.

4. Carefully remove the tomatoes from the grill and stuff with the pesto. If using the pesto, sprinkle with the Parmesan; for cilantro pesto, sprinkle with the Monterey Jack. Serve warm.

Variations: The variations on the theme of stuffed tomatoes are numerous. Two of my favorite replacements for the pesto are an herb-flavored, olive-oil-moistened crumb mixture, or a goat cheese or Boursin cheese filling.

Adapting Recipes to the Grill

Sometimes vegetarian grilling is simply a matter of adapting a favorite recipe to grilling. Why bother? Because the heat of the fire caramelizes the natural sugars in the vegetables, bringing out a sweet flavor you don't get otherwise. It also adds an undertone of smokiness that can be quite pleasant.

Chili-Stuffed Zucchini

Grilling with the lid down gives the zucchini just a little extra smoke flavor, which enhances this dish. However, if you are grilling something else alongside the zucchini and want the lid up, don't worry about it. Just make sure the zucchini is fork tender before removing it from the grill.

SERVES 4 TO 8

4 medium-size zucchini
Salt and black pepper
1 tablespoon extra-virgin olive oil
2 garlic cloves, minced
1½ cups cooked pinto or black beans (or 1 15-ounce can),
    drained
¾ cup grated Monterey Jack cheese
⅓ cup Smoky Tomato Salsa (page 73) or store-bought salsa
¼ cup finely chopped fresh cilantro

1. Prepare a medium-hot fire in the grill.

2. Slice the zucchini in half lengthwise. Scoop out the centers, leaving about ¼ inch of flesh in the shells. (Discard the zucchini flesh or reserve for another use, such as making vegetable stock.) Generously sprinkle the zucchini with salt and pepper. Combine the olive oil and garlic and brush onto the zucchini, inside and out.

3. Combine the beans, ½ cup of the Monterey Jack, the salsa, and cilantro. Season with salt and pepper, if needed. Stuff the mixture into the zucchini shells. Sprinkle the remaining ¼ cup Monterey Jack on top.

4. Grill with the lid down until the zucchini is tender and the stuffing is hot, 10 to 12 minutes. Carefully remove from the grill with a spatula. Serve at once.

Variations: Any leftover chili can be used as a filling for the zucchini. cheddar cheese can replace the Monterey Jack.

Patty Pan Squash Towers

An architectural wonder, these are as delicious to eat as they are beautiful to behold. Patty pan squash are bizarre-looking yellow flying-saucer squash. They are quite similar in taste and feel to the more conventionally shaped yellow or crookneck squash—but they are more fun to work with.

SERVES 4

2 medium-size patty pan squash (about 10 ounces each)
4 large plum tomatoes
3 tablespoons extra-virgin olive oil
1 garlic clove, minced
Salt and black pepper
4 ounces Boursin cheese

1. Prepare a medium-hot fire in the grill. A lightly oiled vegetable grill rack is optional but recommended.

2. Slice the squash about ⅜ inch thick. You should have about 6 slices per squash. Slice the tomatoes about ⅜ inch thick. Combine the olive oil, garlic, and salt and pepper to taste. Brush on the squash and tomatoes.

3. Grill the squash, turning once, until tender and grill-marked, 6 to 10 minutes. Grill the tomatoes until tender and grill-marked on one side, about 5 minutes. Then turn and grill just until lightly grill-marked, 1 to 2 minutes more. Do not overcook, or the tomato slices will fall apart.

4. Spread the grilled squash slices with Boursin.

5. To assemble the towers, make 4 stacks of alternating squash and tomato slices, beginning with the four largest squash slices and ending with smallest squash slices (the ends). Serve at once.

Variations

Patty Pan Goat Cheese Towers. Substitute goat cheese for the Boursin. Proceed with the recipe as above.

Squash Caterpillars. Substitute zucchini or regular yellow squash for the patty pan squash. After building the towers, gently turn them on their sides and spread them out a little (like a row of fallen dominoes).

Fired-Up
Flatbreads and
Pizzas

Grilled Garlic Bread

Once you've tasted garlic bread made on the grill, you may never be satisfied with the foil-wrapped oven version. On a charcoal or gas grill or over a campfire, garlic bread takes on a superior grilled flavor.

MAKES 12 TO 16 SLICES

1 large loaf coarse-textured French or Italian bread
¼ cup extra-virgin olive oil
4 garlic cloves, minced

1. Prepare a medium fire in the grill.

2. Slice the bread in half horizontally. Combine the olive oil and garlic and brush onto the cut sides of the bread.

3. Grill the bread, cut sides up, until lightly toasted, 4 to 6 minutes. Turn and grill the cut sides until lightly toasted, about 4 minutes more.

4. To serve, cut the loaf into individual slices and serve warm. If you can't serve at once, place the bread together so the two grilled sides are touching and wrap in foil for up to 30 minutes before serving.

Garlic Toasts

If you can't justify a steady diet of grilled garlic bread, generously brushed with olive oil, then try this fat-free version. When lightly toasted on the grill, a slice of coarse-crumbed French or Italian bread has lovely little bumps to catch the garlic. How can something this simple taste so fine?

MAKES 12 TO 16 SLICES

1 large loaf coarse-textured French or Italian bread
1 garlic clove, halved

1. Prepare a medium fire in the grill.

2. Cut the bread into ¾-inch-thick slices. If you are slicing a baguette, cut on the diagonal to make the slices as long as possible.

3. Grill one side of each bread slice until lightly toasted, about 2 minutes. Turn and rub the toasted sides with the garlic. Grill the second sides until lightly toasted, about 2 minutes more. Rub that side with garlic. Serve warm.

Naan

Naan is a favorite accompaniment to the tandoori-style grilled foods that are served at many Indian restaurants. The tandoor oven is common throughout Asia and in Africa. It is a dome-shaped clay barrel set over a fire of wood, dung, coal, or gas. The breads are baked on the walls of the oven, resulting in a characteristic well-browned bottom crust. Baking flatbread on the grill rack of a charcoal or gas grill may be as close as most of us will come to replicating those tandoor-baked flatbreads.

MAKES 8 FLATBREADS

4 cups unbleached all-purpose flour
1 teaspoon baking powder
1 teaspoon salt
1 egg
1 tablespoon sugar
1 cup milk
½ cup safflower or canola oil

1. In a food processor fitted with the dough blade, combine the flour, baking powder, and salt. In a small bowl, mix together the egg, sugar, milk, and 4 tablespoons of the safflower or canola oil. With the motor running, slowly pour in the milk mixture and process until a soft dough is formed; add a few tablespoons of water if the mixture is too dry. Add 2 tablespoons of the oil and process briefly. Form the dough into a ball, place in a lightly oiled bowl, cover, and let stand at room temperature for 15 minutes. Knead the dough, cover, and let stand for 2 to 3 hours.

2. Prepare a medium-hot fire in the grill.

3. Divide the dough into 8 balls. Let rest for 15 minutes.

4. Lightly oil a work surface. Pat one of the balls into an oval. Roll out as thinly as possible. Brush the remaining 2 tablespoons oil on both sides. Place on a plate while you finish rolling out each ball of dough. The rolled-out rounds of dough can be stacked on top of each other.

5. Place two or more flatbreads on the grill. Close the grill lid and bake until the bottom is browned and the top begins to puff up, about 1½ minutes. To avoid scorching, check the bottoms after 1 minute and move to a cooler spot on the grill if the breads are cooking too fast. Flip the flatbreads and grill with the lid up for about 30 seconds more. Remove from the grill and stack in a basket while you continue to grill the remaining flatbreads.

6. Serve immediately.

Onion Naan

Here's another version of flatbread, this one with a terrific grilled onion flavor. If you have a gas grill, it's no problem to grill the onion ahead of time. If you have a charcoal grill, either plan ahead and grill the onion ahead of time, or sauté the onion in a little butter or olive oil for a similar, though not as wonderful, flavor. You can also make this recipe without the onion altogether.

MAKES 8 FLATBREADS

1 tablespoon active dry yeast
1 tablespoon honey
½ cup warm (110° to 115°F) water
2½ to 3½ cups unbleached all-purpose flour
1 large onion
6 tablespoons olive oil
½ cup buttermilk
1 tablespoon baking powder
2 teaspoons salt

1. In a food processor fitted with the dough blade, combine the yeast, honey, water, and ½ cup of the flour. Process to mix well. Set aside to rise in the bowl until doubled in bulk, about 30 minutes.

2. Meanwhile, to grill the onion, skewer it, brush it with 1 tablespoon of the olive oil, and grill it over a preheated grill, turning occasionally until tender and well browned, about 10 minutes. Finely chop. Alternatively, finely chop the onion and sauté in oil until tender and well-browned, about 10 minutes. Set aside.

3. Add the onion, buttermilk, 3 tablespoons of the olive oil, the baking powder, and salt to the food processor. Process to mix. Add the remaining flour, ½ cup at a time, and mix until a soft, kneadable dough is formed. Turn out onto a very lightly floured surface and knead until the dough is smooth and elastic. Place in a lightly oiled bowl, cover, and let rise until doubled in bulk, about 1 hour.

4. Prepare a medium fire in the grill.

A Tribute to The Red Front

When you read my cheese pizza recipe, you may think that I've made a mistake and assembled the toppings backward. Who has ever heard of building a pizza with the cheese before the sauce? Well, this is (almost) the pizza of my youth, and it is dedicated to The Red Front restaurant in Troy, New York, which is a classic family-owned upstate Italian-American restaurant. On a recent pilgrimage back to my hometown, I asked if the pizza was still the same. The maitre d', who had been there for more than 30 years, told me the pizza was unchanged, but you had to "ask for it special. Nowadays," he confided *sotto voce*, "people come here from all over, and they want pizza that tastes like everywhere else. They get mad when you give them something different." He shrugged—what can you do?—and left. We ordered our pizza "cheese first," and it was as wonderful as ever. When you build a pizza cheese first, the cheese melts into the crust. Try it.

5. Divide the dough into 8 balls. Lightly oil a work surface. Pat one of the balls into an oval. Roll out as thinly as possible. Brush the remaining olive oil on both sides. Place on a plate while you finish rolling out each ball of dough. The rolled-out rounds of dough can be stacked on top of each other.

6. Place two or more flatbreads on the grill. Grill until the bottom is browned and the top begins to puff up, 2 to 3 minutes. To avoid scorching, check the bottoms after 1 minute and move to a cooler spot on the grill if the breads are cooking too fast. Flip the flatbreads and grill for 1 to 2 minutes more, until golden with brown spots. Remove from the grill and stack in a basket while you continue to grill the remaining flatbreads.

7. Serve immediately.

Cheese-Tomato Pizzas

For these and other grilled pizzas, use a vegetable grill rack or pizza grill rack for an evenly browned crust. Because pizza grilling goes fast, have your tools, rolled-out dough, sauce, and cheese at hand when you begin, along with plates or platters on which to put the finished pizzas. Be sure the sauce is piping hot, which will help ensure that the toppings fully heat through.

SERVES 6

*1 recipe Basic Pizza Dough (page 185) or Quick-Rise
    Pizza Dough (page 186)*
2 cups well-seasoned tomato sauce
4 garlic cloves, minced (optional)
½ cup grated mozzarella cheese
1½ cups freshly grated Parmesan or Asiago cheese
Olive oil

1. Prepare the pizza dough according to the recipe directions. While the dough is resting, prepare a medium fire in the grill. Using a lightly oiled vegetable grill rack or pizza grill and preheating it over the fire will result in a more evenly baked crust, but using a vegetable grill rack is not necessary.

Pizza Grills for Breads and Pizza

You can buy a special round 12-inch pizza grill made of heavy-duty cast iron with a nonstick coating that does a fine job of grilling pizza. The detachable handle enables you to prep the pizza in the kitchen or at a counter near the grill and then carry it to the grill. You detach the handle so the grill lid can be closed. I have a pizza grill and use it alongside my vegetable grill rack; for a two-pizza batch, I make a round pizza on my pizza grill and a rectangular one on my grill rack. They give very similar results, with the pizza grill being slightly more convenient to use because of the handle.

Pizza grills run about $35.00 and are available from King Arthur Flour, The Baker's Catalogue, P.O. Box 876, Norwich, Vermont 05055, or call 800-827-6836.

2. Heat the sauce, with the garlic, if desired, and keep warm. The sauce should be hot when it is spooned onto the pizza, otherwise the cheese won't melt properly.

3. Combine the mozzarella and Parmesan or Asiago in a bowl and mix well.

4. Divide the dough into 6 balls. Roll out the balls to make small pizzas about ⅛ inch thick. Brush both sides with olive oil. Stack the dough rounds on a plate.

5. Place a round of dough on the grill (or on the vegetable grill rack, if using). Grill until the surface of the dough is bubbly and the bottom is browned, 2 to 3 minutes. With a pair of tongs, lift the pizza off the grill and invert onto a plate or baking sheet. Sprinkle ⅙ of the cheese over the browned crust, then spread ⅙ of the sauce on top. Return the pizza to the grill, sauce side up, and grill until the bottom is well browned, 1½ to 2 minutes more. If at any point the pizza seems to be cooking too quickly, reduce the heat on a gas grill or move the pizza to a cooler spot over charcoal or wood to avoid scorching.

6. Place the pizza on a serving plate and keep warm. Repeat with the remaining dough and toppings.

7. Cut each pizza in halves or quarters and serve warm.

Vegetable Lovers' Pizza

You can't beat this combination—grilled vegetables on top of grilled pizza. The double dose of smoke makes this pizza irresistible.

SERVES 6

*1 recipe Basic Pizza Dough (page 185) or Quick-Rise
    Pizza Dough (page 186)
1 medium-size eggplant, peeled and sliced ⅜ inch thick
1 onion, sliced ½ inch thick
1 green bell pepper, halved
1 medium-size zucchini, sliced ⅜ inch thick
2 portobello mushroom caps, sliced ⅜ inch thick
Extra-virgin olive oil
2 cups well-seasoned tomato sauce
1 cup freshly grated Parmesan cheese*

1. Prepare the pizza dough according to the recipe directions. While the dough is resting, prepare a medium-hot fire in the grill.

2. Brush the eggplant, onion, pepper, zucchini, and mushrooms with olive oil.

3. Grill the vegetables, turning occasionally, until tender and grill-marked, 10 to 15 minutes for the eggplant; about 10 minutes for the onion and pepper; and about 5 minutes for the zucchini and mushrooms. As the vegetables become tender, remove from the grill and chop into large dice.

4. Meanwhile, heat the tomato sauce and keep warm.

5. *To make two large pizzas:* Divide the dough into 2 balls. Lightly oil a vegetable grill rack or pizza grill. Stretch 1 ball of dough to fit the oiled grill rack. Place the grill rack over the fire, cover the grill, and grill the pizza until the bottom is browned, about 5 minutes. Remove the grill rack from the grill. Brush the top side with olive oil, then flip the pizza over. Spread about 1 cup of the sauce on the browned crust, top with half of the grilled vegetables, and sprinkle with half of the Parmesan on top. Return the pizza, still on the rack, to the grill. Cover the grill and grill for 5 to 8 minutes, checking the crust after 5 minutes. If at any point the pizza seems to be cooking too quickly, reduce the heat on a gas

grill or move the pizza to a cooler spot over charcoal or wood to avoid scorching. Remove the pizza, place on a serving plate, and keep warm. Repeat with the remaining dough and toppings.

To make individual-size pizzas: Divide the dough into 6 balls. Roll out the balls to make small rounds about ⅛ inch thick. Brush both sides with olive oil. Stack the dough rounds on a plate. Place a round of dough on the grill. Grill until the surface of the dough is bubbly and the bottom is browned, 2 to 3 minutes. With a pair of tongs, lift the pizza off the grill and invert onto a plate or baking sheet. Spread about ⅙ of the sauce on the browned crust, then top with ⅙ of the vegetables, and sprinkle with ⅙ of the Parmesan. Return the pizza to the grill, vegetable side up, and grill until the bottom is browned, 1½ to 2 minutes more. If at any point the pizza seems to be cooking too quickly, reduce the heat on a gas grill or move the pizza to a cooler spot over charcoal or wood to avoid scorching. Remove the pizza, place on a serving plate, and keep warm. Repeat with the remaining dough and toppings.

5. Slice the pizza and serve warm.

Fresh Tomato Pizza

Before I learned to grill pizza, homemade pizza was strictly a winter dish—I wasn't about to crank up the oven to 500° on a hot July evening. But with an outside grill, homemade pizza is easy to enjoy year-round, and in the summer you can take advantage of wonderfully flavored local tomatoes and fresh basil for a simple topping.

SERVES 6

*1 recipe Basic Pizza Dough (page 185) or Quick-Rise
    Pizza Dough (page 186)
3 pounds vine-ripened tomatoes, halved
1 leek, halved lengthwise and cleaned thoroughly
Extra-virgin olive oil
½ cup finely chopped fresh basil
Salt and black pepper
½ cup freshly grated Parmesan cheese
8 ounces fresh mozzarella cheese, thinly sliced*

1. Prepare the pizza dough according to the recipe directions. While the dough is resting, prepare a medium-hot fire in the grill with a lightly oiled vegetable grill rack in place.

2. Brush the cut sides of the tomatoes and both sides of the leeks with the olive oil.

3. Grill the tomatoes, cut side down, until tender and grill-marked, about 10 minutes. Grill the leeks, turning occasionally, until tender and grill-marked, about 10 minutes. Remove the vegetables from the grill and set aside. Remove the grill rack from the grill; you can use this for grilling the pizza.

4. To make the sauce, peel and chop the tomatoes and set aside in a colander or sieve to drain. Press to squeeze out the excess liquid. Finely chop the leek and combine with the drained tomatoes, basil, and salt and pepper to taste. The sauce should be quite thick. If it is not, drain again. A loose sauce will result in a soggy pizza crust.

5. *To make two large pizzas:* Divide the dough into 2 balls. Lightly oil a vegetable grill rack or pizza grill. Stretch 1 ball of dough to fit the oiled grill rack.

Place the grill rack over the fire, cover the grill, and grill the pizza until the bottom is browned, about 5 minutes. Remove the grill rack from the grill. Brush the top side with olive oil, then flip the pizza over. Sprinkle half of the Parmesan over the browned crust, then top with half of the sauce and half of the mozzarella. Return the pizza, still on the rack, to the grill. Cover the grill and grill for 5 to 8 minutes, checking the crust after 5 minutes. If at any point the pizza seems to be cooking too quickly, reduce the heat on a gas grill or move the pizza to a cooler spot over charcoal or wood to avoid scorching. Remove the pizza, place on a serving plate, and keep warm. Repeat with the remaining dough and toppings.

To make individual-size pizzas: Divide the dough into 6 balls. Roll out the balls to make small rounds about 1/8 inch thick. Brush both sides with olive oil. Stack the dough rounds on a plate. Place a round of dough on the grill. Grill until the surface of the dough is bubbly and the bottom is browned, 2 to 3 minutes. With a pair of tongs, lift the pizza off the grill and invert onto a plate or baking sheet. Sprinkle about 1/6 of the Parmesan on the browned crust, then top with 1/6 of the sauce and 1/6 of the mozzarella. Return the pizza to the grill, cheese side up, and grill until the bottom is browned, 1½ to 2 minutes more. If at any point the pizza seems to be cooking too quickly, reduce the heat on a gas grill or move the pizza to a cooler spot over charcoal or wood to avoid scorching. Remove the pizza, place on a serving plate, and keep warm. Repeat with the remaining dough and toppings.

6. Slice the pizza and serve warm.

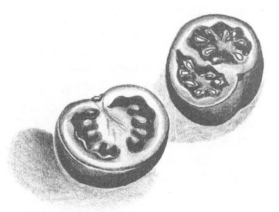

Olivada Pizza

Olivada is a paste made from cured black olives, olive oil, and black pepper. It is intense and pungent, and a little goes a long way. Indeed this pizza is best served as an appetizer or side dish, rather than as a main course, when it might cause sensory overload. The olivada topping is also delicious as a spread on bruschetta or fresh bread. Use the best quality olives you can find.

SERVES 12 TO 18 AS AN APPETIZER

1 recipe Basic Pizza Dough (page 185) or Quick-Rise
    Pizza Dough (page 186)
1 pound imported brine- or oil-cured black olives, pitted
4 garlic cloves, minced
3 tablespoons chopped fresh parsley
2 tablespoon drained capers
2 tablespoons extra-virgin olive oil, plus more for the crust
Black pepper
4 ounces provolone cheese, thinly sliced

1. Prepare the pizza dough according to the recipe directions. While the dough is resting, prepare a medium-hot fire in the grill.

2. Make the olivada topping by combining the olives, garlic, parsley, and capers in a food processor fitted with a steel blade. Process to combine. With the motor running, slowly pour in 2 tablespoons of the olive oil and process until fairly smooth. Season to taste with pepper.

3. Divide the dough into 6 balls. Roll out the balls to make small pizzas about ⅛ inch thick. Brush both sides with olive oil. Stack the dough rounds on a plate.

4. Place a round of dough on the grill. Grill until the surface of the dough is bubbly and the bottom is browned, 2 to 3 minutes. With a pair of tongs, lift the pizza off the grill and invert onto a plate or baking sheet. Spread about ¼ cup of the olivada on the browned crust, then top with ¼ of the provolone. Return the pizza to the grill, cheese side up, and grill until the bottom is browned, 1½ to 2 minutes more. If at any point the pizza seems to be cooking too quickly, reduce the heat on a gas grill or move the pizza to a cooler spot over charcoal

or wood to avoid scorching.

5. Place the pizza on a serving plate and keep warm. Repeat with the remaining dough and toppings.

6. Slice the pizza and serve warm.

White Pizza with Leeks and Peppers

Creamy Italian fontina is a wonderful pizza cheese, with great melting qualities.

SERVES 6

*1 recipe Basic Pizza Dough (page 185) or Quick-Rise
    Pizza Dough (page 186)
1 leek, julienned
1 red bell pepper, julienned
1 green bell pepper, julienned
1 yellow bell pepper, julienned
2 tablespoons extra-virgin olive oil, plus more for brushing
2 tablespoons chopped garlic
1 pound fontina cheese, grated*

1. Prepare the pizza dough according to the recipe directions. While the dough is resting, prepare a medium-hot fire in the grill with a lightly oiled vegetable grill rack in place.

2. Toss the leek and peppers with 2 tablespoons of the olive oil until well coated.

3. Grill the vegetables in two batches, tossing frequently, until tender and grill-marked, about 7 minutes. Remove the vegetables from the grill and set aside. Remove the grill rack from the grill; you can use this for grilling the pizza.

4. *To make two large pizzas:* Divide the dough into 2 balls. Lightly oil the vegetable grill rack or pizza grill. Stretch 1 ball of dough to fit the oiled grill rack. Place the grill rack over the fire, cover the grill, and grill the pizza until the

The Trick Is Not the Dough

Any pizza dough can be grilled directly over fire. You can make grilled pizza with your own standard recipe, you can use my recipes (pages 185 or 186), or you can use refrigerated supermarket dough.

bottom is browned, about 5 minutes. Remove the grill rack from the grill. Brush the top side with olive oil, then flip the pizza over. Scatter 1 tablespoon of the garlic on the browned crust, sprinkle half of the fontina on top, and top with half of the leek mixture. Return the pizza, still on the rack, to the grill. Cover the grill and grill for 5 to 8 minutes, checking the crust after 5 minutes. If at any point the pizza seems to be cooking too quickly, reduce the heat on a gas grill or move the pizza to a cooler spot over charcoal or wood to avoid scorching. Remove the pizza, place on a serving plate, and keep warm. Repeat with the remaining dough and toppings.

To make individual-size pizzas: Divide the dough into 6 balls. Roll out the balls to make small rounds about ⅛ inch thick. Brush both sides with olive oil. Stack the dough rounds on a plate. Place a round of dough on the grill. Grill until the surface of the dough is bubbly and the bottom is browned, 2 to 3 minutes. With a pair of tongs, lift the pizza off the grill and invert onto a plate or baking sheet. Scatter about 1/6 of the garlic on the browned crust, sprinkle 1/6 of the fontina on top, and top with 1/6 of the leek mixture. Return the pizza to the grill, vegetable side up, and grill until the bottom is browned, 1½ to 2 minutes more. If at any point the pizza seems to be cooking too quickly, reduce the heat on a gas grill or move the pizza to a cooler spot over charcoal or wood to avoid scorching. Remove the pizza, place on a serving plate, and keep warm. Repeat with the remaining dough and toppings.

5. Slice the pizza and serve warm.

Spinach Feta Pizza

This flavorful pizza is another perfectly versatile pizza for serving as an appetizer or main course.

SERVES 6 AS A MAIN COURSE;
SERVES 12 TO 18 AS AN APPETIZER

1 recipe Basic Pizza Dough (page 185) or Quick-Rise
 Pizza Dough (page 186)
1 pound spinach, tough stems trimmed
2 tablespoons extra-virgin olive oil
2 tablespoons minced garlic
½ cup freshly grated Parmesan cheese
8 ounces feta cheese, crumbled
½ Vidalia or other sweet onion, thinly sliced

1. Prepare the pizza dough according to the recipe directions. While the dough is resting, prepare a medium-hot fire in the grill.

2. Steam the spinach until just wilted, about 3 minutes. Drain well. Taking a handful of spinach at a time, squeeze out as much water as possible. Coarsely chop.

3. *To make two large pizzas:* Divide the dough into 2 balls. Lightly oil a vegetable grill rack or pizza grill. Stretch 1 ball of dough to fit the oiled grill rack. Place the grill rack over the fire, cover the grill, and grill the pizza until the bottom is browned, about 5 minutes. Remove the grill rack from the grill. Brush the top side with olive oil, then flip the pizza over. Brush the dough with olive oil and scatter 1 tablespoon of the garlic over the browned crust. Sprinkle with half of the Parmesan and top with half of the spinach, half of the feta, and half of the onion. Return the pizza, still on the rack, to the grill. Cover the grill and grill for 5 to 8 minutes, checking the crust after 5 minutes. If at any point the pizza seems to be cooking too quickly, reduce the heat on a gas grill or move the pizza to a cooler spot over charcoal or wood to avoid scorching. Remove the pizza, place on a serving plate, and keep warm. Repeat with the remaining dough and toppings.

To make individual-size pizzas: Divide the dough into 6 balls. Roll out the

Vegetable Grill Racks for Pizza-Making

There are two problems that arise when grilling pizza, and a vegetable grill rack solves both. The first is the problem with hot spots on the grill. Your bottom crust is less likely to scorch in one spot if you grill on a vegetable rack because the metal distributes the heat more evenly.

The second problem has to do with putting toppings on the pizza. On a grill, you cook the bottom crust, flip the pizza over, and put the toppings in place. While you are spooning the toppings over the crust, it continues to cook. If you leave the pizza on the grill, the crust may be completely baked in the time it takes to spoon on the toppings. A better way is to remove the crust from the grill, then assemble the toppings. But this presents the problem of transferring the loaded pizza back to the grill. This maneuver requires a baker's peel and more than a little skill. A simple method is to grill the pizza on a vegetable grill rack, then to remove the pizza, still on the rack, from the grill and set it on a counter or table. Then flip the pizza, load on the toppings, and return the grill rack to the grill. It's easy.

A special pizza rack is also available, the main difference being that the "pizza grill," as it is called, is round and has detachable handles. See the illustration on page 172.

balls to make small rounds about ⅛ inch thick. Brush both sides with olive oil. Stack the dough rounds on a plate. Place a round of dough on the grill. Grill until the surface of the dough is bubbly and the bottom is well-browned, 2 to 3 minutes. With a pair of tongs, lift the pizza off the grill and invert onto a plate or baking sheet. Scatter about 1/6 of the garlic over the browned crust, sprinkle with 1/6 of the Parmesan, and top with 1/6 of the spinach, 1/6 of the feta, and 1/6 of the onion. Return the pizza to the grill, cheese side up, and grill until the bottom is browned, 1½ to 2 minutes more. If at any point the pizza seems to be cooking too quickly, reduce the heat on a gas grill or move the pizza to a cooler spot over charcoal or wood to avoid scorching. Remove the pizza, place on a serving plate, and keep warm. Repeat with the remaining dough and toppings.

4. Slice the pizza and serve warm.

Eggplant Pizza with Goat Cheese

Tangy goat's milk cheese proves to be the perfect foil for smoky herbed eggplant.

SERVES 6 AS A MAIN COURSE;
SERVES 18 AS AN APPETIZER

1 recipe Basic Pizza Dough (page 185) or Quick-Rise
Pizza Dough (page 186)
1 medium-size eggplant, peeled and sliced ⅜ inch thick
1 recipe Basic Herb Marinade and Salad Dressing (page 272)
or ⅓ cup Italian-style salad dressing
1 red bell pepper
Extra-virgin olive oil
8 ounces soft goat cheese

These Recipes Are Different

The pizza-making techniques in this chapter do not rely on the use of a baker's peel for transferring the pizza onto the grill. Most grill recipes call for assembling the pizza on a peel and transferring it to the grill—leaving you vulnerable to the problems of the dough sticking to the peel or sliding off onto the wrong spot on the grill.

The only nonstandard piece of equipment I use is the vegetable grill rack—and that is used in every chapter in this book. With the grill rack, or a pizza rack made specifically for that purpose, you can assemble the pizza right on the surface on which the pizza will be grilled. Individual-size pizzas, by the way, need neither peel nor rack. They are small enough to handle without extra equipment.

1. Prepare the pizza dough according to the recipe directions. While the dough is resting, prepare a medium-hot fire in the grill.

2. In a shallow bowl, combine the eggplant and marinade or salad dressing. Toss well to coat. Let stand for at least 15 minutes to absorb the marinade.

3. Meanwhile, roast the pepper, turning occasionally, until completely charred, about 10 minutes. Place in a plastic or paper bag to steam for 10 minutes to loosen the skin. Peel and seed the pepper, then julienne.

4. Grill the eggplant, turning occasionally, until tender and grill-marked, 10 to 15 minutes.

5. *To make two large pizzas:* Divide the dough into 2 balls. Lightly oil a vegetable grill rack or pizza grill. Stretch 1 ball of dough to fit the oiled grill rack. Place the grill rack over the fire, cover the grill, and grill the pizza until the bottom is browned, about 5 minutes. Remove the grill rack from the grill. Brush the top side with olive oil, then flip the pizza over. Spread half of the goat cheese on the browned crust, then top with half of the eggplant and half of the red pepper strips. Return the pizza, still on the rack, to the grill. Cover the grill and grill for 5 to 8 minutes, checking the crust after 5 minutes. If at any point the pizza seems to be cooking too quickly, reduce the heat on a gas grill or move the pizza to a cooler spot over charcoal or wood to avoid scorching. Remove the pizza, place on a serving plate, and keep warm. Repeat with the remaining dough and toppings.

To make individual-size pizzas: Divide the dough into 6 balls. Roll out the balls to make small rounds about ⅛ inch thick. Brush both sides with olive oil. Stack the dough rounds on a plate. Place a round of dough on the grill. Grill until the surface of the dough is bubbly and the bottom is well-browned, 2 to 3 minutes. With a pair of tongs, lift the pizza off the grill and invert onto a plate or baking sheet. Spread about 1/6 of the goat cheese on the browned crust, then top with 1/6 of the eggplant and 1/6 of the red pepper strips. Return the pizza to the grill, vegetable side up, and grill until the bottom is browned, 1½ to 2 minutes more. If at any point the pizza seems to be cooking too quickly, reduce the heat on a gas grill or move the pizza to a cooler spot over charcoal or wood to avoid scorching. Remove the pizza, place on a serving plate, and keep warm. Repeat with the remaining dough and toppings.

6. Slice the pizza and serve warm.

Broccoli-Gorgonzola Pizza

You may have to be a fan of strong cheese to enjoy this combo (i.e., kids had better step aside), but those who can appreciate Italy's fine, creamy blue cheese will enjoy it. Because of the intense flavor of the cheese, this is a good choice for serving as an appetizer.

SERVES 12 TO 18 AS AN APPETIZER;
SERVES 6 AS A MAIN COURSE

1 recipe Basic Pizza Dough (page 185) or Quick-Rise
*   Pizza Dough (page 186)*
1 pound broccoli, finely chopped
2 garlic cloves
1 teaspoon dried thyme
2 tablespoons extra-virgin olive oil, plus more for brushing
8 ounces Gorgonzola cheese, at room temperature, softened with
*   a fork*
½ cup pine nuts, toasted

1. Prepare the pizza dough according to the recipe directions. While the dough is resting, prepare a medium-hot fire in the grill with a lightly oiled vegetable grill rack in place.

2. Combine the broccoli, garlic, thyme, and olive oil and toss to coat.

3. Grill the broccoli, tossing frequently, until tender and grill-marked, 5 to 8 minutes.

4. Divide the dough into 6 balls. Roll out the balls to make small pizzas about ⅛ inch thick. Brush both sides with olive oil. Stack the dough rounds on a plate. Place a round of dough on the grill. Grill until the surface of the dough is bubbly and the bottom is browned, 2 to 3 minutes. With a pair of tongs, lift the pizza off the grill and invert onto a plate or baking sheet. Spread about 1/6 cup of the Gorgonzola on the browned crust, then top with 1/6 of the broccoli and 1/6 of the pine nuts. Return the pizza to the grill, cheese side up, and grill until the bottom is browned, 1½ to 2 minutes more. If at any point the pizza seems to be cooking too quickly, reduce the heat on a gas grill or move the pizza to a cooler spot over charcoal or wood to avoid scorching. Place the pizza

on a serving plate and keep warm. Repeat with the remaining dough and toppings.

5. Slice the pizza and serve warm.

Basic Pizza Dough

This is my house pizza dough. I make a batch of it every week, whether I'm cooking the pizzas indoors or out.

MAKES 6 INDIVIDUAL-SIZE PIZZAS, TWO 10-INCH TO 12-INCH ROUND PIZZAS, OR TWO 12-INCH BY 15-INCH RECTANGULAR PIZZAS

3 cups all-purpose unbleached flour
2 teaspoons salt
1 package or 1 scant tablespoon active dry yeast
1 cup warm (110° to 115°F) water
3 tablespoons extra-virgin olive oil

1. In a food processor or large bowl, combine the flour and salt.

2. Combine the yeast and water and stir until foamy. Stir in the olive oil.

3. With the food processor motor running, slowly pour in the yeast mixture and process until the dough forms into a ball. Continue processing for 1 minute more to knead the dough. Alternatively, add the yeast mixture to the dough and stir until the dough comes together in a ball. Turn onto a lightly floured surface and knead until the dough is springy and elastic, about 5 minutes. The dough should be firm and just slightly sticky—not dry. Place the dough ball in an oiled bowl and turn to coat with the oil. Cover and let rise until doubled in bulk, about 1 hour.

4. *To shape the dough into individual-size pizzas:* Divide the dough into 6 balls. On the floured work surface, roll out each ball into a circle about 6 inches in diameter and about ⅛ inch thick. Brush both sides with olive oil. You can stack up the dough rounds and they won't stick together if they have been well oiled. The dough is ready for grilling.

To shape the dough into two round or rectangular pizzas: Divide the dough into two balls. Brush the surface of a vegetable and/or pizza grill rack with oil. Stretch the dough to fit onto the rack. The dough is now ready for grilling.

Quick-Rise Pizza Dough

Quick-rising yeast gives you pizza dough with just a 30-minute rising time—just enough time to get the grill prepared and the toppings assembled.

**MAKES 6 INDIVIDUAL-SIZE PIZZAS,
TWO 10-INCH TO 12-INCH ROUND PIZZAS, OR
TWO 12-INCH BY 15-INCH RECTANGULAR PIZZAS**

*3 cups all-purpose white bread flour
1 package quick-rising yeast
2 teaspoons salt
½ teaspoon sugar
1 cup water
2 tablespoons extra-virgin olive oil*

1. In a food processor fitted with the dough blade, combine the flour, yeast, salt, and sugar. Process to mix.

2. In a small saucepan or in a microwave-safe container, combine the water and olive oil. Heat until an instant-read thermometer registers 125° to 130°F.

3. With the food processor motor running, slowly pour in the heated water mixture and process until the dough forms into a ball. Continue processing for 1 minute more to knead the dough. Turn onto a lightly floured surface, cover with plastic wrap, and let rise for 30 minutes.

4. *To shape the dough into individual-size pizzas:* Divide the dough into 6 balls. On the floured work surface, roll out each ball into a circle about 6 inches in diameter and about ⅛ inch thick. Brush both sides with olive oil. You can stack up the dough rounds and they won't stick together if they have been well oiled. The dough is ready for grilling.

To shape the dough into two round or rectangular pizzas: Divide the dough into two balls. Brush the surface of a vegetable and/or pizza grill rack with oil. Stretch the dough to fit onto the rack. The dough is now ready for grilling.

Flame-Kissed Pasta

CHAPTER 8 • FLAMED-KISSED PASTA

Fettuccine with Charred Tomato and Leek Sauce

Grilling tomatoes and leeks brings out their natural sweetness. They are then combined in a food processor and processed briefly to make a sauce that is just slightly warmer than room temperature. This is a great warm-weather dinner.

SERVES 4 TO 6

1 large leek (white part only), halved lengthwise
2½ pounds vine-ripened tomatoes, halved
Extra-virgin olive oil
4 large garlic cloves
1 cup loosely packed fresh basil leaves
Salt and black pepper
1½ pounds fresh fettuccine, or 1 pound dried
½ cup freshly grated Parmesan cheese

1. Prepare a medium fire in the grill.

2. Begin heating a large pot of salted water for the pasta.

3. Brush the leeks and the cut sides of the tomatoes with olive oil. Skewer the garlic and brush with olive oil.

4. Grill the leek, turning occasionally, until tender and lightly charred, 8 to 10 minutes. Grill the tomatoes, cut side down, until tender and lightly charred, about 10 minutes. Grill the garlic, turning occasionally, until well browned, about 12 minutes.

5. Peel the tomatoes and discard the cores. In a food processor fitted with a steel blade, combine the tomatoes, leeks, garlic, and basil. Process to make a fairly smooth sauce. Pour into a large pasta serving bowl. Season generously with salt and pepper. Set aside.

6. Add the pasta to the boiling water and cook until just tender. Drain. Place the pasta in a large serving bowl.

7. Toss the pasta with the sauce and Parmesan. Serve at once.

Fettuccine with Charred Tomatoes and Arugula

Arugula is one of the early spring greens. Its distinctively peppery and smoky flavor is well matched by the flavor of the grilled tomatoes. The tomatoes aren't at their best at this time of the year—all the more reason to grill them and coax out as much flavor as possible.

SERVES 4 TO 6

3 pounds vine-ripened tomatoes, halved
Extra-virgin olive oil
3 large garlic cloves
1 bunch arugula, stemmed and leaves torn
Salt and black pepper
1½ pounds fresh fettuccine or linguine, or 1 pound dried
½ cup freshly grated Parmesan cheese

1. Prepare a medium fire in the grill.
2. Begin heating a large pot of salted water for the pasta.
3. Brush the cut sides of the tomatoes with olive oil. Skewer the garlic and brush with olive oil.
4. Grill the tomatoes, cut side down, until tender and lightly charred, about 10 minutes. Grill the garlic, turning occasionally, until well browned, about 12 minutes.
5. Peel the tomatoes and discard the cores. In a blender or food processor fitted with a steel blade, combine the tomatoes and garlic. Process to make a fairly smooth sauce. Pour into a medium-size saucepan and bring to a boil. Stir in the arugula and cook just until the arugula is wilted, 1 to 2 minutes. Remove from the heat and season generously with salt and pepper. Set aside.
6. Add the pasta to the boiling water and cook until just tender. Drain. Place the pasta in a large serving bowl.
7. Toss the pasta with the sauce and Parmesan. Serve at once.

Pasta with Grilled Tomato-Fennel Sauce

Fennel is a very under-appreciated vegetable in the United States. Its sweet, delicate flavor combines beautifully with tomatoes, and it takes well to grilling. Look for clean, crisp bulbs with crisp leaves. When you get it home, store it in a tightly sealed plastic bag in the refrigerator for up to 5 days. In this recipe, grilling enhances the sweetness in the vegetables—fennel, tomatoes, and leeks. The addition of Parmesan at the table is essential for bringing all the flavors together.

SERVES 4 TO 6

1 fennel bulb
1 leek (white part only), thinly sliced
4 tablespoons extra-virgin olive oil
2 large garlic cloves, minced
1½ pounds plum tomatoes, halved
Salt and black pepper
1 pound rotini or corkscrew pasta
Freshly grated Parmesan cheese

1. Prepare a medium fire in the grill with a lightly oiled vegetable grill rack in place.

2. Begin heating a large pot of salted water for the pasta.

3. Thinly slice the fennel bulb and chop a few tablespoons of the leaves. Place the chopped fennel bulb in a bowl and set the chopped leaves aside. Place the leeks in another bowl.

4. Combine 3 tablespoons of the olive oil and the garlic. Brush on the cut side of the tomatoes. Divide the remaining olive oil between the fennel and leeks and toss to coat. Sprinkle salt and pepper to taste on all the vegetables.

5. Grill the tomatoes cut side down, until charred and soft, about 10 minutes. Remove from the grill, peel, chop, and place in a large bowl.

6. Grill the fennel, tossing frequently, until tender and lightly charred, about 6 minutes. Combine with the tomatoes.

7. Grill the leeks, tossing frequently, until tender and lightly charred, about 4 minutes. Combine with the tomatoes and fennel.

8. Add the pasta to the boiling water and cook until just tender. Drain. Place the pasta in a large serving bowl.

9. Toss the pasta with the remaining 1 tablespoon olive oil and the vegetable mixture. Garnish with the chopped fennel leaves. Serve at once, passing the Parmesan at the table.

Fusilli with Marinated Summer Vegetables

Pasta and vegetables make for healthy eating in the summer. Feel free to substitute whatever vegetables you have on hand for the squash, beans, and mushrooms. The grilled tomatoes and peppers provide a necessary moisture, while the salty olives and Parmesan bring all the flavors together.

SERVES 4 TO 6

1 zucchini, julienned
1 yellow summer squash, julienned
1 small onion, cut into slivers
4 ounces green beans, cut into 2-inch lengths
4 ounces mushrooms, sliced
1 recipe Basic Herb Marinade and Salad Dressing (page 272)
2 red bell peppers
1 pint cherry or yellow pear tomatoes, halved
½ cup imported brine- or oil-cured black olives
½ to 1 cup freshly grated Parmesan cheese

1. In a large bowl, combine the zucchini, summer squash, onion, green beans, and mushrooms. Add the marinade and set aside. (The vegetables can marinate for up to a day in the refrigerator.)

2. Prepare a medium-hot fire in the grill with a lightly oiled vegetable grill rack in place.

Long Marinating Is Not Necessary

While meat is often marinated for a long time before grilling, it just isn't necessary with vegetables because most vegetables don't absorb much marinade. Tossing the vegetables with a marinade and grilling immediately yields the same results as leaving the vegetables in the marinade for an hour or more.

3. Begin heating a large pot of salted water for the pasta.

4. Roast the peppers off to the side of the grill until completely charred, about 10 minutes. Place in a plastic or paper bag to steam for 10 minutes to loosen the skins.

5. Meanwhile, lift the vegetables out of the marinade and grill, tossing frequently, until tender and grill-marked, about 7 minutes. Set aside and keep warm.

6. Toss the cherry tomatoes with the remaining marinade. Lift out with a slotted spoon and grill, tossing frequently, until tender, about 5 minutes. Set aside with the other vegetables and keep warm.

7. Add the pasta to the boiling water and cook until just tender. Drain. Place the pasta in a large serving bowl.

8. Cut slits in the peppers, then drain briefly into the bowl with the pasta to catch any juices. Quickly peel and seed the peppers, then julienne and add to the pasta. Toss to mix. Add the grilled vegetables along with the olives and Parmesan and toss to mix. Season with salt and pepper, if needed. Serve at once.

**Variation: Marinated
Summer Vegetable Sauté.**
Skip the pasta; these
vegetables are great on their
own. Without the pasta, this
dish will serve three as a
vegetarian vegetable feast or
six as a side dish.

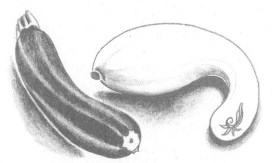

Mixed Grilled Vegetable Pasta with Pesto Cream Sauce

Stock or broth is used to extend the pesto cream sauce without diluting the flavors. The best canned chicken broths add a rich flavor without a strong chicken presence. Unfortunately, most canned vegetable broths add a dominant flavor, like tomatoes or carrots. I stock Westrae Natural's "Un-Chicken Broth" for its neutral, rich flavor. If your homemade or canned vegetable stock is not neutral in flavor, it is better to use water or cream.

SERVES 6

3 tablespoons olive oil
2 garlic cloves, minced
1 small zucchini, julienned
1 small yellow summer squash, julienned
4 ounces snow peas or sugar snap peas
4 ounces green beans, cut into 2-inch lengths
1 carrot, julienned
1 cup chicken or neutral-tasting vegetable stock or broth
¾ cup half-and-half
¾ cup Pesto (page 282)
Salt and black pepper
1½ pounds fresh or 1 pound dried linguine or fettuccine
Freshly grated Parmesan cheese (optional)

1. Prepare a medium fire in the grill with a lightly oiled vegetable grill rack in place.

2. Begin heating a large pot of salted water for the pasta.

3. Combine the olive oil and garlic in a large bowl. Add the zucchini, summer squash, peas, green beans, and carrot and toss to coat.

4. In a small saucepan, combine the stock, half-and-half, and pesto and heat just until simmering. Season to taste with salt and pepper. Keep warm while you grill the vegetables and cook the pasta.

5. Grill the vegetables, tossing frequently, until tender and grill-marked, 5 to 8 minutes. Remove from the grill and keep warm.

6. Add the pasta to the boiling water and cook until just tender. Drain. Arrange on a large serving platter.

7. Spoon the sauce over the pasta and toss to coat. Arrange the vegetables on top. If you wish, toss to mix in the vegetables. Sprinkle with Parmesan, if desired, and serve at once.

Roasted Garlic and Pepper Linguine

The strong flavor of roasted peppers dominates in this simple pasta dish, with garlic and basil providing the background flavors and tomatoes contributing moisture and a balancing sweetness. This is simple to prepare, despite the rather lengthy instructions.

SERVES 4 TO 6

1 garlic bulb
4 tablespoons extra-virgin olive oil
4 bell peppers (a combination of red, green, purple, yellow,
*   orange, etc.)*
4 medium-size vine-ripened tomatoes, halved
½ cup loosely packed fresh basil leaves
Salt and black pepper
1½ pounds fresh linguine or 1 pound dried
Freshly grated Parmesan cheese

1. Prepare a medium fire in the grill.

2. Begin heating a large pot of salted water for the pasta.

3. Remove as much of the outer papery skin from the garlic as possible. Using a sharp knife or a pair of kitchen scissors, snip off the tips of the cloves to expose the garlic within. Place the bulb on a square of heavy-duty foil. Drizzle 1 tablespoon of the olive oil over the bulb and wrap to form a tightly sealed packet.

4. Grill the garlic and peppers on the grill with the lid closed, turning the peppers occasionally until blackened all over, for about 10 minutes. Remove the peppers from the grill and place in a plastic or paper bag to steam for 10

Tomatoes: To Peel or Not to Peel

A vine-ripened tomato that has been lightly grilled is eager to shed its skin. Indeed, the skins will slip off, whether you want them to or not. With many supermarket tomatoes, however, the skins will be resistant to peeling. Generally, I peel off the skins when they can be removed by hand. If I have to take a knife to the tomato to peel it, I don't usually bother.

minutes to loosen the skins. Check the garlic. If the bulb is easy to squeeze, remove from the heat. Otherwise continue grilling until the garlic is softened, about 5 minutes more.

5. Brush the cut side of the tomatoes with a little of the olive oil. Grill until lightly charred and softened, about 10 minutes.

6. While the tomatoes are grilling, open the garlic packet and allow the garlic to cool. Separate the bulb into individual cloves. Peel the cloves or gently squeeze to force out the cooked pulp. Place the pulp in a food processor fitted with a steel blade. Add the basil leaves and process until finely chopped. Alternatively, you can chop on a cutting board or macerate in a mortar with a pestle. Set aside.

7. Core the tomatoes, peel, seed, and chop. Place in a large serving bowl.

8. Cut slits in the peppers, then drain briefly into the bowl to catch any juices. Peel and seed the peppers, then cut into long, thin strips. Add to the bowl along with the remaining olive oil and the basil and garlic mixture. Season generously with salt and pepper.

9. Add the pasta to the boiling water and cook until just tender. Drain.

10. Add the pasta to the sauce mixture in the serving bowl and toss well to combine. Sprinkle with plenty of Parmesan and serve hot.

Fusilli with Mixed Peppers and Fresh Mozzarella

Fresh Italian mozzarella is readily available these days in supermarkets as well as specialty food stores. It is worth seeking out for its delicate flavor.

SERVES 4 TO 6

8 ounces fresh mozzarella, diced
1 sun-dried tomato, minced
2 tablespoons finely chopped fresh basil
4 garlic cloves, minced
4 tablespoons extra-virgin olive oil
Salt and black pepper
4 large bell peppers (a combination of red, green, purple, yellow,
*   orange, etc.)*
1 pound fusilli
½ cup freshly grated Parmesan cheese

1. In a large bowl, combine the mozzarella, sun-dried tomato, basil, garlic, olive oil, and salt and pepper to taste. Toss to mix well. Set aside.

2. Prepare a medium-hot fire in the grill.

3. Begin heating a large pot of salted water for the pasta.

4. Roast the peppers, turning occasionally, until completely charred, about 10 minutes. Place in a plastic or paper bag to steam for 10 minutes to loosen the skins. Cut slits in the pepper, then drain briefly into the bowl with the mozzarella mixture. Peel, seed, and dice the pepper, and add to the bowl. Toss to mix.

5. Add the pasta to the boiling water and cook until just tender. Drain.

6. Add the pasta to the bowl with the mozzarella and vegetables. Add the Parmesan and toss to mix. Season with more salt and pepper if needed. Serve at once.

Serving Suggestions: Since it is hard to justify lighting a fire just for roasting some peppers, consider serving this with Grilled Garlic Bread (page 167), perhaps along with a plate of sliced tomatoes seasoned with coarse salt and freshly ground pepper.

Orzo with Lemon-Grilled Asparagus and Feta Cheese

The bright, fresh flavors of the lemon-accented asparagus are a wonderful contrast against the salty, earthy flavors of feta cheese. This is a marvelously light pasta dish.

SERVES 4 TO 6

1 red bell pepper
1 pound asparagus, sliced into 2-inch lengths
1 recipe Lemon-Garlic Marinade (page 273)
1 pound orzo
1 tablespoon extra-virgin olive oil
4 ounces feta cheese, crumbled
2 tablespoons chopped fresh parsley
1 tablespoon chopped fresh mint
Salt and black pepper

1. Prepare a medium fire in the grill with a lightly oiled vegetable grill rack in place.

2. Begin heating a large pot of salted water for the orzo.

3. Roast the pepper, turning occasionally, until completely charred, about 10 minutes. Place in a plastic or paper bag to steam for 10 minutes to loosen the skin.

4. Meanwhile, place the asparagus in a bowl. Add the marinade and toss to coat.

5. Add the orzo to the boiling water and cook until tender. Drain. Place in a large serving bowl, toss with the oil, feta, parsley, and mint. Set aside and keep warm.

6. Remove the asparagus from the marinade with a slotted spoon. Grill, tossing frequently, until tender and grill-marked, about 8 minutes.

7. Peel, seed, and chop the pepper. Add to the orzo along with the asparagus and salt and pepper to taste. Serve at once.

Penne with Grilled Vegetables and Goat Cheese

Lightly grilling the tomatoes adds a slight smoky flavor, without taking away from the fresh taste of vine-ripened tomatoes. When the hot pasta is combined with the tomatoes and goat cheese, a creamy sauce is formed that is perfectly complemented by the slightly charred sweet vegetables. This is a pasta dish of outstanding flavors—and it can be made in the time it takes to heat the pasta water.

SERVES 4 TO 6

2 tablespoon extra-virgin olive oil
2 large garlic cloves, minced
1 pound vine-ripened tomatoes, halved
1 small yellow summer squash, julienned
1 small zucchini, julienned
1 green or red bell pepper, julienned
Salt and black pepper
¼ cup loosely packed chopped fresh basil
1 pound penne
4 ounces soft goat cheese, crumbled

1. Prepare a medium-hot fire in the grill with a lightly oiled vegetable grill rack in place.

2. Begin heating a large pot of salted water for the pasta.

3. Combine the olive oil and garlic. Brush on the cut side of the tomatoes. Toss the remaining olive oil with the summer squash, zucchini, and peppers. Sprinkle all the vegetables with salt and pepper.

4. Grill the tomatoes, cut side down, until charred and soft, about 10 minutes.

5. When cool enough to handle, peel and seed the tomatoes. Combine in the blender with the basil and process until smooth. Season to taste with salt and pepper. Set aside.

6. Grill the summer squash, zucchini, and peppers, tossing frequently, until tender and lightly charred, about 5 minutes. Set aside.

7. Add the pasta to the boiling water and cook until just tender. Drain. Place the pasta in a large serving bowl.

8. Toss the pasta with the goat cheese. Add the tomato-basil sauce and toss. Add the grilled vegetables and toss once more. Serve at once.

Linguine with Red Pepper Pesto and Grilled Vegetables

Grill roasted peppers have hundreds of wonderful uses. Here they add a touch of smoky sweetness to a basil pesto.

SERVES 4

2 red bell peppers
3 garlic cloves
1 cup loosely packed fresh basil leaves
½ cup loosely packed fresh parsley leaves
½ cup freshly grated Parmesan cheese
6 tablespoons extra-virgin olive oil
Salt and black pepper
1 small zucchini, julienned
1 carrot, julienned
2 scallions, julienned
1 tablespoon balsamic vinegar
1½ pounds fresh linguine or 1 pound dried

1. Prepare a medium fire in the grill with a lightly oiled vegetable grill rack in place.

2. Begin heating a large pot of salted water for the pasta.

3. Roast the peppers, turning occasionally, until completely charred, about 10 minutes. Place in a plastic or paper bag to steam for 10 minutes to loosen the skins.

4. Cut slits in the peppers, then drain briefly into the bowl of a food processor fitted with a steel blade, to catch any juices. Peel and seed the pepper, then

Much Depends on Ripeness

A vine-ripened tomato will grill to a softened, sweetly charred state in about half the time of a rock-hard supermarket-reddened orb. A greenhouse-grown tomato will grill in less time than a supermarket tomato, but it requires more time than a homegrown tomato.

To grill a tomato, simply cut in half, brush with olive oil, and grill cut side down until the tomato is softened and lightly charred. A vine-ripened tomato will reach that tender state in 8 to 10 minutes; a supermarket tomato can take as long as 20 minutes.

coarsely chop. Add to the food processor along with the garlic, basil, and parsley. Process until you have a smooth paste. Add the Parmesan and process until well mixed. With the motor running, slowly add 4 tablespoons of the olive oil and continue processing until you have a smooth paste. Season with salt and pepper to taste. Set aside.

5. Toss the zucchini, carrot, and scallions with the remaining 2 tablespoons olive oil and the vinegar. Grill, tossing constantly, until tender and grill-marked, about 5 minutes. Set aside and keep warm.

6. Meanwhile, add the pasta to the boiling water and cook until just tender. Drain, reserving a few tablespoons of the cooking water, and transfer to a large serving bowl.

7. Thin the pesto with the reserved cooking water. Pour over the pasta and toss to coat. Add the grilled vegetables and toss again. Season with salt and pepper to taste. Serve at once.

Penne with Grilled Butternut Squash and Pine Nuts

Incredibly rich and delicious, this is a special occasion pasta. The added fillip of smoke flavoring adds greatly to its appeal.

SERVES 4 TO 6

1 medium-size butternut squash (1½ to 2 pounds)
2 tablespoons extra-virgin olive oil
3 garlic cloves, minced
1 teaspoon chopped fresh sage, or ½ teaspoon dried
¼ cup pine nuts
1 pound penne
⅓ cup dry white wine
1 cup crème fraîche
½ cup grated Parmesan cheese
Salt and black pepper

1. Peel the squash, cut in half horizontally, remove the fibers and seeds, and cut into ½-inch cubes. Steam over boiling water until barely fork tender, about 7 minutes. Transfer to a bowl and toss with the olive oil, garlic, and sage to coat well.

2. Prepare a medium-low fire in the grill with a lightly oiled vegetable grill rack in place.

3. Begin heating a large pot of salted water for the pasta.

4. Grill the squash, tossing frequently, until tender and grill-marked, about 8 minutes. Check frequently as squash chars easily. Remove from the grill and keep warm.

5. Place a square of heavy-duty foil on the grill rack. Add the pine nuts and grill, stirring often, until the nuts begin to color, about 2 minutes. Set aside.

6. Add the pasta to the boiling water and cook until just tender. Drain.

7. To make the sauce, bring the wine to a boil in a large saucepan. Boil for 1 minute, then add the crème fraîche and squash. Let the sauce return to a boil, then stir in the pasta and Parmesan. Season to taste with salt and pepper.

8. Divide the pasta among serving plates, sprinkle the toasted nuts on top, and serve.

Mixed Smoked Vegetable Lasagna

This rich-tasting lasagna bears only a passing resemblance to the watery spinach lasagna that served as many people's introduction to vegetarian lasagna. Smoky vegetables add delicious flavor and texture to the traditional tomato sauce. It's a good idea to enhance the smoked flavor of the vegetables with wood chips (see page 10).

SERVES 6 TO 9

⅓ cup extra-virgin olive oil
4 garlic cloves, minced
½ teaspoon dried rosemary, or more to taste
½ teaspoon dried thyme, or more to taste
1 onion, quartered
1 large eggplant, peeled and sliced ⅜ inch thick
1 red or green bell pepper, quartered
1 small zucchini, sliced ½ inch thick
8 ounces mushrooms, trimmed
4 cups well-seasoned tomato sauce
Salt and black pepper (optional)
1 pound ricotta cheese
1 egg, lightly beaten
1 teaspoon dried basil
12 no-boil lasagna noodles
1 pound mozzarella cheese, shredded
1 cup freshly grated Parmesan cheese

1. Prepare a medium fire in the grill.
2. Combine the olive oil, garlic, ½ teaspoon rosemary, and ½ teaspoon

thyme in a small bowl. Skewer the onion. Brush the flavored oil on the onion, eggplant, pepper, zucchini, and mushrooms.

3. Grill the vegetables, turning occasionally, until tender and well browned, 10 to 15 minutes for the eggplant, pepper, and onion; 5 to 8 minutes for the zucchini and mushrooms. Because a lot of vegetables are being grilled all at once, some vegetables will be more directly over the hot spots than others, so check carefully and remove the vegetables from the grill as they are done. It is better to overcook than undercook the vegetables in this recipe.

4. Place the grilled vegetables on a cutting board and chop into ½-inch pieces. Combine with the tomato sauce. Taste and add more rosemary and thyme and salt and pepper, if desired.

5. Combine the ricotta, egg, and basil and mix well. Set aside.

6. Preheat the oven to 350°F.

7. Spread about 1¼ cups of the grilled vegetables and sauce in a 9-inch by 13-inch baking pan. Arrange 3 of the lasagna noodles on top. (The noodles should not touch or overlap.) Spread a third of the ricotta mixture evenly over the noodles. Top with a quarter of the remaining sauce (about 1½ cups). Sprinkle a quarter of the mozzarella and a quarter of the Parmesan on top. Repeat the layers two more times. Top with the remaining 3 lasagna noodles. Spread the remaining sauce on top. Sprinkle with the remaining mozzarella and Parmesan. Cover with foil.

8. Bake the lasagna for 30 minutes. Remove the foil and bake until hot and bubbly, 10 to 15 minutes more.

9. Let stand for 5 minutes before cutting and serving.

Make Ahead Notes: The lasagna can be assembled and held for up to 8 hours in the refrigerator. Add 15 minutes to the baking time if it is cold when placed in the oven. Or the lasagna can be baked in advance and frozen for up to a month. Bake it still frozen and covered, adding 30 minutes to the baking time.

Variation: **Baked Ziti with Mixed Smoked Vegetables.** Grill the vegetables and combine with the tomato sauce as directed above. Combine in a 9-inch by 13-inch baking dish with 1 pound ziti, cooked until tender but firm. Mix in 2 cups shredded mozzarella cheese and 1 cup freshly grated Parmesan cheese. Omit the lasagna noodles and ricotta-egg-basil mixture. Bake as directed above.

White Lasagna with Smoked Vegetables

Layers of smoky vegetables, noodles, and a Parmesan cream sauce make up this white lasagna. The vegetables should be strongly flavored with smoke or the dish will be bland, so get out the wood chips for this one (see page 10).

SERVES 6 TO 9

LASAGNA

⅓ cup extra-virgin olive oil
4 garlic cloves, minced
½ teaspoon dried rosemary
½ teaspoon dried thyme
1 zucchini, diced
1 yellow summer squash, diced
1 red bell pepper, diced
1 green bell pepper, diced
1 small leek (white part only), sliced ¼ inch thick
1 small fennel bulb, diced
12 lasagna noodles

BÉCHAMEL SAUCE

6 tablespoons butter
6 tablespoons all-purpose flour
2¾ cups skim or low-fat milk
½ cup dry white wine
Salt and black pepper

1⅓ cups freshly grated Parmesan cheese
¾ cup Pesto (page 282) or store-bought pesto (optional)

1. Prepare a medium fire in the grill with a lightly oiled vegetable grill rack in place.
2. Begin heating a large pot of salted water for the pasta.
3. Combine the olive oil, garlic, rosemary, and thyme in a large bowl. Add

Tossing Tips

Many recipes call for tossing ingredients with oil or a marinade to coat them. A rubber spatula does the best job of tossing and turning the vegetables without crushing them. This is especially important with tofu, which is very fragile.

the zucchini, summer squash, peppers, leek, and fennel and toss to coat.

4. Divide the vegetables into two batches. Grill each batch, tossing frequently, until tender and grill-marked, 5 to 8 minutes. Set aside.

5. Add the lasagna noodles to the boiling water and cook according to the package directions. Drain and set aside.

6. To make the béchamel sauce, melt the butter in a heavy-bottomed saucepan over medium heat. Whisk in the flour to make a smooth paste. Cook, whisking constantly, for 1 minute. Add the milk and whisk until smooth. Bring to a low boil and stir in the wine. Season with salt and pepper to taste. Remove from the heat.

7. Preheat the oven to 350°F.

8. Spread about ½ cup of the béchamel in a 9-inch by 13-inch baking pan. Place 3 of the lasagna noodles on top. Spread about one-third of the pesto (about ¼ cup), if using, over the noodles. Pour about ½ cup of the sauce evenly over the noodles. Spread about a third of the vegetables evenly over the sauce. Sprinkle about a quarter of the Parmesan on top. Repeat the layers two more times. Top with the remaining 3 lasagna noodles. Spread the remaining sauce on top and sprinkle with the remaining Parmesan. Cover with foil.

9. Bake the lasagna for 30 minutes. Remove the foil and bake until hot and bubbly, 10 to 15 minutes more.

10. Let stand for 5 minutes before cutting and serving.

Make Ahead Notes: The lasagna can be assembled and held for up to 8 hours in the refrigerator. Add 15 minutes to the baking time if it is cold when placed in the oven. Or the lasagna can be baked in advance and frozen for up to a month. Bake it still frozen and covered, adding 30 minutes to the baking time.

Grilled Mushroom Stroganoff with Egg Noodles

I like to include at least some fresh shiitake mushrooms in the mushroom mixture as their flavor is particularly well suited to the cream sauce. This is a very rich dish.

SERVES 4

½ cup extra-virgin olive oil
½ cup finely chopped mixed fresh herbs (such as parsley,
*   oregano, thyme, mint, basil)*
3 garlic cloves, minced
2 pounds mixed wild and domestic mushrooms, sliced
12 shallots, sliced
2 tablespoons dry sherry
1 cup crème fraîche
Salt and freshly ground black pepper
12 ounces egg noodles
1 to 2 tablespoons butter
2 tablespoons chopped fresh parsley

1. Prepare a medium fire in the grill with a lightly oiled vegetable grill rack in place.

2. Begin heating a large pot of salted water for the noodles.

3. Combine the olive oil, mixed fresh herbs, and garlic in a large bowl. Add the mushrooms and shallots and toss to coat.

4. Grill the mushrooms and shallots, tossing frequently, until browned and tender, about 8 minutes. Remove from the grill and place in a large saucepan.

5. Stir the sherry, crème fraîche, and salt and pepper to taste into the saucepan with the mushrooms. Keep warm over low heat.

6. Meanwhile, add the noodles to the boiling water and cook until just tender. Drain. Toss with the butter.

7. Serve the warm mushroom mixture over the noodles and garnish with a little parsley.

Wok-Grilled
Vegetable Lo Mein

I love it when a Chinese restaurant has a kitchen that is open to the dining customers. The flames always seem to leap high around the huge woks and steaming cauldrons. Back home, I am never able to make the same delicious foods because my stove just can't put out the BTUs required to sear the food quickly. When I bought a grill-wok, it was with the hope that I could replicate the Chinese restaurant fare—it comes close. Make as hot a fire as you can in your grill, have all the ingredients assembled and close at hand, and see what you think.

By the way, a small amount of the ingredients will fall through the holes in the wok and land in the fire—the burning of these stray food bits adds to the flavor of the dish.

SERVES 4

1 pound lo mein noodles or capellini
10 fresh shiitake mushrooms, stems removed and caps sliced
1 onion, cut into slivers
2 garlic cloves, minced
1 teaspoon minced fresh ginger
2 tablespoons toasted sesame oil
3 tablespoons soy sauce, or more to taste
2 small bok choy, stems and greens sliced
¼ cup oyster sauce (see Note)
⅛ teaspoon black pepper

1. Bring a large pot of salted water to a boil. Add the noodles and cook until just tender. Drain and set aside.

2. Prepare a medium-hot fire in the grill with a lightly oiled grill-wok in place.

3. In a medium-size bowl, combine the mushrooms, onion, garlic, ginger, sesame oil, and 2 tablespoons of the soy sauce. Toss well to coat.

4. Add the mushrooms and onion to the wok and stir-fry until just tender

and grill-marked, about 4 minutes. Add the bok choy and stir-fry until limp, about 1 minute more. Add the noodles and toss to combine. Pour in the oyster sauce and continue to stir-fry until well-coated and heated through, 4 to 7 minutes.

5. Place in a serving bowl. Season to taste with more soy sauce, if desired, and the black pepper. Serve at once.

Note: Not all oyster sauces have oysters in them, but most have some form of fish extract. You can find bottles labeled "vegetarian oyster sauce," which do not contain any fish extracts.

Chinese Barbecued Noodles with Tofu and Broccoli

Chinese hoisin sauce—sometimes called Chinese barbecue sauce—stars in the marinade that flavors this truly delicious and healthy dish.

SERVES 4 TO 6

1 pound firm or extra-firm tofu
2 or 3 stalks broccoli, cut into bite-size florets, stems julienned
2 carrots, julienned
4 scallions, julienned
1 recipe Chinese Barbecue Marinade (page 278)
1 pound dried linguine
1 tablespoon soy sauce

1. Wrap the tofu in a clean cotton kitchen towel. Place a heavy weight on top (such as a cutting board weighted with a heavy juice can). Set aside for at least 30 minutes to allow the excess water to drain from the tofu.

2. Prepare a medium-hot fire in the grill with a lightly oiled vegetable grill rack in place.

3. Begin heating a large pot of salted water for the pasta.

Save Your Life with Soy

The way I figure it, you just can't have too many tofu recipes—and it's great that tofu takes so well to the grill. A growing body of evidence suggests that eating soy foods may help prevent certain cancers, slow calcium loss from the bones, and moderate the symptoms of menopause. Researchers believe that a natural substance in soy called isoflavones, which resembles the hormone estrogen, may replicate the many protective effects of estrogen, without any negative side effects.

4. Combine the broccoli, carrots, and scallions in a medium-size bowl. Drizzle about ¼ cup of the marinade over the vegetables and toss to coat.

5. Slice the tofu into ⅜-inch-thick slices. Brush some of the marinade on both sides.

6. Add the pasta to the boiling water and cook until just tender. Drain and transfer to a large serving bowl. Toss with the remaining marinade and the soy sauce. Set aside and keep warm.

7. Grill the broccoli, carrots, and scallions, tossing frequently, until tender and grill-marked, about 5 minutes. Grill the tofu until browned and a slight crust forms, about 5 minutes per side.

8. Toss the vegetables with the noodles. Slice the tofu into bite-size pieces and arrange on top of the pasta. Serve at once.

Variation: When asparagus is in season, replace the broccoli with 1 pound of asparagus.

9

Kabobs, Couscous, and Other Compelling Combinations

CHAPTER 9 • KABOBS, COUSCOUS, AND OTHER COMPELLING COMBINATIONS

Tandoori-Style Vegetable Kabobs

These vegetables are marinated in the yogurt-based sauce typical of tandoori foods often served in Indian restaurants. The vegetables are a trifle dry, but the accompanying raita (relish) adds moisture and mouth-cooling refreshment. Naan (page 168) makes the perfect complement, but you can serve these vegetables with hot white rice, if you prefer.

SERVES 4

1 pound new potatoes, halved, quartered, or cut into wedges
½ head cauliflower, broken into florets
2 medium-size carrots, sliced 2 inches thick
1 medium-size onion, cubed
1 recipe Tandoori Marinade (page 276)
1 recipe Raita (page 287)

1. Bring a medium-size pot of lightly salted water to a boil. Add the potatoes and boil for 3 minutes. Add the cauliflower to the potatoes and boil for 3 minutes. Add the carrots to the potatoes and cauliflower and boil for 2 minutes more. Drain immediately, plunge into cold water to stop the cooking, and drain again.

2. Place the vegetables, including the onion, in a large bowl. Add the marinade and toss to coat. Let stand at room temperature while you prepare the fire. (Alternatively, the marinating vegetables can be refrigerated for up to 12 hours.)

3. Prepare a medium-hot fire in the grill. Thread the vegetables onto skewers.

4. Grill the vegetables, turning occasionally, until browned and tender, about 8 minutes.

5. Serve hot, passing the raita on the side.

Teriyaki Vegetable Kabobs

The challenge to making vegetarian kabobs is to choose vegetables that cook in the same amount of time. If you use vegetables with different cooking times, you will need to precook some of them, as with the broccoli in this recipe.

SERVES 4 TO 6

1 pound firm or extra-firm tofu
1 broccoli stalk, florets cut into bite-size pieces and stalks sliced ½
inch thick
1 recipe Teriyaki Marinade and Dipping Sauce (page 277), at
room temperature
4 ounces snow peas
1 red bell pepper, cubed
2 small onions, cubed
4 ounces button mushrooms, trimmed
Hot cooked white or brown rice

1. Wrap the tofu in a clean cotton kitchen towel. Place a heavy weight on top (such as a cutting board weighted with a heavy juice can). Set aside for at least 30 minutes to allow the excess water to drain from the tofu. Cut into 1-inch cubes.

2. Cook the broccoli in a microwave or in boiling water on top of the stove until just tender, about 2 minutes. Plunge into cold water to stop the cooking, then drain.

3. Prepare a medium-hot fire in the grill.

4. Pour about half of the marinade into a shallow dish. Add the tofu, broccoli, snow peas, pepper, onions, and mushrooms and toss gently to coat. Thread onto skewers.

6. Grill the kabobs, turning occasionally, until the vegetables are cooked through, about 10 minutes.

7. Spoon a bed of rice onto a serving platter or individual plates. Top with the vegetables, on or off the skewers, and serve. Pass the additional dipping sauce at the table.

*Kabobs,
Couscous, and
Other
Compelling
Combinations*

215

Presoaking Bamboo Skewers

Before threading vegetables onto bamboo skewers, place the skewers in a shallow dish and cover with water. Let soak for at least 30 minutes. This is to prevent them from incinerating on a hot grill. If you forget to presoak the skewers, you can still use them, but you run the risk of having them break on the grill.

Couscous with Grilled Vegetable Kabobs

These kabobs are marinated in flavors typical of the Middle East—cumin, cinnamon, and pepper—and served on a bed of couscous. A topping of a yogurt-based sauce completes the dish. Indeed, without the sauce, the vegetables and couscous are just too dry, so don't think of skipping it, though you could substitute Raita (page 287) instead.

SERVES 4

*1 teaspoon ground cumin
1 teaspoon sweet or hot paprika
½ teaspoon ground cinnamon
½ teaspoon salt
¼ teaspoon black pepper
2 tablespoons fresh lemon juice
¼ cup extra-virgin olive oil
8 ounces okra, trimmed
1 medium-size yellow summer squash, halved and
    sliced ¾ inch thick
1 red bell pepper, cubed
1 green bell pepper, cubed
1½ cups instant couscous
2¼ cups boiling water
Grilled Onion Dip (page 288)*

1. Combine the cumin, paprika, cinnamon, salt, pepper, lemon juice, and olive oil in a large bowl. Mix well. Add the vegetables and toss to coat.

2. Prepare a medium fire in the grill.

3. Thread the okra, summer squash, and peppers onto skewers.

4. Combine the couscous and boiling water. Cover tightly and set aside.

5. Grill the kabobs, turning occasionally, until the vegetables are tender and grill-marked, about 10 minutes.

6. Fluff the couscous with a fork and transfer to a large serving platter or individual serving plates. Place the kabobs on the couscous and serve, passing the onion dip on the side.

An Attitude About Kabobs

Whenever I mentioned that I was working on a book on vegetarian grilling, people would nod, and say, "Ah, kabobs." It's the first thing people think of. That's because whenever they have been to a barbecue where meat kabobs were grilled, the vegetarians made do with the meatless ones.

Vegetables threaded on a skewer with meat are delicious because they are basted by the juices the meat releases as it cooks. Vegetarian kabobs are not quite as delicious without the meat juices, but they are still good if the marinade is flavorful.

However, kabobs are probably the most labor-intensive, inefficient way to cook vegetables on the grill. First, there's the fussy business of threading all the vegetables onto the skewers. Then each skewer must be handled individually as it cooks. One vegetable may cook faster than another, and you may find yourself choosing between overcooking or undercooking.

A vegetable kabob is pleasant on occasion, but it isn't the ultimate vegetarian grill experience.

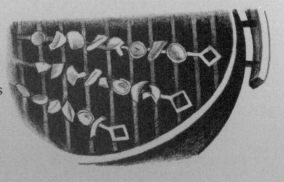

Tofu Kabobs with Tomato-Peanut Sauce

*Kabobs,
Couscous, and
Other
Compelling
Combinations*

217

The flavors are American barbecue goes East. Serve over hot steamed white rice. The recipe makes 12 to 16 skewers, enough for 4 people as a main dish. But the skewers also make fine appetizers or side dishes, in which case allow 1 to 2 skewers per serving.

SERVES 4

1½ pounds firm or extra-firm tofu
½ cup Barbecue Glaze (page 280) or store-bought tomato-based barbecue sauce
2 tablespoons soy sauce
1 tablespoon toasted sesame oil
3 tablespoons smooth or chunky peanut butter
2 garlic cloves, minced
¼ teaspoon red pepper flakes (optional)
1 green bell pepper, cut into 1-inch squares
1 medium-size zucchini, cut into 1-inch cubes
16 pearl onions, peeled
Hot cooked white or brown rice

1. Wrap the tofu in a clean cotton kitchen towel. Place a heavy weight on top (such as a cutting board weighted with a heavy juice can). Set aside for at least 30 minutes to allow the excess water to drain from the tofu. Cut into 1-inch cubes.

2. Combine the barbecue glaze, soy sauce, sesame oil, peanut butter, garlic, and red pepper flakes.

3. Thread the tofu, peppers, zucchini, and onions onto skewers. Brush generously with the barbecue sauce. Set aside.

4. Prepare a medium fire in the grill. Lightly oil the grill grate or vegetable grill rack.

5. Grill the kabobs, turning occasionally, until the vegetables are tender, about 7 minutes.

6. Spoon a bed of rice onto a serving platter or individual plates. Top with the vegetables, on or off the kabobs, and serve.

Metal or Bamboo Skewers?

Believe it or not, the answer is both—each has value for grilling vegetables. Metal skewers are the skewers of choice when you are grilling vegetables that take a little longer to cook, especially potatoes and root vegetables. The metal conducts heat and cooks the vegetables from the inside out. Bamboo skewers, which are thinner and don't conduct heat, are preferable for delicate, quick-cooking items, such as cherry tomatoes or tofu.

Metal skewers are usually longer, which means they may hang over the edge of the grill, making it hard to close the lid on some grills. The extra length does make them easier to handle over a campfire, where a short skewer forces you to reach awkwardly over the hot coals.

Sesame-Grilled Tofu

It is the nature of tofu to readily absorb the flavors of a marinade, and this marinade packs a lot of flavor. It gets a little heat from Chinese chili paste with garlic. If you have a fresh jar of chili paste, you may find that 1 teaspoon adds enough spicy flavor. Those who love their food spicy-hot, and those who found their jar of chili paste at the back of the refrigerator where it has been since who knows when, will want to add more.

SERVES 4

2 pounds firm or extra-firm tofu
2 tablespoons toasted sesame oil
2 tablespoons canola oil
2 tablespoons mirin (sweet rice wine)
1 tablespoon soy sauce
1 to 3 teaspoons chili paste with garlic (available where Asian
    foods are sold)
2 garlic cloves, minced

1 teaspoon minced fresh ginger
1 recipe Sesame Dipping Sauce (page 285)

1. Wrap the tofu in a clean cotton kitchen towel. Place a heavy weight on top (such as a cutting board weighted with a heavy juice can). Set aside for at least 30 minutes to allow the excess water to drain from the tofu.

2. Combine the sesame oil, canola oil, mirin, soy sauce, chili paste, garlic, and ginger, and mix well.

3. Slice each block of tofu lengthwise into 4 slices and brush on the marinade. Let marinate for at least 1 hour at room temperature or up to 8 hours in the refrigerator.

4. Prepare a medium-hot fire in the grill. Lightly oil the grill grate or a vegetable grill rack.

5. Grill the tofu until browned and a slight crust forms, about 5 minutes per side.

6. Serve hot, passing the sesame dipping sauce at the table.

A Simple Grill-Wok Stir-Fry

Grilling adds much flavor to the ordinary stir-fry. You can adapt this recipe to most vegetables—just be sure the vegetables are cut to a uniform size.

SERVES 4

3 tablespoons tamari
3 tablespoons mirin (sweet rice wine)
3 tablespoons toasted sesame oil
20 fresh shiitake mushrooms, stemmed
8 scallions, cut into 2-inch lengths
2 carrots, julienned
8 ounces snow peas, trimmed
2 broccoli stalks, broken into florets and stems julienned
Hot cooked rice

1. Prepare a medium-hot fire in the grill with a lightly oiled grill-wok or vegetable grill rack in place.

2. In a large bowl, combine the tamari, mirin, and sesame oil. Mix well to combine. Add the mushrooms, scallions, carrots, snow peas, and broccoli. Toss to coat.

3. Lift half the vegetables out of the marinade with a slotted spoon. Grill the vegetables, tossing frequently, until tender and grill-marked, 5 to 8 minutes. Set aside and keep warm. Repeat with the remaining vegetables.

4. Spoon a bed of rice onto a serving platter or individual plates. Top with the grilled vegetables. Drizzle the remaining marinade on top and serve.

Grill-Woks

A grill-wok is a curious hybrid. It is shaped like a squared-off wok with handles. But instead of being solid, the metal is dotted with holes to allow smoke to flavor the contents. Grill-woks are somewhat less versatile than flat vegetable grill racks because less of their surface is in contact with the grill. However, you can stir-fry in them and create dishes with wonderful grilled flavor. Just resist the temptation to grill too much at one time, or the vegetables will end up tasting steamed rather than grilled.

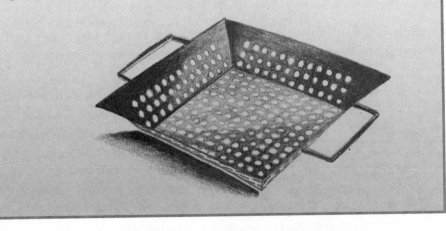

Spicy Grill-Wok Stir-Fry

*Kabobs,
Couscous, and
Other
Compelling
Combinations*

221

I took this dish to a potluck recently and mischievously called it "Chinese take-out." The dish held up surprisingly well; the vegetables were bedded on freshly cooked white rice, which kept them warm enough. When pressed for the restaurant name, I had to confess, "It's Chinese and I took it out of my house."

SERVES 4

1 pound firm or extra-firm tofu
*3 tablespoons sweet bean sauce (available where Asian foods
    are sold)*
2 tablespoons plus 1 teaspoon soy sauce
1 tablespoon dry sherry
1 carrot, diced
1 onion, diced
1 broccoli stalk, broken into florets and stems diced
4 ounces green beans, diced
2 garlic cloves, minced
2 tablespoons peanut oil
*2 teaspoons chili paste with garlic (available where Asian foods
    are sold)*
¾ cup dry-roasted peanuts
Hot cooked white rice

1. Wrap the tofu in a clean cotton kitchen towel. Place a heavy weight on top (such as a cutting board weighted with a heavy juice can). Set aside for at least 30 minutes to allow the excess water to drain from the tofu. Dice.

2. Prepare a medium-hot fire in the grill with a lightly oiled grill-wok or vegetable grill rack in place.

3. Combine the sweet bean sauce, 2 tablespoons of the soy sauce, and the sherry in a small bowl. Set aside.

4. Combine the carrot, onion, broccoli, and green beans in a large bowl. Add the garlic, peanut oil, chili paste, and the remaining 1 teaspoon soy sauce and toss to coat. Add the tofu and toss again.

5. Divide the vegetable-tofu mixture into 2 batches. Stir-fry or grill, tossing

The Secret to Stir-Frying on the Grill

Stir-frying on the grill results in dishes that are surprisingly close to what you get in restaurants where they have sufficient BTUs to quickly sear the vegetables in a conventional wok. Indeed, I prefer the flavor of my grill stir-fries over stovetop stir-fries, even when I use a gas grill and the smoke flavor is minimized. The reason is the way the grill sears the vegetables without steam.

The method is simple: Toss the vegetables with the cooking oil (toasted sesame oil or peanut oil give the best flavor) and a little seasoning, such as ginger, garlic, and/or a touch of soy sauce. Then grill in small batches (this part is critical) in a preheated grill-wok or on a vegetable grill rack. It will take longer to cook over high heat on a grill than it does in a high-powered wok, but the vegetables do not get soggy from overcooking. After removing the crisp-tender vegetables from the grill, toss with a prepared flavoring sauce. The flavoring sauces can be adapted from any Chinese cookbook—generally they are what is added to the wok to finish the dish. If the sauces require thickening with cornstarch, they must first be cooked in a pot on the side of the grill or on the kitchen stove.

frequently, until the vegetables and tofu are tender and grill-marked, about 8 minutes. Remove to a large bowl and keep warm.

6. Add the sweet bean sauce mixture and peanuts to the grilled vegetables and toss to coat.

7. Serve at once over hot cooked rice.

Wok-Grilled Chinese Fried Rice

Fried rice over the grill? In a wok that has holes on the bottom? Am I crazy? Well, I tried it on a lark and I loved what I tasted. Yes, you do get some food falling onto the coals, but it's probably the smoke from these bits burning that adds so much flavor to the dish. Although the dish cooks a little slower than it would in a restaurant setting, the flavor is remarkably similar.

SERVES 4 TO 6

2 eggs
1 tablespoon water
6 teaspoons soy sauce, or more to taste
3 teaspoons peanut oil
¼ cup diced onion
1 large carrot, diced
2 garlic cloves, minced
4 cups very thinly sliced green or Chinese cabbage
6 cups cooked white rice
5 tablespoons oyster sauce, or more to taste (see Note)
2 cups bean sprouts
1 cup fresh or frozen peas
3 or 4 scallions, chopped

1. Beat the eggs, water, and 1 teaspoon of the soy sauce.

2. Heat 1 teaspoon of the peanut oil in a large skillet or wok over high heat. Pour in the eggs and swirl the pan over the heat to make a large omelet. When the bottom has set, flip over and cook on the other side. Remove from the skillet. Dice into ½-inch pieces and set aside.

3. Prepare a medium fire in the grill with a lightly oiled grill-wok in place.

4. In a large bowl, combine the onion, carrot, garlic, the remaining 2 teaspoons peanut oil, and 1 teaspoon of the soy sauce and toss to coat well.

5. Grill the vegetables in the grill-wok, tossing constantly, until the vegetables are tender, about 2 minutes. Add the cabbage and stir-fry until limp, about

2 minutes. Add the rice, oyster sauce, and remaining 4 teaspoons soy sauce to the grill-wok. Grill, continuously stirring and tossing, until the rice is heated through, 4 to 7 minutes.

6. Taste and add more oyster sauce or soy sauce, if desired. Carefully mix in the bean sprouts, peas, scallions, and egg. Grill, carefully tossing and stirring, until heated through, about 2 minutes. Serve hot.

Note: Not all oyster sauces have oysters in them, but most have some form of fish extract. You can find bottles labeled "vegetarian oyster sauce," which do not contain any fish extracts.

Risotto with Grilled Mushrooms

If you are in any doubt that grilling adds flavor, try tasting this recipe with a side-by-side version of a mushroom risotto in which the mushrooms are sautéed rather than grilled. That extra lick of grilled flavor makes all the difference.

SERVES 4 TO 6

½ cup dried porcini mushrooms (½ ounce)
8 cups water
1 pound portobello mushrooms, trimmed
4 ounces fresh shiitake mushrooms, stemmed
1 tablespoon butter, melted
3 tablespoons extra-virgin olive oil

Kabobs,
Couscous, and
Other
Compelling
Combinations

225

1 tablespoon chopped fresh sage, or 1 teaspoon dried
Salt and black pepper
½ cup dry white wine
2 shallots, minced
3 garlic cloves, minced
1½ cups Arborio rice
½ cup grated Parmesan cheese

1. Combine the dried porcini mushrooms and water in a medium-size saucepan. Bring to a boil, then reduce the heat and simmer the broth, uncovered, for 30 minutes.

2. Meanwhile, prepare a medium-hot fire in the grill with a lightly oiled vegetable grill rack in place.

3. Trim off the dirty part of the portobello mushroom stems and wipe the remainder clean with a damp cloth. Slice about ⅜ inch thick. Combine with the shiitakes in a large bowl.

4. Combine the butter, 2 tablespoons of the olive oil, sage, and salt and pepper to taste in a small bowl. Drizzle over the mushrooms and toss to coat.

5. Grill the mushrooms, turning occasionally, until tender and browned, 10 to 12 minutes. Remove from the grill and keep warm.

6. Strain the porcini broth into a clean saucepan. Avoid transferring any grit from the bottom of the pan. Discard the porcini. Return the broth to a simmer. Add the wine and salt and pepper to taste.

7. Heat the remaining 1 tablespoon olive oil in a large nonstick skillet over medium heat. Add the shallots, garlic, and rice and toss to coat with the oil. Cook, stirring, until the rice appears toasted, 3 to 5 minutes. Add 1 cup of the simmering broth to the rice and reduce the heat to medium. Stir until almost all the liquid is absorbed. Continue adding more broth, 1 cup at a time, and cooking and stirring until most of the liquid is absorbed. It will take about 6 cups of broth and a total of about 18 to 35 minutes for the liquid to be absorbed and the rice to become tender and creamy.

8. Stir in the Parmesan and the grilled mushrooms. Season to taste with salt and pepper, if needed. Serve hot.

Saffron Rice with Grilled Vegetables

This recipe was inspired by the great paellas of Spain, those wonderful rice dishes redolent with saffron, the world's most expensive spice. In Spain, it is not unusual to see paella prepared over an open fire for large crowds on festive occasions. Vegetarian versions, however, are quite uncommon. The final step, cooking the paella on the grill, is not essential, but it adds an extra touch of smoke and a pleasing dryness to the rice.

SERVES 4 TO 6

1½ cups long-grain white rice
3 cups water
1 teaspoon salt
⅛ teaspoon crushed saffron threads
1 red bell pepper
1 cup green beans, cut into 2-inch lengths
1 carrot, julienned
1 zucchini, julienned
3 tablespoons extra-virgin olive oil
2 garlic cloves, minced
Salt and black pepper

1. Prepare a medium-hot fire in the grill with a lightly oiled vegetable grill rack in place.

2. Rinse the rice in several changes of water until the water runs clear. In a large saucepan, combine the rice, water, salt, and saffron. Cover and bring to a boil, then reduce the heat and boil gently until the rice is tender and the liquid is absorbed, about 2 minutes. Fluff the rice with a fork. Crumple a clean kitchen towel or paper towel and place over the rice. Set aside and keep warm.

3. Roast the pepper, turning occasionally, until completely charred, about 10 minutes. Place in a plastic or paper bag to steam for 10 minutes to loosen the skin. Peel, seed, and dice.

4. Toss the green beans, carrot, and zucchini with the olive oil and garlic. Grill, tossing frequently, until tender and grill-marked, 5 to 8 minutes.

5. Add the roasted peppers and grilled vegetables to the rice and toss to mix well. Season to taste with salt and pepper.

6. Place the rice in an ovenproof casserole or cast-iron skillet and set on the grill. Grill, with the lid down, until heated through and slightly dry, 5 to 15 minutes. This step will add a smoky essence. Serve hot.

Cumin-Scented Grilled Vegetable Couscous

The flavors of the Middle East make a rich marinade for the grilled vegetables, which are served on a bed of couscous. This tasty one-dish meal provides the grains, beans, and vegetables for healthy, hearty eating.

SERVES 4

6 tablespoons extra-virgin olive oil
2 tablespoons balsamic vinegar
2 garlic cloves, minced
1 tablespoon ground cumin
1 tablespoon minced fresh parsley
1 onion, thickly sliced
1 green bell pepper, quartered
2 small zucchini, sliced ¼ inch thick
1 large eggplant, peeled and sliced ⅜ inch thick
1½ cups cooked chickpeas (or 1 15-ounce can), drained
1½ cups diced tomatoes
Salt and black pepper
1½ cups instant couscous
2¼ cups boiling water

1. Prepare a medium-hot fire in the grill.

2. In a large bowl, combine the olive oil, vinegar, garlic, cumin, and parsley. Add the onion, pepper, and zucchini and toss to coat. Brush the remaining marinade on the eggplant.

3. Grill the vegetables, turning occasionally, until well browned, 10 to 15

That Old Smoky Magic

Casual browsers might observe that many of the recipes in this chapter could be adapted to stovetop cooking, but they would be missing the point. Good cooking has to do with enhancing the natural flavors of high-quality ingredients. In no way is this done better or easier than with a grill.

The intense dry heat of the grill caramelizes the natural sugars contained within the vegetables, which enhances their flavor. Stovetop cooking inevitably introduces the element of steam as water trapped within the cells of the vegetables releases and collects in the pan. The resulting flavors are just that much less intense.

Meateaters often add a bit of bacon or prosciutto to enhance the flavor of the foods they cook. For vegetarians, the grill can perform that smoky magic.

minutes for the eggplant and onion; 10 minutes for the pepper; and 5 to 8 minutes for the zucchini.

4. Chop the grilled vegetables into bite-size pieces and combine in a saucepan with the chickpeas and tomatoes. Add a little water if the tomatoes are not very juicy and season to taste with salt and pepper. Keep warm over low heat.

5. Combine the couscous and boiling water. Cover and let steam until the water is all absorbed and the grains are tender, about 10 minutes. Uncover and fluff with a fork.

6. To serve, spoon the vegetables over the couscous.

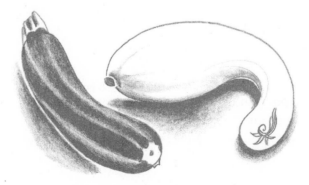

Mixed Grill with Spicy Peanut Sauce

*Kabobs,
Couscous, and
Other
Compelling
Combinations*

229

A grill-wok enables you to stir-fry with ease. This recipe is for a basic grilled veggie stir-fry. The peanut sauce adds much flavor to this otherwise simple dish.

SERVES 4

*1 pound firm or extra-firm tofu
3 tablespoons toasted sesame oil
3 tablespoons soy sauce
3 tablespoons dry sherry or Chinese rice wine
2 garlic cloves, minced
1 teaspoon minced fresh ginger
4 ounces green beans, cut into 2-inch lengths
1 carrot, julienned
8 fresh shiitake mushrooms, stemmed and caps thinly sliced
1 broccoli stalk, florets cut into bite-size pieces and stems
    julienned
4 ounces snow peas, trimmed
2 bok choy stems, thinly sliced
2 scallions, cut into 2-inch lengths
Hot cooked rice
1 recipe Spicy Peanut Sauce (page 286)*

1. Wrap the tofu in a clean cotton kitchen towel. Place a heavy weight on top (such as a cutting board weighted with a heavy juice can). Set aside for at least 30 minutes to allow the excess water to drain from the tofu.

2. Prepare a medium-hot fire in the grill with a lightly oiled grill-wok in place.

3. Combine the sesame oil, soy sauce, sherry or rice wine, garlic, and ginger in a small bowl.

4. Set out three medium-size bowls. In the first, place the green beans, carrot, and shiitakes; in the second, the broccoli and snow peas; and in the third, the bok choy, scallions, and tofu. Spoon 3 tablespoons of the marinade into

each of the first two bowls; pour the remaining marinade into the third bowl. Toss the vegetables in each bowl to coat with the marinade.

5. Lift the green beans, carrot, and shiitakes out of the marinade with a slotted spoon, place in the grill-wok, and cook for 4 minutes, tossing frequently. Lift the broccoli and snow peas out of the marinade and add to the grill-wok. Continue to grill, turning and tossing, until the vegetables are tender and browned, about 10 minutes. Remove to a serving bowl and keep warm.

6. Lift the bok choy and tofu out of the marinade and place in the grill-wok. Grill until tender and slightly grill-marked, about 5 minutes, tossing frequently. Add to the vegetables in the serving bowl and toss to mix. Pour any remaining marinade over the vegetables.

7. Serve the grilled vegetables with hot cooked rice, passing the peanut sauce on the side.

Mediterranean Mixed Grill
with Aïoli

A bountiful assortment of grilled vegetables artfully arrayed on a platter with a knock-your-socks-off sauce of garlicky mayonnaise—this is a feast! The vegetables suggested here can be replaced by other vegetables in season.

SERVES 4

⅓ cup extra-virgin olive oil
2 tablespoons lemon juice
2 garlic cloves, minced
*1 to 2 tablespoons chopped fresh rosemary, thyme, basil, or
    oregano*
Salt and black pepper
1½ pounds potatoes, peeled, if desired, and sliced ¼ inch thick
4 ounces green beans, trimmed
4 ounces baby carrots
1 red bell pepper, sliced
*1 small zucchini, cut into quarters or eighths and sliced into
    3-inch spears*

*Kabobs,
Couscous, and
Other
Compelling
Combinations*

231

*1 small yellow summer squash, cut into quarters or eighths and
 sliced into 3-inch spears*
12 imported brine- or oil-cured black olives
1 recipe Aïoli (page 284)

1. Prepare a medium fire in the grill with a lightly oiled vegetable grill rack in place.

2. Combine the olive oil, lemon juice, garlic, fresh herbs, and salt and pepper to taste in a large bowl. Add the potatoes and toss to coat.

3. Lift the potatoes out of the marinade with a slotted spoon. Grill, turning occasionally, until browned and tender, 15 to 25 minutes. Arrange the potatoes on a serving platter.

4. Add the green beans, carrots, pepper, zucchini, and summer squash to the marinade and toss to coat well. Lift the vegetables out of the marinade with a slotted spoon. Grill, tossing frequently, until tender and grill-marked, about 10 minutes. Remove the vegetables from the grill as they are done and arrange on top of the potatoes.

5. To serve, scatter the olives on top of the vegetables. Pass the aïoli on the side.

Serving Suggestions: You can serve the vegetables with the aïoli as an hors d'oeuvre or main course. It makes a wonderful summery meal with the addition of bread and cheese. A first course of soup or a side dish of a grain-based salad may be necessary to satisfy hearty appetites.

The 20-Degree Rule

Winter is no reason to stop grilling, but it may require some changes in technique. I have found that when the outside temperature dips below 20 degrees Fahrenheit, I must grill with the lid down and add significantly to the time it takes to grill the vegetables. The slower rate of grilling does no harm to the dish, and the smoky flavor is generally increased. When the temperature is below 10 degrees Fahrenheit, I usually don't attempt to grill.

Jerk Vegetables

A visit to Jamaica would be incomplete without a stop at a roadside jerk joint—a barbecue shack that serves a specialty of jerk pork or chicken. The cooking method can be traced back to the Cormantee hunters of preslavery West Africa, who roasted pork over hot coals in earthen pits covered with green tree branches. The cooking method was brought to Jamaica and evolved into a roadside industry. Today chicken, and even fish, are grilled with a jerk paste. So why not vegetables?

Jerk flavors are a complex mixture of sweet, spicy, and hot. The heat comes from the Scotch bonnet (or habanero) chile, a *very* hot chile. You can make a milder paste by using a different chile, such as *aji dulce,* a small, sweet mild chile that contributes some of the fruity notes of the Scotch bonnet without much heat at all. The potatoes are steamed before grilling as it is difficult to grill the potatoes without charring when there is sugar in the marinade.

SERVES 4

JERK PASTE

4 scallions, chopped
2 garlic cloves
1 Scotch bonnet chile (or substitute a milder chile), seeded
3 tablespoons canola oil
2 tablespoons sugar
1 tablespoon soy sauce
1 tablespoon dried thyme
1 tablespoon ground allspice

VEGETABLES

1½ pounds potatoes, cut into wedges
4 ears of corn
1 onion, cut into wedges
12 cherry tomatoes, halved
*1 medium-size zucchini, cut into quarters or eighths and
    sliced into 4-inch spears*
Lime wedges

*Kabobs,
Couscous, and
Other
Compelling
Combinations*

233

1. To make the jerk paste, combine the scallions, garlic, chile, canola oil, sugar, soy sauce, thyme, and allspice in a food processor and process until you have a paste.

2. Steam the potatoes over boiling water until just tender, about 12 minutes. Drain well.

3. Prepare a medium-hot fire in the grill. A vegetable grill rack is optional but recommended.

4. Peel back the husks from the corn cobs and remove the silks. Brush the jerk paste onto the ears. Bring the husks back over the cobs and secure with kitchen twine. Skewer the onion and cherry tomatoes and brush with the paste. Toss the zucchini and potatoes with the remaining paste.

5. Grill the vegetables, turning occasionally, until tender and well browned, 15 to 25 minutes for the corn, 10 to 15 minutes for the onion, and about 5 minutes for the tomatoes, zucchini, and potatoes. Remove the vegetables as they are done and keep warm.

6. Arrange the vegetables on a large platter, garnish with lime wedges, and serve.

Serving Suggestions: Grilled pineapples (page 257) make an excellent accompaniment to this tropical feast. Add a loaf of French bread (plates will be mopped clean) and you have a very satisfying dinner.

Precooking Vegetables

Some cookbooks—and articles about grilling—suggest you precook most every vegetable before grilling, but it usually isn't necessary. Vegetables that are often eaten raw (such as tomatoes, onions, and peppers) or that have a quick cooking time (such as summer squash, snow peas, broccoli, cauliflower, and leeks) don't require it. Vegetables that generally require about 10 minutes of cooking time (such as sliced potatoes, sliced beets, sliced rutabagas, and sliced eggplant) can be precooked, but it isn't required as long as the fire isn't too hot. Vegetables that usually require longer cooking times (such as artichokes and winter squash) all benefit from precooking.

Harvest Grill

A terrific cool-weather grilled supper.

SERVES 4

2 tablespoons Dijon mustard
2 garlic cloves, minced
1 teaspoon chopped fresh rosemary
⅓ cup Classic Vinaigrette (page 271) or Basic Herb Marinade
*   and Salad Dressing (page 272) or store-bought Italian-style*
*   salad dressing*
Salt and freshly ground black pepper
1½ pounds red new potatoes, cut into quarters or eighths
1 pound beets, cut into wedges
2 onions, cut into wedges
1 red or yellow bell pepper
2 pounds sauerkraut

1. Prepare a medium-hot fire in the grill. A vegetable grill rack is optional but recommended. (However, not all the vegetables will fit.)

2. Combine the mustard, garlic, rosemary, vinaigrette or dressing, and salt and pepper to taste in a small bowl. Whisk until well combined.

3. Place the potatoes in one bowl and the beets in another. Toss the potatoes with 3 tablespoons of the marinade. Toss the beets with 3 tablespoons of the marinade. Skewer the onions and brush with the remaining marinade.

4. Roast the pepper, turning occasionally, until completely charred, about 10 minutes. Place in a plastic or paper bag to steam for 10 minutes to loosen the skin.

5. Meanwhile, grill the vegetables, turning occasionally, until tender and grill-marked, 20 to 25 minutes for the potatoes and beets, about 10 minutes for the onions.

6. Peel, seed, and cut the grilled pepper into thin strips. Combine with the sauerkraut in a medium saucepan and heat through.

7. To serve, drain the sauerkraut and place on a serving platter. Arrange the grilled vegetables on top. Serve hot.

Serving Suggestions: This makes a one-dish meal that is great with a chewy, rustic loaf of rye or pumpernickel bread. Beer is an excellent accompaniment. Meateaters might want to add a few sausages to the grill.

Grilled Ratatouille

Ratatouille from southern France is a standard in the American vegetarian repertoire. It is difficult to make an unappealing version—but a truly great ratatouille is special indeed. A generous dose of garlic and a lovely touch of smoke elevate this recipe out of the ordinary. This tastes better the day after it is made. It will keep in the refrigerator for up to 5 days.

SERVES 6 TO 8

1 large onion, quartered
½ garlic bulb, separated into cloves and peeled
⅓ cup extra-virgin olive oil
1 large eggplant, peeled and sliced ⅜ inch thick
1 green bell pepper, halved
6 medium-size tomatoes, halved
2 medium-size zucchini, sliced ⅜ inch thick
2 tablespoons chopped fresh basil
1 teaspoon dried oregano
1 teaspoon dried thyme
1 bay leaf
Salt and black pepper

1. Prepare a medium-hot fire in the grill.
2. Skewer the onion and garlic. Brush the olive oil on the onion, garlic, eggplant, pepper, tomatoes, and zucchini.
3. Grill the vegetables, turning occasionally, until tender and grill-marked, 10 to 15 minutes for the eggplant, onion, and garlic; about 10 minutes for the pepper and tomatoes; and 5 to 8 minutes for the zucchini. Remove the vegetables from the grill as they are done.

Extra-Virgin Olive Oil Makes a Difference

Most of the recipes in this book that require moistening the vegetables with olive oil specify extra-virgin olive oil. The fruity, peppery flavor of a high-quality oil really does add flavor that complements the smoky flavor the grill imparts. Extra-virgin olive oil is made from the first cold-pressing of the olives. It extracts the most olive flavor; lesser grades of oil have less olive flavor. You can substitute a less flavorful oil, but the results may be a little disappointing.

4. Chop the grilled vegetables into ½-inch dice and combine in a saucepan with the basil, oregano, thyme, bay leaf, and salt and pepper to taste. Simmer for 30 minutes on the grill or on the stove. Taste and adjust the seasonings.

5. Serve hot, at room temperature, or cold.

Serving Suggestions: It's hard to go wrong with this summertime classic. Serve it hot or cold, as a side dish or as an appetizer with crackers. It's also great as a main dish, served with couscous, pasta, or rice.

Grilled Chakchouka

Chakchouka is to North Africa what ratatouille is to France—a rich mélange of summer vegetables. In both dishes, the vegetables are the same, but cumin and harissa in the North African version replace the basil and oregano. Harissa is a spicy hot pepper paste that can be found where African foods are sold. A good mail-order source is Sultan's Delight (800-852-5046). In a pinch, you can substitute Chinese chili paste with garlic, but the flavor will be significantly different. This dish tastes even better the day after it is made. It will keep in the refrigerator for up to 5 days.

SERVES 6 TO 8

*Kabobs,
Couscous, and
Other
Compelling
Combinations*

237

1 large onion, quartered
8 garlic cloves
⅓ cup extra-virgin olive oil
2 teaspoons ground cumin
1 large eggplant, peeled and sliced ⅜ inch thick
6 medium-size tomatoes, halved
1 green bell pepper, halved
1 red bell pepper, halved
1 medium-size yellow summer squash, sliced ⅜ inch thick
1 tablespoon harissa, or to taste
Salt and black pepper

1. Prepare a medium-hot fire in the grill.

2. Skewer the onion and garlic. Combine the olive oil and cumin and brush on the onion, garlic, eggplant, tomatoes, peppers, and summer squash.

3. Grill the vegetables, turning occasionally, until tender and grill-marked, 10 to 15 minutes for the onion, garlic, and eggplant; about 10 minutes for the peppers and tomatoes; and 5 to 8 minutes for the summer squash. Remove the vegetables from the grill as they are done.

4. Chop the grilled vegetables into ½-inch dice and combine in a saucepan with the harissa and salt and pepper to taste. Simmer for 30 minutes on the grill or on the stove. Taste and adjust seasonings.

5. Serve hot or at room temperature.

Serving Suggestions: In North Africa, Chakchouka is often served with a topping of poached or fried eggs. This vegetable stew also makes a delicious topping for couscous. My favorite way to serve Chakchouka is with pita pockets or another Arabic flatbread and feta cheese.

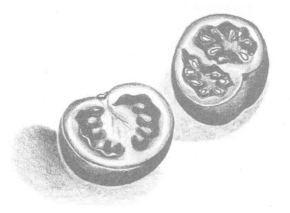

Italian-Style Grilled Vegetable Casserole

This is a great dish for a party or potluck because you can make it in advance and then bake it in a regular oven, and still get the rich grill flavor.

SERVES 4 TO 6

1 garlic bulb
⅓ cup extra-virgin olive oil
½ teaspoon dried rosemary
½ teaspoon dried marjoram
1 medium-size eggplant, peeled and sliced ⅜ inch thick
1 medium-size yellow summer squash, sliced ⅜ inch thick
1 bell pepper (any color), quartered
1 onion, quartered (keep stem end intact)
8 ounces mushrooms, trimmed
4 medium-size vine-ripened tomatoes, halved
½ cup loosely packed fresh basil leaves
1 tablespoon capers, rinsed and drained
Salt and black pepper
½ cup freshly grated Parmesan cheese
½ cup grated mozzarella cheese

1. Prepare a medium fire in the grill.

2. Remove as much of the outer papery skin from the garlic as possible. Using a sharp knife or a pair of kitchen scissors, snip off the tips of the cloves to expose the garlic within. Place the bulb on a square of heavy-duty foil. Drizzle 1 tablespoon of the olive oil over the bulb. Wrap the bulb in the foil to form a tightly sealed packet.

3. Grill for about 10 minutes. If the bulb is easy to squeeze, remove from the heat. Otherwise continue grilling until the garlic is softened, about 5 minutes more.

4. Meanwhile, combine the remaining olive oil with the rosemary and marjoram. Brush onto the eggplant, summer squash, pepper, onion, and mushrooms.

*Kabobs,
Couscous, and
Other
Compelling
Combinations*

239

5. Place as many of the vegetables on the grill grate as possible. Grill, turning occasionally, until well-browned, tender, and grill-marked, 10 to 15 minutes for the eggplant, pepper, and onion; about 10 minutes for the mushrooms; and 5 to 8 minutes for the summer squash. Remove the vegetables from the grill as they are done. As space becomes available, add more vegetables and continue grilling. It is better to overcook than undercook the vegetables in this recipe. Place the vegetables on a cutting board and chop into bite-size pieces.

6. Brush the cut side of the tomatoes with the remaining olive oil–herb mixture and grill until lightly charred and softened, about 10 minutes.

7. While the tomatoes are grilling, preheat the oven to 350°F. Unwrap the garlic and separate into cloves. Gently squeeze each clove to force out the pulp. Place in a food processor fitted with a steel blade. Add the basil leaves and process until finely chopped. Alternatively, you can chop on a cutting board or macerate in a mortar with a pestle. Set aside.

8. Peel, core, and chop the tomatoes. Combine with the garlic-basil mixture. Add the capers and mix well. Season to taste with salt and pepper.

9. Place the chopped grilled eggplant, summer squash, pepper, onion, and mushrooms in a 2-quart casserole dish. Add the tomato mixture and mix well. Add the Parmesan and mozzarella and toss again. Season to taste with salt and pepper.

10. Cover and bake in the oven for 15 minutes. Uncover, then continue baking until the cheese is melted and bubbling, about 15 minutes more. Or place over indirect heat on the grill, close the lid, and bake until heated through, 20 to 30 minutes. Serve hot.

Serving Suggestions: Serve this with a good French or Italian bread for sopping up the extra vegetable juices. This vegetable casserole can be served on top of pasta or along with an undressed pasta, such as fresh cheese-stuffed tortellini.

Smoky Eggplant Parmesan

You can't bread eggplant if you are grilling it, but the loss of the coating seems significant. A fine solution is to layer the eggplant with thinly sliced grilled bread. It gives the eggplant a heft and mouth-feel that would otherwise be missing. This delicious rendering of smoky eggplant, sauce, and cheese is a great way to make Eggplant Parmesan without frying.

Because of the relatively long cooking times, and because eggplant acts like a sponge for picking up flavors, the eggplant will acquire a smoky flavor as it cooks. However, I think the dish is improved with heavy smoke flavor, so use presoaked wood chips on the fire (see page 10).

SERVES 6 TO 9

3 pounds eggplant (about 2 large), peeled and sliced ⅜ inch thick
⅓ cup extra-virgin olive oil
1 small loaf French or Italian bread (about 1 pound), thinly
*   sliced*
1 garlic clove, halved

*Kabobs,
Couscous, and
Other
Compelling
Combinations*

241

4 cups well-seasoned tomato sauce
8 ounces mozzarella cheese, grated
¼ cup freshly grated Parmesan cheese

1. Prepare a medium-hot fire in the grill. Use presoaked wood chips, if desired.

2. Brush the eggplant with the olive oil.

3. Grill the eggplant, turning occasionally, until tender and grill-marked, 10 to 15 minutes. Set aside. Grill the bread until lightly toasted, about 2 minutes per side. Rub the toasted bread with the garlic.

4. Preheat the oven to 350°F.

5. To assemble the casserole, spoon about ¾ cup of the tomato sauce in the bottom of a 9-inch by 13-inch baking dish. Place a single layer of bread on the sauce. Top with a layer of half the eggplant. Spoon about 1¼ cups sauce over the eggplant. Sprinkle with half of the mozzarella and half of the Parmesan. Repeat the layers once more, ending with the cheese.

6. Cover the casserole with foil and bake for 30 minutes. Remove the foil and bake until the cheese is golden and bubbly, 10 to 15 minutes more.

7. Let stand for 5 to 10 minutes before serving.

Smoked Cheese, Mushroom, and Leek Quiche

The recipe includes directions for making a quiche crust from scratch, but a frozen or refrigerated pie shell will work just as well.

SERVES 6 TO 8

CRUST

1¼ cups unbleached all-purpose flour
1 teaspoon salt
2 tablespoons butter
4 tablespoons solid vegetable shortening
3 tablespoons cold water

FILLING

8 ounces mushrooms, halved
1 leek (white part only), thinly sliced
2 tablespoons extra-virgin olive oil
1 cup shredded smoked Gouda or cheddar cheese
1 tablespoon all-purpose flour
3 eggs
1 cup whole milk
1 teaspoon fresh thyme leaves
Salt and black pepper

1. To make the crust, combine the flour and salt in a bowl. Cut in the butter and shortening until the mixture resembles coarse crumbs. Sprinkle the cold water over the mixture and gather the dough into a ball. Transfer to a lightly floured work surface and roll into a circle. Transfer the dough to a 9-inch pie pan and trim the edges. Place in the refrigerator until you are ready to fill it.

2. Prepare a medium-hot fire in the grill with a lightly oiled vegetable grill rack in place. Preheat the oven to 350°F.

3. Toss the mushrooms and leek with the olive oil.

4. Grill the vegetables, tossing frequently, until tender and grill-marked, about 8 minutes.

5. In a medium-size bowl, combine the grilled leeks and mushrooms with the cheese and flour. Toss to mix. Spoon into the prepared pie crust.

6. In another bowl, whisk together the eggs, milk, thyme, and salt and pepper to taste. Pour over the vegetables.

7. Bake the quiche until set, 35 to 45 minutes.

8. Let stand for 20 to 30 minutes before serving.

Fall Vegetable Tart

Goat cheese is a wonderful foil for the grilled winter squash, mushrooms, and leeks that fill this tart. Add a green salad for a delicious light supper. Normally,

I prefer to make my pie crusts from scratch, but the store-bought refrigerated pastry sheets are easy to handle for this free-form tart, and the texture is flaky and lovely.

SERVES 6

½ butternut squash, peeled and cut into ½-inch cubes
3 portobello mushrooms, sliced ¼ inch thick
2 leeks (white part only), sliced ¼ inch thick
1 red bell pepper, diced
6 garlic cloves, thinly sliced
2 tablespoons extra-virgin olive oil
Salt and black pepper
8 ounces soft goat cheese
2 large eggs
1 15-ounce package refrigerated pie crust sheets (contains 2 pie crusts), not in tins

1. Prepare a medium fire in the grill with a lightly oiled vegetable grill rack in place. Preheat the oven to 375°F. Line two baking sheets with foil.

2. Meanwhile, steam the squash over boiling water until just tender, 5 to 7 minutes. Drain well.

3. In a large bowl, combine the squash, mushrooms, leeks, pepper, garlic, olive oil, and salt and pepper to taste. Toss to coat well.

4. Divide the vegetables into two batches. Grill each batch, tossing frequently, until tender and lightly charred, 5 to 8 minutes.

5. In a medium-size bowl, combine the goat cheese and egg. Beat until well blended.

6. Place one pie crust on each baking sheet. Unfold the crust and pinch together any tears. Divide the goat cheese mixture between the two crusts and spread carefully, leaving a 2-inch border around the edges. Arrange the grilled vegetables on top. Fold the dough border up to partially cover the filling and crimp the edges together.

7. Bake, reversing the pans halfway through baking, until the crust is golden, about 35 minutes.

8. Serve warm.

Grilled Fall Vegetable Packets

Foil packets capture my kids' imaginations, enticing them to eat vegetables they normally avoid. This particular vegetable combination tastes great and is simple to prepare. The packets are completely transportable, which makes them a definite possibility for a picnic.

SERVES 4

1 pound red potatoes, thinly sliced
1 small winter squash (¾ to 1 pound), peeled, seeded, and thinly
*   sliced*
½ rutabaga, peeled and thinly sliced
1 onion, thinly sliced
4 garlic cloves, thinly sliced
Salt and black pepper
4 tablespoons butter
4 tablespoons dry white wine
4 tablespoons freshly grated Parmesan cheese

1. Prepare a medium fire in the grill.

2. Mist 4 large pieces of heavy-duty foil with nonstick spray. Divide the potatoes, squash, rutabaga, onions, and garlic among the foil pieces. Sprinkle generously with salt and pepper. Place a tablespoon of butter on and drizzle a tablespoon of wine over each packet, then sprinkle each with a tablespoon of Parmesan. Seal the packets so no liquid or steam escapes (see box, page 245).

3. Grill with the lid down until the vegetables are tender, 20 to 25 minutes. Check one package after 20 minutes to be sure it isn't scorching on the bottom. Remove from the grill when the vegetables are completely tender if serving at once; remove when slightly underdone if you are holding for a while.

4. The packets are well-insulated and will hold their heat for up to 30 minutes after removing from the grill. Serve hot.

Serving Suggestions: Serve this dish with soup and a salad for a comforting at-home supper, or serve with bread and cheese on a picnic.

*Kabobs,
Couscous, and
Other
Compelling
Combinations*

245

Foil-Wrapped Vegetables

As every camper knows, cooking in foil over hot coals can greatly extend the menu and reduce the need for various pots and pans. Vegetables cut to a uniform size and dotted with a little butter or olive oil, sprinkled with a little wine, if you have it, and topped with fresh herb sprigs, if desired, steam in their own juices and taste delicious. Just shift the packets around occasionally and turn them over so the vegetables cook evenly.

To make a packet that will hold in the juices, use heavy-duty foil. Cut the foil large enough to hold one or two servings. Place the vegetables and any flavorings in the center. Fold the long sides of the foil up and over the vegetables. Fold the long edges over about three times to seal them. Then fold the short ends over about three times. This should form a tightly sealed packet.

Grilled Polenta

Grilling polenta brings out more corn flavor. I think unembellished grilled polenta tastes a good deal like popcorn. But the texture is completely different—crusty on the outside, creamy inside.

This is a foolproof method for making polenta in a double boiler; its only drawback is that it requires about an hour of cooking time. I can guarantee that it will taste great and never feel gummy in texture, which is the bane of careless polenta cooks.

SERVES 6 AS A SIDE DISH

4 cups boiling water
1 teaspoon salt
1 cup medium-grind cornmeal
About 2 tablespoons extra-virgin olive oil

1. Pour the boiling water into the top of a double boiler set over simmering water. Add the salt. Gradually sprinkle in the cornmeal, whisking constantly to prevent lumps. Cover and cook over the simmering water until the polenta is soft and fluffy, about 1 hour. Stir for about 1 minute every 15 minutes or so.

2. Brush some of the olive oil into a 9-inch by 13-inch baking dish. Scrape the polenta into the pan. Smooth the top and let cool. Cover and chill for 2 to 4 hours. The polenta will solidify as it cools. (At this point, the polenta can be stored in the refrigerator, covered, for up to 1 day.)

3. Prepare a medium fire in the grill.

4. Brush the top of the polenta with the remaining olive oil and slice into 12 squares.

5. Grill the squares, turning once, until browned and crisp, 20 to 30 minutes. Serve hot.

Variations: You can embellish the polenta in many different ways by adding flavoring during the last few minutes of cooking. Pesto or Parmesan cheese are good choices to stir in, as are a few tablespoons of chopped fresh herbs, some minced garlic, scallions, sun-dried tomatoes, or grilled or sautéed mushrooms.

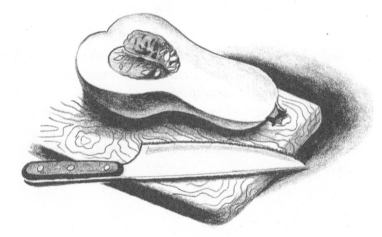

Grilled Cheesy Grits

Kabobs,
Couscous, and
Other
Compelling
Combinations

247

Grits vs. polenta: Grits are grittier, polenta smoother. Grits have a stronger corn flavor, polenta is more refined. Grits are also easier to cook. These grilled rectangles of grain make a fine accompaniment to most grilled vegetables.

SERVES 4 AS A SIDE DISH

3 cups water
½ teaspoon salt
¾ cup yellow or white quick-cooking (not instant) grits
1 cup packed grated cheddar cheese
3 scallions, finely chopped
½ red bell pepper, finely chopped
Salt and black pepper
Melted butter

1. Bring the water and salt to a boil in a large saucepan. Stir in the grits, cover, and reduce the heat to a simmer. Simmer, stirring occasionally, until thickened, about 15 minutes. Remove from the heat. Stir in the cheddar, scallions, and peppers. Season to taste with salt and pepper.

2. Line an 8-inch square baking dish with plastic wrap. Spoon the grits into the dish. Smooth the top, cover, and chill for 2 to 4 hours. The grits will solidify as they cool. (At this point, the grits can be stored in the refrigerator, covered, for up to 1 day.)

3. Prepare a medium fire in the grill.

4. Invert the dish onto a cutting board. Lift off the dish and remove the plastic wrap. Cut the grits into 8 rectangles. Brush both sides of each piece with butter.

5. Grill the rectangles, turning once, until browned and crisp, 20 to 30 minutes. Serve hot.

10

Grilled Fruit and Desserts

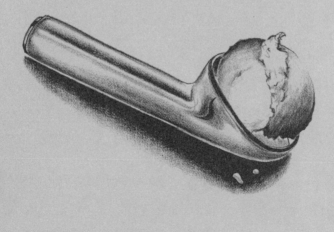

Grill-Baked Apples

Apples wrapped in foil and baked over the dying embers of a fire are a classic camping experience. It is very important that these are baked over a low, low fire so you don't char the apples.

SERVES 4

4 apples
¼ cup finely chopped walnuts
¼ cup brown sugar
1 teaspoon ground cinnamon

1. Prepare a low fire in the grill.

2. Slice off the top ½ inch of the apples and set these "hats" aside. Core the apples and peel them to about one-third of the way down from the stem end.

3. Combine the walnuts, brown sugar, and cinnamon in a small bowl and mix well. Stuff the mixture into the hollowed-out apples. Replace the hats. Wrap each apple in a piece of heavy-duty foil.

4. Grill the apples with the grill lid down until the apples are soft when squeezed or pierced with a fork, 20 to 30 minutes.

5. Serve hot or warm.

Variations: You can play around with the fillings, but whatever combination of ingredients you use, make about 1/2 cup of filling. You can use any type of nuts, or replace the nuts with raisins or cookie crumbs. Pure maple syrup, white sugar, or honey can be used in place of the brown sugar.

Foil-Wrapped
Apple Brown Betty

Normally this recipe would serve four, but two hungry campers will have no trouble consuming all of this delicious, easily prepared dessert. One note of caution: Be sure to grill this over a low fire—one that has died down considerably. Over a hot fire, the apples will scorch and their flavor will be bitter.

SERVES 2 TO 4

4 apples, peeled and thinly sliced
½ cup crushed graham cracker crumbs, preferably, or crushed
*   cookie crumbs*
¼ cup brown sugar
4 tablespoons butter, melted
1 teaspoon ground cinnamon

1. Prepare a low fire in the grill.

2. Combine the apples, cookie crumbs, brown sugar, butter, and cinnamon in a bowl and mix well. Divide the mixture between 2 large pieces of heavy-duty foil and seal the packets so no liquid or steam will escape (see page 245).

3. Grill the packets, turning once, until the apples are soft, about 20 minutes.

4. Open the packets very carefully and serve warm.

Serving Suggestions: Like many old-fashioned fruit desserts, this version of apple brown betty is delicious served with ice cream or a dollop of barely sweetened whipped cream.

Caramelized Bananas

The faint flavor of smoke and caramelized brown sugar do exquisite things to a simple banana. A drizzling of rum or liqueur gives this simple dessert

A Very Simple Grilled Banana

The simplest grilled banana is made by putting a whole, unpeeled banana over a fire or in the coals of a dying fire and roasting it for 15 to 30 minutes, turning occasionally. The skin will turn black, but don't let the banana char completely. Inside, the banana will turn into a custardlike pudding. Open the peel and sprinkle a little cinnamon and sugar on top, if desired. Eat the cooked, softened banana with a spoon. Sip hot chocolate on the side. This is the kind of fare that makes a camping trip memorable.

"gourmet" status. Tips for success: Choose firm, just-ripe bananas so they don't fall apart, do cut the bananas as instructed for ease of handling, and do use a clean grill rack or a fresh piece of heavy-duty foil to cover the grill.

SERVES 4 TO 6

2 tablespoons butter, melted
2 tablespoons brown sugar
4 bananas
1 to 2 tablespoons rum or liqueur (such as Frangelico, Kahlúa,
Cointreau, or kir), optional

1. Prepare a medium fire in the grill.

2. Combine the butter and brown sugar in a shallow dish. Peel the bananas, slice in half lengthwise, then again crosswise. Add the bananas to the butter mixture and toss very gently to coat.

3. Grill the bananas, turning once, until a crispy brown coating of caramelized sugar forms on the surface, about 5 minutes per side. Watch carefully; don't allow the sugar to char.

4. Remove from the grill and, if desired, drizzle the rum or liqueur on top. Serve hot.

Aluminum Foil: Don't Leave the Kitchen Without It

If you suspect your grill might be less than clean, or if you are grilling dessert after a meal's worth of grilled onions and garlic, line the grate with foil.

Grilled Figs with Orange Cream

Should a treat as rare as fresh figs be grilled at all? The answer is a resounding "Yes!" Grilling—really roasting—brings out the fruit's delicate flavor. While the figs are delicious served plain, hot off the grill, I especially like them with the mascarpone-based dip.

SERVES 4

½ cup mascarpone cheese
*1 tablespoon Grand Marnier, Cointreau, or other orange-
    flavored liqueur*
1 tablespoon honey
12 ripe fresh figs

1. Prepare a low fire in the grill.

2. To make the orange cream, combine the mascarpone, liqueur, and honey and mix well.

3. Skewer the figs.

4. Grill the figs, turning occasionally, until the skins blacken and become somewhat glossy, about 10 minutes.

5. To serve, make a mound of the orange cream on each plate and surround with the grilled figs, sliced open if desired.

Grilled Pears with Chocolate Nut Sauce

Pears and chocolate are such a magical combination, it's hard to understand why it is so infrequently encountered. This is a great dessert, although a little on the rich side. Some would say that one pear half per serving is sufficient, but dessert lovers will insist that a whole pear is only fair.

SERVES 4 TO 8

2 ounces unsweetened chocolate
2 tablespoons butter
2 cups firmly packed light brown sugar
½ cup half-and-half
1 tablespoon Frangelico or amaretto or 1 teaspoon
*   vanilla extract*
4 pears, halved lengthwise and cored
½ cup chopped toasted hazelnuts, almonds slivers,
*   walnuts, or pecans (see Note)*

1. In the top of a double boiler set over simmering water, melt the chocolate and butter. Stir in the brown sugar. Add the half-and-half and cook until the mixture is blended and smooth. Stir in the liqueur. Remove from the heat and cover to keep warm.

2. Prepare a medium-low fire in the grill.

3. Grill the pears, cut side down, until tender and grill-marked, about 10 minutes.

4. To serve, place the pears, cut side up, on dessert plates. Spoon the chocolate sauce over and sprinkle the nuts on top.

Note: To toast nuts, place the nuts in a dry skillet and toast, stirring constantly, over medium heat until golden and fragrant, about 5 minutes. Do not allow the nuts to scorch.

Pears Stuffed with Hazelnut Cream

Mascarpone cheese, a rich cream cheese from Italy, has a particular affinity to grilled fruit. In this recipe it is lightly flavored with hazelnuts and stuffed inside grilled pears.

SERVES 4

4 ripe pears
1 cup mascarpone cheese
2 tablespoons Frangelico
2 tablespoons superfine sugar
½ cup chopped toasted hazelnuts (see Note)

1. Prepare a medium-low fire in the grill.

2. Cut the pears in half lengthwise. Scoop out the cores and fibers running from the core to the stem. (A melon baller is an excellent tool for this job.)

3. Grill the pears cut side down until tender and grill-marked, about 10 minutes.

4. In a small bowl, combine the mascarpone, Frangelico, and sugar.

5. Just before serving, stuff the mascarpone mixture into the cores of the pears. Sprinkle the nuts on top. Serve at once.

Note: To toast hazelnuts, place the nuts in a dry skillet and toast, stirring constantly, over medium heat until golden and fragrant, 5 to 7 minutes. Do not allow the nuts to scorch. Place the hot nuts in a clean kitchen towel and rub vigorously to remove the bitter skins.

Basic Grilled Pineapple

Grilling brings out the natural sweetness of pineapple. The outsides of the slices become slightly dry, but the insides become even sweeter and juicier than you might expect. You'll want to grill this fruit over a low fire, which makes pineapple ideal to put on the grill after the main course has been served and the fire is beginning to die down. If you want to serve grilled pineapple as a side dish, grill it on the outer perimeter of the fire, not directly over the coals.

SERVES 4

1 pineapple

1. Prepare a low fire in the grill.

2. On a cutting board, cut off the crown and bottom of the pineapple so it can stand. Slice down the sides, removing the peel and eyes. Cut into quarters and remove the core. Slice each quarter into ½-inch-thick slices.

3. Grill the pineapple slices, turning once, until lightly browned, about 15 minutes. Serve hot.

Serving Suggestions: The pineapple makes a fine dessert, served without any embellishment. It also makes a very interesting side dish for Jerk Vegetables (page 232) or any spicy vegetable dish.

Rum-Soaked Pineapple

Dark rum seems to overpower the delicate pineapple flavor, so light rum is preferred in this dessert.

SERVES 4

½ cup light rum
¼ cup lime juice
½ cup brown sugar
1 pineapple

1. Combine the rum, lime juice, and brown sugar in a small saucepan or microwave-safe container. Heat just enough to dissolve the sugar. Set aside to cool.

2. On a cutting board, cut off the crown and bottom of the pineapple so it can stand. Slice down the sides, removing the peel and eyes. Cut into quarters and remove the core. Slice each quarter into ½-inch-thick slices. Combine the pineapple and rum mixture in a large glass or stainless steel bowl and let stand for at least 1 hour or up to 4 hours.

3. Prepare a low fire in the grill.

4. Grill the pineapple slices, turning once, until lightly browned, about 15 minutes. Serve hot.

Summer Fruit Compote

Fruit baked in foil can be tricky: You don't want to open the packet prematurely and let all the steam escape, but you certainly don't want to scorch the fruit. Your nose can be of great help to you—if you smell something burning, remove the packets from the fire instantly. This compote will satisfy two people if served plain; it is enough for four if served as a topping for vanilla ice cream. The flavor intensifies if you can let the fruit sit for an hour or more after grilling.

SERVES 2 TO 4

4 plums, thinly sliced
2 nectarines, thinly sliced
1 cup berries (such as raspberries, blueberries, blackberries)
¼ cup fruit liqueur (such as Cointreau, Framboise, or
  Chambord)
Sugar

Instant Desserts

Foil-wrapped fruit is a great way to cook fruit over coals, especially when you have a grate that is not clean. Simply cut the fruit into uniform-size pieces and place on a sheet of heavy-duty foil. Add butter or a little fruit liqueur, sweeten with granulated sugar, brown sugar, pure maple syrup, or honey, and add a little ground cinnamon or even a splash of lemon juice for extra flavor. Then seal the packets tightly (see page 245). Cook until the fruit is softened and heated through, usually 10 to 15 minutes. Apples, bananas, nectarines, peaches, plums, pears, pineapple, and oranges are all well-suited to this type of cooking. Serve the fruit with cookies or over ice cream.

1. Prepare a low fire in the grill.

2. Divide the fruit between 2 large pieces of heavy-duty foil. Drizzle 2 tablespoons of the liqueur over each packet of fruit. Seal the packets so no liquid or steam will escape (see page 245).

3. Grill the packets, turning once, until the fruit is softened, 15 to 20 minutes.

4. Open the packets carefully over a bowl; the fruit will have formed a syrup. Sprinkle with sugar to taste. Serve warm.

Variations: Experiment with other fruits and sweeteners. Also try substituting fruit juice for the liqueur.

Brandied Fruit Parfaits

Here's another elegant dessert for the trail: Grill the fruit in foil, then layer it with vanilla pudding. The pudding can be homemade or even (gasp!) from a package. The fruit can be fresh or canned. Just choose fruits of a similar soft (not crunchy) consistency.

SERVES 6

4 cups mixed sliced fruit (such as peeled peaches, pineapple
chunks, nectarines, plums, mangoes) or berries
2 tablespoons butter, melted
2 tablespoons brandy
4 cups vanilla pudding or yogurt (see Note)

1. Prepare a medium-low fire in the grill with a lightly oiled grill rack in place.

2. Divide the fruit between 2 large pieces of heavy-duty foil. Add 1 tablespoon of butter and 1 tablespoon of brandy to each packet of fruit. Seal the packets so no liquid or steam will escape (see page 245).

3. Grill the packets, turning once, until the fruit is softened and hot, 15 to 20 minutes.

4. Open the packets carefully over a bowl; the fruit will have formed a syrup. Layer the pudding and fruit with syrup in 6 parfait glasses, large stemmed wine glasses, or dessert bowls. (Do not layer hot pudding into delicate wine glasses, as the glasses may break.)

5. Serve at once or chill for several hours before serving.

Note: To make vanilla pudding, in the top of a double boiler, combine ½ cup sugar, 6 tablespoons cornstarch, and ¼ teaspoon salt. Gradually stir in 4 cups milk. Set the pan over boiling water and cook, stirring constantly, until the mixture begins to thicken, 8 to 12 minutes. Cover and cook for 10 minutes more. Remove 1 cup of the thickened mixture and slowly stir in 2 well-beaten eggs. Return to the pot and continue to cook, stirring constantly, for 2 minutes more. Do not overcook; the pudding will thicken as it cools. Remove from the heat and stir in 1 teaspoon vanilla extract. Let cool slightly before layering with the fruit.

Grilled Nectarines with Mascarpone Cream

Nectarines and peaches both take well to the grill. The advantage of nectarines is they don't require peeling.

SERVES 4

8 ounces mascarpone cheese
¾ cup heavy cream
4 tablespoons Grand Marnier, Cointreau, or other orange-
flavored liqueur
1 tablespoon sugar
3 tablespoons butter, melted
4 large nectarines, sliced about ½ inch thick
Freshly grated nutmeg

1. Combine the mascarpone, ¼ cup of the heavy cream, and 2 tablespoons of the liqueur. Stir until smooth.
2. Combine the remaining ½ cup heavy cream and the sugar in another bowl and beat until soft peaks form. Fold the cream into the mascarpone. Set aside in the refrigerator.
3. Prepare a medium-low fire in the grill.
4. Combine the butter and the remaining 2 tablespoons liqueur and brush onto the nectarines.
5. Grill the nectarines until softened and lightly grill-marked, about 4 minutes per side.
6. Fold the nectarines into the mascarpone mixture. Spoon into dessert bowls and top each serving with a grating of fresh nutmeg.

Variations: Any stone fruit can be substituted for the nectarines. If you select peaches, make it easier to peel them by dipping them into boiling water for about 30 seconds to loosen their skins.

Maple-Grilled Pound Cake
with Peaches

The light maple glaze adds an appealing crust to the cake, while the maple and smoke enhance the flavor of the peaches. Choose a densely crumbed pound cake—the frozen kind works well for a quick dessert.

SERVES 8

8 peaches or 16 canned peach halves
¼ cup orange juice
2 tablespoons butter, melted
2 tablespoons pure maple syrup
1 8-inch loaf pound cake (homemade or store-bought),
*   sliced 1 inch thick*
Pure maple syrup (optional)

1. If you are using fresh peaches, dip them into boiling water for about 30 seconds to loosen their skins. With a sharp paring knife, pull away the skin and discard. Halve and pit each peach. If you are using canned peaches, drain well.

2. Prepare a medium fire in the grill.

3. Combine the orange juice, butter, and maple syrup and mix well. Brush onto the peaches and both sides of the cake slices.

4. Grill the peaches and cake slices until golden brown, about 5 minutes per side for the peaches and about 3 minutes per side for the cake.

5. Place a slice of cake and 2 peach halves on each plate. Drizzle additional maple syrup over the cake and peaches, if desired. Serve at once.

Clean Grill Racks Are Essential

Delicately flavored fruit must be grilled on scrupulously clean grill racks or it will pick up flavors from the grill. You might consider keeping a grate or grill rack just for fruit so you won't ever have to deal with onion-flavored peaches.

Angel Bites

"Oooh! Toasted marshmallow cake!" was my son Sam's delighted cry when he first tasted grilled angel food cake. His description was remarkably accurate. This is a dessert for the young at heart and palate.

SERVES 4

¼ cup apple or raspberry jelly
¼ cup apple or orange juice
1 11-ounce angel food cake
3 bananas

1. Prepare a medium fire in the grill.

2. In a small pan or microwave-safe container, heat the jelly and juice together until the jelly is melted.

3. Cut the cake into 2-inch cubes. Slice the banana crosswise about 1½ inches thick. Arrange the cake and banana slices on 8 skewers. Brush generously with the jelly mixture.

4. Grill the cake skewers until golden brown, about 3 minutes per side. Serve at once.

Variations: Omit the bananas altogether or use peaches, nectarines, or pineapple chunks instead.

Piña Colada Kabobs

Watch out! That coconut is flammable! And the cake wants to roll around on the skewers, which is why I recommend using two skewers for each kabob. This dessert requires a vigilant eye and a careful hand—but it's also delicious and fun.

SERVES 6

1 6-ounce carton lemon yogurt
½ cup pineapple juice
1 tablespoon rum
1 tablespoon lime juice
2 cups sweetened flaked dried coconut
1 11-ounce angel food cake, cut into 2-inch cubes
15 to 20 pineapple chunks

1. Prepare a low fire in the grill.

2. Combine the yogurt, pineapple juice, rum, and lime juice in a shallow bowl and mix well. Place the coconut in a second bowl.

3. One piece at a time, roll the cake in the yogurt mixture, then in the coconut. Alternating the cake and pineapple cubes, thread 2 skewers side by side through each cube. (This will reduce the tendency of the cake pieces to roll around when you turn the kabobs.)

4. Grill the cake until golden brown, 1 to 3 minutes per side. Serve at once.

Honey-Nut Fruit Kabobs

Cookies are a nice accompaniment to this dessert.

SERVES 4 TO 8

1 pineapple
2 large bananas, peeled and sliced 1½ inches thick
2 oranges, peeled and sectioned
3 tablespoons butter
2 tablespoons honey
1 tablespoon Grand Marnier, Cointreau, or other orange-
    flavored liqueur
1 cup finely chopped nuts (such as almonds, walnuts, or pecans)

1. Prepare a medium-low fire in the grill.

2. On a cutting board, cut off the crown and bottom of the pineapple so it can stand. Slice down the sides, removing the peel and eyes. Cut into quarters and remove the core. Slice each quarter into chunks 1½ inches thick.

3. Arrange the pineapple, bananas, and oranges on skewers.

4. Combine the butter and honey in a small pan or microwave-safe container and heat until the butter is melted. Stir in the liqueur. Brush onto the fruit and sprinkle the nuts on top.

5. Grill, turning occasionally, until the nuts are golden brown, 5 to 10 minutes. Serve warm.

Grilled Apple Corn Cakes

The jury's out as to whether these delicious warm, grilled polenta slices are better topped with maple syrup or ice cream. My kids go for both.

SERVES 6

4 cups boiling water
1 teaspoon salt
1 cup medium-grind cornmeal
2 Granny Smith apples, peeled and finely chopped
¼ cup sugar
⅛ teaspoon ground nutmeg
2 tablespoons butter, melted
Warm pure maple syrup, frozen vanilla ice cream, or frozen
*   vanilla yogurt*

1. Pour the boiling water into the top of a double boiler set over simmering water. Add the salt. Gradually sprinkle in the cornmeal, whisking constantly to prevent lumps. Cover and cook until soft and fluffy, about 1 hour. Stir for about 1 minute every 15 minutes or so. Stir in the apples, sugar, and nutmeg.

Menu Planning Tip

Sometimes more is just more. If your whole meal is to be grilled, it is probably wise to go with a foil-wrapped dessert so as not to overwhelm the palate with smoke flavor. On the other hand, if the meal starts with a grilled salad or appetizer and then progresses to a main course off the grill, a smoke-touched grilled dessert may be just the perfect finishing touch.

Cook for 15 minutes more.

2. Mist a 9-inch by 13-inch baking dish with nonstick spray.

3. Scrape the corn mush into the baking dish. Smooth the top, cover, and chill for 2 to 4 hours. The corn mush will solidify as it cools. (At this point, the mush can be stored in the refrigerator, covered, for up to 1 day.)

4. Prepare a medium fire in the grill.

5. Slice the corn mush into 12 squares. Brush the melted butter on both sides of the squares.

6. Grill the squares, turning once, until golden and heated through, about 8 minutes.

7. Serve hot, passing warm maple syrup on the side or topping each slice with ice cream or frozen yogurt.

Variations: Substitute other fruits for the apples, especially finely chopped peaches, nectarines, or pears.

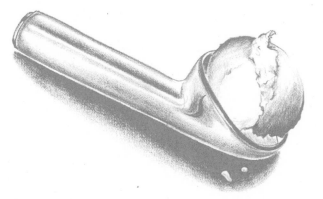

Campfire Cinnamon Toast Treats

Breakfast or dessert? These cinnamon-coated cubes of bread skewered with strawberries and banana make a delicious and unusual addition to brunch, but they would not be at all out of place as a dessert. My family likes them as a breakfast treat when we are camping.

SERVES 4

¼ cup sugar
1 teaspoon ground cinnamon
8 brown-and-serve rolls, cut into quarters
4 tablespoons butter, melted
1 pint strawberries, hulled, halved if large
2 firm bananas, peeled and sliced

1. Prepare a low fire in the grill.
2. Combine the sugar and cinnamon in a medium-size bowl.
3. Brush the rolls with the butter, then toss in the bowl with the cinnamon and sugar. Thread the bread onto skewers, alternating with the strawberries and bananas.
4. Grill the kabobs, turning occasionally, until the bread is browned and toasted, 8 to 10 minutes. Serve hot.

11

Marinades, Glazes, Pestos, and Dipping Sauces

CHAPTER 11 • MARINADES, GLAZES, PESTOS, AND DIPPING SAUCES

Classic Vinaigrette

This is a classic vinaigrette, a simple combination of oil and vinegar, perfect to drizzle over grilled vegetables—or a green salad. Because it is so simple, it is best to use high-quality olive oil and vinegar. The recipe makes enough to dress about a pound of grilled asparagus, green beans, carrots, leeks, or mushrooms.

MAKES ABOUT 1/4 CUP

> *1 tablespoon red wine vinegar*
> *1 garlic clove, minced*
> *½ teaspoon Dijon mustard*
> *3 tablespoons extra-virgin olive oil*
> *Salt and black pepper*

1. In a small bowl, combine the vinegar, garlic, and mustard and whisk until smooth. Slowly pour in the olive oil and whisk constantly until the oil is emulsified. Stir in salt and pepper to taste.

2. Use immediately or store airtight in the refrigerator for up to 2 weeks.

Variation: Balsamic Vinaigrette. Balsamic vinegar is often the perfect complement to the sweet smoky flavor of grilled vegetables. Substitute balsamic vinegar for the red wine vinegar.

Marinating Mushrooms

Mushrooms are one of the few vegetables that will absorb a marinade. Indeed, toss a pound of mushrooms in marinade and you can watch the marinade disappear. Once the marinade has been completely absorbed, there is no need to marinate longer; one hour is generally enough time to allow. One pound of mushrooms will absorb 1/3 to 1/2 cup of marinade.

Basic Herb Marinade and Salad Dressing

This basic dressing is similar in flavor to a bottled Italian salad dressing. The herbs give it great clinging ability, making it an ideal marinade for grilled vegetables. This recipe is sufficient for marinating or dressing 1 to 1½ pounds of vegetables.

MAKES ABOUT 1/3 CUP

4 garlic cloves, minced
¼ cup chopped fresh basil
2 tablespoons chopped fresh oregano, or 2 teaspoons dried
2 tablespoons red wine vinegar
1 teaspoon salt
½ teaspoon black pepper
¼ cup extra-virgin olive oil

1. In a small bowl, combine the garlic, basil, oregano, vinegar, salt, and pepper. Slowly pour in the olive oil and whisk constantly until the oil is emulsified.

2. Use immediately or store airtight in the refrigerator for up to 4 days.

Lemon-Garlic Marinade

When you make a vinaigrette, you mix together the flavoring agents—the herbs and lemon juice (or vinegar), then you beat in the oil. Because oil won't naturally mix with water, it must be emulsified, which is where the beating action comes in. The emulsified marinade is thickened and does an excellent job of coating each piece of vegetable with moisturizing oil infused with flavorings. This recipe is sufficient for marinating or dressing a pound of vegetables and is an excellent choice for asparagus, broccoli, carrots, and summer squash.

MAKES ABOUT 1/2 CUP

3 garlic cloves, minced
½ teaspoon grated lemon zest
¼ cup chopped fresh parsley
1 teaspoon sugar
Juice of 1 lemon
½ teaspoon Dijon mustard
¼ cup extra-virgin olive oil
Salt and black pepper

1. In a food processor fitted with a steel blade, combine the garlic, lemon zest, parsley, and sugar. Process until the parsley is very finely chopped and the mixture is fairly smooth. Add the lemon juice and mustard and process again. With the motor running, slowly pour in the olive oil and continue to process until the oil is emulsified. Stir in salt and pepper to taste.

2. Use immediately or store airtight in the refrigerator for up to 2 weeks.

Garlic-Herb Marinade

The coarse mustard and sweet apple juice enhance the garlic and herb flavors in this very versatile marinade. Use it with all manner of vegetables—especially zucchini, eggplant, onions, peppers, potatoes, and cherry tomatoes. This amount of marinade is sufficient for marinating or dressing 1 to 2 pounds of vegetables.

MAKES ABOUT 1/2 CUP

2 garlic cloves, minced
1 tablespoon chopped fresh basil leaves, or 1 teaspoon dried
1 teaspoon minced fresh oregano leaves, or ¼ teaspoon dried
1½ teaspoons coarse-grained mustard
1½ tablespoons unfiltered apple juice or cider
1½ tablespoons cider vinegar or wine vinegar
⅓ cup canola or extra-virgin olive oil
¼ teaspoon salt
Freshly ground black pepper

1. Combine the garlic, basil, oregano, mustard, apple juice or cider, and vinegar in a small bowl. Slowly pour in the oil and whisk constantly until the oil is emulsified. Stir in the salt and add pepper to taste.

2. Use immediately or store airtight in the refrigerator for up to 2 weeks.

Maple-Lime Marinade

This marinade adds a Southeast Asian flavor, with maple syrup standing in for the less readily available tamarind. It is particularly good on sweet potatoes and winter squash.

MAKES ABOUT 1/2 CUP

3 tablespoons fresh-squeezed lime juice
3 tablespoons pure maple syrup
2 teaspoons soy sauce
½ teaspoon Dijon mustard
2 garlic cloves, minced
3 tablespoons toasted sesame oil

1. Combine the lime juice, maple syrup, soy sauce, mustard, and garlic in a small bowl. Whisk in the mustard. Slowly pour in the sesame oil and whisk constantly until the oil is emulsified.

2. Use immediately or store airtight in the refrigerator for up to 2 weeks.

Tandoori Marinade

This yogurt-based marinade is a traditional Indian marinade. The acid in yogurt works to tenderize meat. While it doesn't perform that function for vegetables, it does coat the vegetables, adding to both their texture and their flavor. There is a recipe for Tandoori-Style Vegetable Kabobs (see page 213), but you can use this marinade with any vegetable or combination of vegetables.

MAKES ABOUT 1 CUP

1 cup plain yogurt
2 garlic cloves, minced
1 teaspoon minced fresh ginger
1 teaspoon ground cumin
1 teaspoon ground coriander
1 teaspoon salt
¾ teaspoon garam masala
⅛ teaspoon ground red pepper

Tandoori Cooking

Tandoori-style cooking is the Indian way of barbecuing. Tandoori food gets its name from the tandoor, the clay oven in which the food is cooked. This style of cooking was introduced to India by Mogul conquerors, who brought their Middle Eastern cooking methods with them. When Middle Eastern barbecue was combined with traditional Indian spices, the result was tandoori barbecue.

The tandoor itself is a beehive-shaped oven sunk into the ground, the bottom of which is lined with glowing goals. Food on skewers is lowered through an opening and the food is quickly cooked in the intense heat of the tandoor. Although restaurants typically offer chicken and shrimp cooked tandoori-style, the marinade is very compatible with vegetables as well.

> ## If You Eat Meat
>
> The marinades and sauces in this chapter need not be restricted to vegetables. All can be used with meats, chicken, and seafood as well.

1. Stir together the yogurt, garlic, ginger, cumin, coriander, salt, garam masala, and red pepper.

2. Use immediately.

Teriyaki Marinade and Dipping Sauce

This marinade is thickened with cornstarch so it has good vegetable-clinging characteristics and makes an excellent dipping sauce. It is particularly good on tofu.

MAKES ABOUT 1 1/4 CUPS

2 tablespoons toasted sesame oil
1 tablespoon canola or peanut oil
1 tablespoon minced fresh ginger
2 garlic cloves, minced
½ cup tamari
¼ cup dry sherry
3 tablespoons brown sugar
2 tablespoons lime juice
¼ cup orange or pineapple juice
1 tablespoon cornstarch

1. In a saucepan over medium-high heat, heat the sesame oil and canola or peanut oil. Add the ginger and garlic and cook, stirring, until fragrant, about 1 minute. Add the tamari, sherry, brown sugar, and lime juice and bring to a boil.

2. Mix together the orange or pineapple juice and cornstarch until you

have a smooth paste. Stir into the tamari mixture and cook until the sauce is thickened, about 5 minutes. Set aside to cool.

3. Use immediately or store airtight in the refrigerator for up to 1 week.

Lemon-Soy Marinade and Salad Dressing

There's always a jar of this marinade in the door of my refrigerator. It doubles as a great salad dressing. I particularly like it with broccoli.

MAKES ABOUT 1 1/4 CUPS

½ cup soy sauce
¼ cup water
¼ cup toasted sesame oil
6 tablespoons fresh lemon juice
4 garlic cloves, minced

1. Combine the soy sauce, water, sesame oil, lemon juice, and garlic in an airtight jar and shake well. This dressing separates quickly, so be sure to shake it just before using.

2. Use immediately or store airtight in the refrigerator for up to 3 months.

Chinese Barbecue Marinade

Chinese hoisin sauce forms the basis of this marinade. Hoisin sauce is a sweet, red-brown sauce made from fermented soybean paste, sugar, garlic, and spices, which are usually Chinese five-spice powder and a little ground chile. It's often used as a glaze for poultry and pork, but you haven't tasted paradise until you've had it on grilled broccoli. It is also delicious on other vegetables and tofu.

Tips for Tofu

Tofu will be easier to handle on the grill if you use firm or extra-firm tofu and drain it first. Wrap the block of tofu in a clean cotton kitchen towel or several paper towels. Place a heavy weight on top, such as a cutting board with a full juice can on top of it. Let stand for 30 minutes. Excess water will be forced out (and absorbed by the towels). The resulting tofu will be significantly compressed and drier in texture. It will absorb a marinade more readily in this state and it will hold together better on the grill.

Tofu will stick on the grill unless the grill and/or the tofu is generously brushed with oil.

MAKES ABOUT 1 CUP

½ cup hoisin sauce
¼ cup dry sherry
2 tablespoons soy sauce
2 tablespoons peanut oil
1 tablespoon toasted sesame oil
2 garlic cloves, minced
*1 teaspoon chili paste with garlic (available where Asian
    foods are sold)*
1 teaspoon chopped fresh ginger (optional)

1. Combine the hoisin sauce, sherry, soy sauce, peanut oil, sesame oil, garlic, chili paste, and, if desired, ginger in an airtight jar and shake well.

2. Use immediately or store airtight in the refrigerator for up to 3 weeks.

Chinese Soy–Black Bean Marinade and Dressing

The black beans in the bean sauce are dried fremented black soybeans. They add a special salty, nutty flavor to any dish. I find the flavor somewhat addictive.

MAKES ABOUT 2/3 CUP

> ¼ cup toasted sesame oil
> 3 tablespoons soy sauce
> 2 tablespoons mirin
> 1 tablespoon rice vinegar
> 3 garlic cloves, minced
> 1 teaspoon black bean sauce with chili (available where Chinese foods are sold)
> 1 teaspoon sugar

1. Combine the sesame oil, soy sauce, mirin, vinegar, garlic, black bean sauce, and sugar in an airtight jar and shake well.
2. Use immediately or store airtight in the refrigerator for up to 3 months.

Variation: Spicy Chinese Marinade and Dressing. Substitute chili paste with garlic for the black bean sauce with chili. Increase the soy sauce to 1/4 cup. Add 1 tablespoon chopped fresh cilantro.

Barbecue Glaze

This is a simple but classic tomato-based barbecue glaze. It is not cooked, as it cooks after it has been spread on burgers or veggies on the grill. If you want a sauce to serve as a condiment, see the Variation.

Smoke in a Jar

Forget about liquid smoke. Chipotles, which are smoke-dried jalapeños, add smoke flavor and more to barbecue sauces, beans, soups, salad dressings, and sautés. If you simmer the dried chiles in a cooked dish then remove them, they will add smoke flavor but not much heat. Chop the flesh and return the chile to the cooked dish if you want to enjoy the heat. Without the seeds, the flesh adds a modest heat; with the seeds, the punch is greater. Chipotles en abodo, chipotles in a tomato-vinegar base, can be added to any dish, without cooking. You can find this magic ingredient wherever Mexican foods are sold. A good mail-order source is: Nancy's Specialty Market, P.O. Box 530, Newmarket, NH 03857; 800-462-6291.

MAKES ABOUT 1/2 CUP

¼ cup ketchup
2 tablespoons brown sugar
1 tablespoon soy sauce
4 garlic cloves, minced
1 tablespoon minced onion
2 teaspoons ground cumin

1. Combine the ketchup, brown sugar, soy sauce, garlic, onion, and cumin and mix well.

2. Use immediately or store airtight in the refrigerator for up to 1 week.

Variation: **Barbecue Sauce.** For serving this flavor combination as a condiment—it is great on veggie burgers, both store-bought and home-made—I prefer to cook the onion first. To do so, heat 1 tablespoon of canola oil in a small saucepan. Add the onion and garlic and cook, stirring, until fragrant, about 3 minutes. Add the ketchup, brown sugar, soy sauce, and cumin and simmer for 5 minutes. Cool before serving. You can double, triple, or even quadruple the recipe, but don't use more than 2 tablespoons oil (it just isn't needed). The sauce will keep in an airtight container in the refrigerator for up to 3 weeks.

A Love Affair with Pesto

Pesto and grilled food is a marriage made in heaven. Here are eight ways to celebrate the union. You can use Pesto or Cilantro Pesto in any of the suggestions below, depending on whether you want to go Mediterranean or Tex-Mex.

1. Pesto-Vegetable Foil Packets: Substitute pesto for the butter or olive oil and herbs in a foil packet of vegetables.

2. Pesto Pasta Salads: Toss pasta with grilled vegetables and dress with pesto thinned with extra-virgin olive oil.

3. Pesto Crostini: Brush pesto on grilled bread.

4. Pesto Polenta: Stir a tablespoon or two of pesto into just-cooked polenta before chilling it in a pan. Grill as usual.

5. Pesto Pasta: Toss pasta with pesto then top with grilled vegetables.

6. Pesto Vegetable Sandwiches: Split open a loaf of French or Italian bread. Brush with pesto. Fill with grilled vegetables. Close the loaf, wrap in foil, and reheat on grill.

7. Pesto Pizza: Top a grilled pizza shell with pesto and sliced tomatoes.

8. Pesto Corn: Pull back the husks of corn that has been soaked in water for 10 minutes. Spread pesto on the kernels. Replace the husks and grill as usual.

Pesto

Pesto—the heavenly paste made from basil, Parmesan, olive oil, and pine nuts—is an incredibly versatile flavoring agent that works especially well with grilled vegetables. Each summer, I stock up on Parmesan and pine nuts and spend a few hours making pesto from the basil that grows so easily in my garden. I freeze the pesto in small batches in recycled yogurt containers and use it year-round.

MAKES ABOUT 2/3 CUP

1½ cups tightly packed fresh basil leaves
2 garlic cloves
3 tablespoons pine nuts
¼ cup extra-virgin olive oil
3 tablespoons grated Parmesan cheese
Salt and black pepper

1. Combine the basil, garlic, and pine nuts in a food processor fitted with a steel blade. Process until finely chopped. With the motor running, slowly pour in the olive oil and continue to process until you have a paste. Add the Parmesan and salt and pepper to taste and pulse to combine.

2. Let stand for at least 20 minutes before serving to allow the flavors to develop. Store airtight in the refrigerator for up to 1 week.

Cilantro Pesto

Cilantro pesto makes a delicious spread for grilled bruschetta or quesadillas—or try it inside a grilled cheese and tomato sandwich. We like to brush it on grilled cauliflower, zucchini, corn, and tomatoes. It can also be spread on pizza or inside a tortilla, or it can be used to dress a Tex-Mex inspired pasta dish.

MAKES ABOUT 2/3 CUP

1½ cups fresh cilantro leaves or 1 cup fresh cilantro leaves
*   and ½ cup fresh parsley leaves*
¼ cup freshly grated Parmesan cheese
3 tablespoons pine nuts
1 teaspoon grated lime zest
1 large garlic clove
5 tablespoons extra-virgin olive oil
Salt and freshly ground black pepper

1. Combine the cilantro, Parmesan, pine nuts, lime zest, and garlic in a food processor fitted with a steel blade. Process until well mixed. With the motor running, slowly pour in the olive oil. Season to taste with salt and pepper and process to the desired consistency.

2. Let stand for at least 20 minutes before serving to allow the flavors to develop. Store airtight in the refrigerator for up to 1 week.

Maple-Lime Glaze

Butter-based glazes are excellent for vegetables that are somewhat dry and fibrous, such as sweet potatoes and winter squash. Brush onto vegetables just before and during grilling. Check frequently as this sweet glaze will cause charring.

MAKES ABOUT 1/4 CUP

2 tablespoons butter, melted
1 tablespoon pure maple syrup
1 tablespoon lime juice
⅛ teaspoon ground cinnamon
Salt and freshly ground black pepper

1. Combine the butter, maple syrup, lime juice, cinnamon, and salt and pepper to taste and mix well.

2. Use immediately or store airtight in the refrigerator for up to 1 week.

Aïoli

Heady stuff this aïoli, a garlicky mayonnaise from southern France. It is made with a raw egg, so exercise all due caution in warm weather and keep aïoli refrigerated when not in use. It is a good idea to make this early in the day, then chill well. This gives the raw garlic a chance to mellow and allows you to serve a chilled dip, which will spoil less quickly.

MAKES ABOUT 1 1/2 CUPS

4 garlic cloves
1 egg
¾ cup extra-virgin olive oil
Juice of ½ lemon
Salt and black pepper

1. In a food processor fitted with a steel blade, mince the garlic. Add the egg and process until completely mixed. With the motor running, slowly pour in ¼ cup of the olive oil. Stop the machine and add the lemon juice. Then, with the motor running, slowly add the remaining ½ cup olive oil, and process until the mixture is thickened and the oil is emulsified. Add salt and pepper to taste.

2. Refrigerate for at least 30 minutes and up to 8 hours before serving to allow the raw garlic flavor to mellow a little.

Serving Suggestions: Traditionally a dip for vegetables, meat, and fish, aïoli makes a wonderful accompaniment to many grilled vegetables, especially asparagus, carrots, green beans, peppers, summer squash, and tomatoes.

Sesame Dipping Sauce

With this dipping sauce passed at the table, any manner of grilled vegetables can be served over rice and made into an interesting meal with Asian flavors. It is also great as a dressing for noodles or as a dip for raw vegetables.

MAKES ABOUT 1 CUP

½ cup tahini (sesame paste)
¼ cup warm water, or more if needed
2 tablespoons soy sauce
2 tablespoons rice vinegar
2 tablespoons mirin (sweet rice wine)
2 garlic cloves, minced
1 tablespoon minced fresh ginger

1. Combine the tahini, water, soy sauce, vinegar, mirin, garlic, and ginger and mix well. Add more water, if needed, to achieve the desired consistency.

2. Let stand for at least 30 minutes before serving to allow the flavors to blend. Store airtight in the refrigerator for up to 3 weeks. Mix well before serving.

Spicy Peanut Sauce

As with the previous recipe, which is made with sesame paste, this delicious peanut sauce can be used served with any grilled or stir-fried vegetables. It can be used as a dip for raw or steamed vegetables or tossed with noodles.

MAKES ABOUT 1 1/2 CUPS

1 scallion, trimmed
2 garlic cloves
½ cup smooth peanut butter
1 cup vegetable stock or broth, or weak brewed green tea
1 teaspoon rice vinegar
1 teaspoon soy sauce
1 teaspoon chili paste with garlic (available where Asian foods
     are sold), or more to taste
½ teaspoon sugar
1 tablespoon chopped fresh cilantro

1. Combine the scallion and garlic in a food processor and process until finely chopped. Add the peanut butter and stock, broth, or tea to the vinegar, soy sauce, chili paste, and sugar and process until well mixed. Stir in the cilantro.

2. Cover and let stand at room temperature for at least 1 hour to allow the flavors to develop. Store airtight in the refrigerator for up to 1 week.

Garlic Math

1 medium clove = 1/2 teaspoon minced

Raita

Raita is a traditional Indian relish, which can provide mouth-cooling refreshment with spicy foods. It is essential to serve this with Tandoori-Style Vegetable Kabobs (page 213) as the sauce complements and moistens the fairly dry vegetables. It also makes a great topping for any burger or for Falafel (page 133) instead of the usual relish and tahini sauce.

MAKES ABOUT 2 1/2 CUPS

1 cucumber, peeled, seeded, and chopped fine
1 cup plain yogurt
1 tablespoon finely chopped fresh cilantro
1 tablespoon finely chopped fresh mint
Salt and black pepper

1. Combine the cucumber, yogurt, cilantro, mint, and salt and pepper to taste and mix well.

2. Let stand for about 10 minutes before serving to allow the flavors to develop.

Grilled Onion Dip

For adding moisture to grilled vegetables and burgers and for heightening the grilled flavor, nothing beats this simple combination of grilled onions, yogurt, and herbs.

MAKES ABOUT 3 CUPS

3 onions, thinly sliced
2 tablespoons extra-virgin olive oil
1½ cups plain yogurt
¼ cup chopped fresh parsley
2 tablespoons chopped fresh mint, or 2 teaspoons dried
Salt

1. Prepare a medium-hot fire in the grill with a lightly oiled vegetable grill rack in place.

2. Toss the onions with the olive oil.

3. Grill the onions, tossing frequently, until well browned and tender, about 10 minutes.

4. Combine the onions with the yogurt, parsley, mint, and salt to taste.

5. Let stand for at least 30 minutes before serving to allow the flavors to develop.

Index